RUMO
BETTER

RUMOURS OF A BETTER COUNTRY

RUMOURS OF A BETTER COUNTRY

Searching for trust and community in a time of moral outrage

Marsh Moyle

INTER-VARSITY PRESS
SPCK Group, Studio 101, The Record Hall, 16–16A Baldwin's Gardens,
London EC1N 7RJ, England
Email: ivp@ivpbooks.com
Website: www.ivpbooks.com

First published 2023

British Library Cataloguing-in-Publication Data
A catalogue record for this book is available from the British Library.

ISBN: 978–1–78974–467–5
eBook ISBN: 978–1–78974–469–9

Set in Minion 11/14 pt
Typeset in Great Britain by Fakenham Prepress Solutions,
Fakenham, Norfolk

Printed in Great Britain by Clays Ltd

Produced on paper from sustainable forests

Inter-Varsity Press publishes Christian books that are true to the Bible and that communicate the gospel, develop discipleship and strengthen the church for its mission in the world.

IVP originated within the Inter-Varsity Fellowship, now the Universities and Colleges Christian Fellowship, a student movement connecting Christian Unions in universities and colleges throughout Great Britain, and a member movement of the International Fellowship of Evangelical Students. Website: www.uccf.org.uk. That historic association is maintained, and all senior IVP staff and committee members subscribe to the UCCF Basis of Faith.

To the Angel
who wrestles
through the night

and

Tuula
wise woman
who tends the wound
with love and grace

Advice to the reader

This book was written under the influence of coffee.
It will reward you most if you read it slowly,
with reflection,
and discuss it in the company of friends,
with drinks of your choice.
Speed reading is not recommended.

Contents

Prologue

In the early 1980s, when the Iron Curtain[1] was a permanent part of Europe, I was in Czechoslovakia meeting people who distributed literature that had been smuggled into the country.

One winter evening, I went with a friend to a crowded pub. We found space at the last remaining table. Soon, three men, more Middle Eastern than Czech, took the last remaining seats. We introduced ourselves as the waiter brought beer. They were from Palestine, sent to study in Czechoslovakia by the Palestinian Liberation Organization. In those days, we thought of the PLO as a terrorist organisation and could imagine the training they were receiving. In hindsight, they were probably learning to be accountants or town planners. Cigarette smoke hung as thick as the heavy snowfall we watched through a perspiring window.

We were soon deep in conversation, and I asked about their hopes for a liberated Palestine. Their passion was infectious. They spoke eagerly of their dreams: self-determination, of having their own state, personal responsibility, and the freedom to think and act for themselves. It seemed slightly ironic that some of the freedoms they wanted were denied in the country where they studied, but we agreed with them. We wanted the same for our friends in Czechoslovakia, though it would have been unwise to say it aloud.

As we listened, a question was forming in my mind. 'Your dream is rich, and I hope you achieve it,' I said, 'but is your dream large enough?'

They were shocked; what could be more important than what they had described? So they asked what I meant.

'If you get your dream, and I hope you do, what will make your country any different from those around it? Will your communities be more trusting? Will a few powerful people dominate everyone

1

else? Will people be able to trust each other, or will they have to look over their shoulders? You will have freedom from external oppression, but little freedom from our common universal struggles. There will still be murders, theft and corruption. My country enjoys many freedoms you want, but I am still seeking a better country.'

The laughter and chatter in the pub grew as the evening wore on. We talked for a while about what a vision of a good country might be. Our conversation meandered to other themes, and then we went into the snow.[2]

Could there be a better country?

I was cynical. Untethered utopian dreams lead to totalitarianism. Beware the impatience of idealists who cannot live with less than their ideal, who seek to save humanity but have little time for humans. Wasn't the world torn apart by romantic idealism in the twentieth century? Didn't Hitler, Lenin and Stalin want heaven on earth? Mao Zedong said, 'All political power comes from the barrel of a gun.'[3] A better country should be better for everyone.

But how do we know what makes a better country? What does it mean to live together well?

What would it take to be a thriving community of unique people who get along well – communities of trust, where difference does not threaten, and power is not abused? What would make people safe to be vulnerable enough to have deep and meaningful relationships?

These are the questions for our age.

We live in a time of moral outrage and judgement, and there is much to be outraged about. Is it not tragic that companies need policies on modern slavery or that women should walk in fear at night? People speak of cancelling each other in the search for a new moral order of left or right. We are polarised in a way we have not been for generations. Every day one hears of people withdrawing from public discussion or ceasing to talk deeply with friends, afraid to cross the invisible lines where minds have closed. Tech giants monopolise our data in exchange for previously unimagined convenience. But they influence our opinions and fragment us into silos of hostility. Fear replaces trust in our public discourse, which cannot bode well for society. So, we must ask if the new moral dream will produce a better country.

Maybe a country is too big to think about; perhaps it is enough to imagine a local community sitting in our teashops or pubs, visiting the mosque or church, or when we eat together around the table. We must ask: what is the foundation of a better community?

Our moral imagination is the ability to conceive fruitful alternatives to present realities. Mine was awakened in that Czech pub. The hunger for a better country and thriving communities has stayed with me.

In an age where the call for justice is strong again, we should ask the question I asked my Palestinian friends: is our dream big enough?

This book is about the search for trust and trustworthiness, the meaning of goodness, and why it matters. It is not about moralism but about the possibilities and failures of love. It aims to arouse the moral imagination to the possibilities of the good life; to encourage the search for that better country.

Now let me invite you to a café somewhere in Central Europe to drink some coffee and explore the ideas with friends.

The café was often open in many cultures and continents. I have listened for nearly three decades, like a fly on the wall, to people whose lives and prospects have been very different. It has continually surprised me to hear our guests make similar observations about how they would like to be treated and their desires for a better country, regardless of culture, colour, class or creed. I suppose it is because we are human before anything else, and we all feel the longing for trust in our homes and society.

Let's join the Café Now and Not Yet...

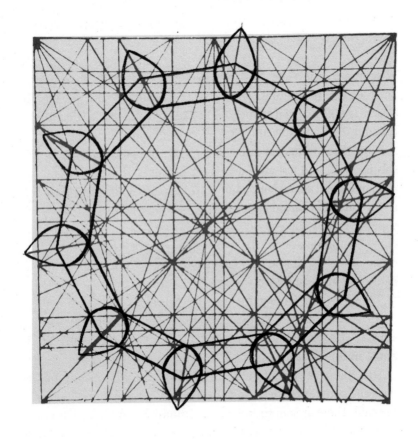

1

An Invitation to the Café Now and Not Yet

Welcome to the Café Now and Not Yet! The original owner, a philosopher by training, called it the 'Café Being and Becoming', which is still its legal name, but some patron, time out of mind, called it the Café Now and Not Yet, and the name stuck.

I am the doorkeeper and collector of tickets, because this is a special event and not an ordinary evening.

I have spent many happy hours reading, observing and thinking in the cafés of Central Europe. In Vienna, where the coffee can be expensive, they say you do not buy the coffee so much as rent the table. So, tonight, people have come in anticipation. The café has a menu of ideas to ignite our imagination as we think about our city. These evening events are always stimulating.

There is a hatstand by the door. Let me take your coat.

It's windy outside – rain streams down the large glass windows. I am glad you came; I hope it did not take long for you to travel from home in this weather.

Streetlight reflects off the damp cobblestones of the town square. A young couple are sheltering together in a shop doorway opposite the café. There are ten round tables, each with a candle and flowers, surrounded by five cane chairs. Take a seat and get to know others at your table. Feel the hum of conversation and laughter as we await the night's diversions, and other guests arrive.

The music is soft, and candlelight illuminates the faces of the guests, reflecting from an ornate and overbearing mirror – the taste of a previous generation. It hangs on the wall alongside old pictures of the city. People dressed in sepia hurrying to important business long forgotten. Newspapers hang on a rack, daily news from time immemorial.

The café is old and the tables are well worn. It has been here for as long as there have been memories of coffee. It has watched the automobile replace the horse and cart; mud, manure and the acid bite of horse pee exchanged for petrol fumes and tar. The café has seen men off to war and watched inflation price coffee out of reach. Customers used to chat as they read the news. These days, they are more often lost in their pocket icons, though they have turned them off tonight and put them in a basket on the counter.

In the centre of the room sits a sculpture on a low round table. A card beside it says 'The Invitation'. Ten bronze pillars, each about 25 cm high and 2.5 cm apart, rise in a circle from a heavy green marble base about 50 cm in diameter. The pillars appear sharp-edged like the clawed back of some disturbing fish from the outside. They are scarred and green and feel cold and harsh. On the inside, they are round like fingers and polished and reflect the candlelight. Not many people pay much attention to the sculpture, though a few stop to look.

The waiters are busy serving food and drink. The café has a fine cellar, and the Turkish chef is well known for his generous portions. People huddle around their tables, hesitant at first, exchanging small talk, shrugging off the weight of the day, getting into the mood.

The head waiter taps a glass. He is short and slightly round, and has long grey hair tied behind his neck. He is old-fashioned and very formal and is wearing a dinner jacket. People turn toward him and listen.

'Good evening. My name is Marco. We are delighted that you have joined us this evening.' He lights a small candle and places it in the centre of the sculpture as his colleagues dim the lights and blow out the other candles. It is rather dark as he says, 'I would like to draw your attention to this sculpture.'

We look at the sculpture in silent anticipation as our eyes adjust to the darkened room.

The candle flickers as the bronze pillars cast giant shadows onto the walls and across the high, white ceiling. Their ghoulish reflections dance off the mirror onto the window, evoking memories of ancient stone circles.

'What do you see?' Marco smiles and gestures to the sculpture.

Most are hesitant to speak at first, unfamiliar with works of art and unsure how to think about them. They do not want to seem foolish. You may be feeling this too.

A Finnish woman in a yellow dress, Anna-Liisa, is the first to speak. 'The bronze objects are in a circle. They look a bit like frogs' legs sticking up from a pond.'

Maria, who works at a local bank, observes, 'On the inside, they shine; the bronze is smooth, round and polished.'

There's a long pause, but Marco is in no hurry and lets the silence linger.

'They look a little bit like fingers on the inside,' says Samat, from central Asia.

'They look like claws on the outside, like a razor,' says Silvio from Brazil, who lives next door and often comes for breakfast. His hair is long and bound in a ponytail, and he wears a red shirt and a red-and-white-striped jacket. He has handed out a card that announces his design studio. 'They are green on the outside and splashed with acid.'

'I wouldn't want to meet them on a dark night!' Samat suggests, and there is a ripple of laughter.

'The candlelight reflects brightly off the bronze,' says Aaron, leaning in; he does not know it, but the candle also reflects in his dark eyes. He continues, 'The fingers are simultaneously ugly and beautiful, fearful and inviting.'

Anna-Liisa speaks again. 'Light reflects off each pillar to the others. All the fingers are visible in each finger, creating a kind of grid or matrix of light.'

'Where is the sculpture from, and who made it?' asks Beata from Bratislava.

'Liviu Mocan, a Romanian artist, created it,' replies Marco. 'It is called *The Invitation/Decalogue*. We chose it for the café because it reflects our desire to explore the possibility of a better life.'

'Who commissioned it?' asks Tibor, a journalist who has arrived late.

Marco replies, 'This is a model of a much larger work commissioned for the city of Geneva. In full scale, each finger is five metres high. When he set it up, the artist sat in the circle and said he felt almost blinded by the light of the sun as it reflected from finger to finger...

How does it make you feel?' Marco asks us.

'Conflicted,' Maria replies. 'It is beautiful but strange.'

Anna-Liisa thinks it is ugly – a risky statement, but you can feel people pause and then relax. They appreciate her honesty.

'It *is* offensive, and inviting at the same time. Can you feel the tension?' asks Marco. There is a sigh of relief. We can be honest and open. He will not be offended if we do not like the sculpture.

'Why is it called *The Invitation* when the green claws and the shadows are off-putting?' asks Silvio.

'What do *you* think?' Marco asks us all.

Silvio responds, 'On the inside, the fingers are inviting. I feel drawn into the warmth and light, like watching the fire glowing through the window as I approach home after a long walk in the snow.'

People are leaning forward from their chairs and call out.

'The pillars appear threatening on the outside,' Samat comments. 'Maybe they create a protective ring around the inner space.'

Marco suggests that we come up and feel it, look closely, and lift it. 'Feel the weight,' he says. A few courageous guests venture from their seats.

A bearded man in a dark formal suit, Ramone, feels the smooth surface, then tries to lift it, but it is too heavy. 'It is an immovable object,' he sighs. 'Some realities do not bend to our will!'

Maria makes a feeble attempt to lift it too, then she squats down and looks closely through the pillars. She wonders aloud what it would be like to sit inside. She runs her fingers over the sharp edges of the pillars and comments on how cool the marble base feels.

People speak freely. The sculpture appeals to the senses, with its hard edges and curved surfaces. Some find the sculpture inviting; something draws them to the centre. The inside is light, but heavy with meaning. The outside is flat, dark and two-dimensional; the flickering grey shadows feel chaotic, fragmented and hollow.

8

The shadows of the fingers loom above us on every wall. Marco speaks again. 'We become so used to the shadows that we barely notice them. But what is a shadow?'

We ponder the question. What do you think?

'Shadows are flat,' says Aaron. 'A two-dimensional projection of a three-dimensional reality.' As an architect, he is used to thinking about the impact of shadow.

Tibor says, 'They are a distortion, almost a misrepresentation, but they point to the real thing.'

'The closer you get to the real object, the darker the shadows become,' Marco adds. 'The mind plays tricks in the dark; the shadows seem more prominent than the pillars, but the pillars are more substantial. Life can be like that sometimes. The real hides in the illusion, the signified lost in the sign.'

The sculpture feels familiar, but no one can say why until Mehran from Iran recognises it in the logo on the menu. The sign also hangs over the door outside the café and is on the invitation people have received. They pick up their menus and look. No one has noticed the circle outlining the sculpture engraved on the door until now. It is strange how much information we process without it coming fully to the conscious mind. Did you notice it on the way into the chapter?

Marco asks what the sculpture might symbolise. Someone says, 'There are ten fingers.' No one has noticed this before.

'Is the number significant?' asks Tibor.

'Have you heard of the Decalogue?' says Marco. 'Each finger represents one of the *Deca Logoi*, in Greek, or "Ten Words".'[1]

'Do you mean the Ten Commandments?' someone asks.

'The word "commandment" can seriously mislead modern people,' Marco responds. 'You could translate it as "instruction", a less intimidating phrase to modern ears. What is your reaction when you hear the word "commandment" or "law"?' he asks. A quick word association reveals that we think of limits, restrictions, submission, punishment and loss of freedom. 'For that reason,' he says, 'I resisted the idea for the longest time; it is hard for people conditioned to think of obedience as servitude to understand it as a way of freedom. Then I remembered that I learned to enjoy playing the trumpet through submission to practice. But you have to want it.

'Then one time as I read the introduction to the Decalogue, "out of Egypt, out of the land of slavery", I heard an invitation to freedom and wondered if I was looking at an organising principle that would allow the enslaved people to stay free in their new country.'

Marco asks if anyone knows the Ten Words, and a few try to guess, but no one remembers. It is the sort of information you think you know but, when asked, discover that you do not. The audience tries to guess a little longer but must admit defeat. Perhaps you want to try – how many can you remember?

He continues. 'I began to see it as a framework for trust. If you are going to trust other people, it is wise to know the basis for their trustworthiness. Though we sometimes use the language of Good and Evil, it is a relic of a past that believed in a universe with a moral beginning. This belief has faded, because it is not justifiable in an impersonal universe of time, matter and chance. We think of goodness as "better or worse", "pleasure or pain", "being decent, equal or fair", categories that give little guidance or foundation for trusting relationships or the moderation of power.

'We want a category called evil because we see its fruit everywhere, but the idea of goodness raises questions of transcendence, which we are ill equipped to answer. Nevertheless, though we may find describing it difficult, we intuit that goodness matters. We feel it keenly when someone steals something, or someone is humiliated. We are angry and demand justice when violated. That demand comes from somewhere deep. It is easy to imagine *evil*, because the media deliver a daily diet of catastrophe and sadness. We recognise evil by the anxiety that surrounds it and how it turns us inward and separates us from each other when trust breaks. We know the tedious work to repair the damage and destruction left in its path.

'On the other hand, an environment of *goodness* enables a liberating self-forgetfulness that allows for the discovery of the fascinating world beyond us. But the good life is harder to describe.

We lose sight of what life could be. Just imagine eating a grey and gritty porridge day after day, year in year out, for breakfast, lunch and supper, spiced on special days with a bit of honey or maybe some cinnamon, while knowing nothing of the joys of French or Indian cooking. So, we must awaken our moral imagination to find greater possibilities. Then perhaps we can give our compliments to the chef.' Marco pauses. 'Talking of food, would anyone like something to eat or drink?'

A few people signal to the waiters, who silently and efficiently meet their needs with minimal disruption.

'Inside the circle,' Marco continues, pointing to the sculpture, 'there is freedom from behaviours and attitudes that destroy both love and freedom. One finger says *Do not murder*. It keeps the person with murderous intent outside but invites those who refuse to consider murder an option. The space inside is free of murder and, as we will discover, of all attitudes and actions that lead to it. What remains is life that can be lived to the full.'

He points to the sculpture. 'On the inside, there is the freedom to trust. Another finger says *Do not lie*. The confusion and waste that lies cause are not present inside the circle. Within the circle, people are free because they have a commitment to truth and a shared sense of reality. Only a fool trusts blindly; the Ten Words lay the foundation for trustworthiness, which in turn leads to greater openness and intimacy.

'Everyone, including those in authority, submits to it. The pillars humble us because they expose our need, and humility makes power safe. Those who would lie will not want to enter. The goodness of the place would make them uncomfortable, even unstable. Goodness takes time to get used to. On the outside, there is distrust and suspicion; everyone is distant. Power roams wildly and, without direction, rival wills fight and have no means of reconciliation. Eventually, power destroys those who abuse it. These old habits were necessary for the survival of the fittest in a world without purpose, but they are devoid of love.'

Marco gestures to the shadows. 'Feel the chaos and disorder, the quivering uncertainty of a two-dimensional world, the lifeless loneliness of shadows and darkness, but long for a richer three-dimensional fullness.' He pauses, and the café is quiet as we reflect in silence.

'Who is that?' John, from California, calls out suddenly. He points to a bronze figure of a man with a beard, looking up intensely into the middle of the circle. Unnoticed until now, he sits on a ledge inside one of the pillars. The man seems lost in his thoughts. More people gather around the sculpture to look at him. Some squat down and look at him through the pillars and then from above, like birds flying overhead.

Marco asks, 'What does the man see in his mind's eye, as he follows the light from one finger to the next? What is he thinking about? What would it be like to sit on the inside amid those glowing reflections? What does he allow into his circle? What does he exclude?'

'Who is the man?' asks Tibor.

'I am not sure,' replies Marco. 'There are several possibilities. It might be Moses, who first received the Ten Words. It might be you or me! It could be the ancient poet-king David, who once wrote that his delight was in the instruction of the Lord, and on his instruction he meditated day and night.[2] For a long time I wondered what he was seeing that I was not, because I couldn't delight in them at all. So I began to ask myself what he might be thinking about. Then I asked myself what would change if we all kept them. The light started to go on when I began to see the levels of trust we might have if we were all committed to them.

'In his songs, David said they were "more to be desired than gold… sweeter also than honey". Not usually an association you make with law unless you are a lawyer preparing the bill! So I decided to think about them until they tasted like honey and seemed as weighty as gold, as if this might be an interpretive principle. It was some time after that that I came across the sculpture.'

'Do you mean that the logo of the café is a recent addition?' asks Anna-Liisa.

'That is the strange thing,' says Marco. 'We used the logo for generations and had forgotten what it meant. When I saw the sculpture fit it perfectly, I began to explore the origins of the logo in the writings of the founder of the café.'

'How curious,' says Anna-Liisa, intrigued and puzzled.

Marco continues, 'I was thinking about them some years ago while sitting on an early morning bus on the way to an airport. I was watching the red sunrise through the autumn fog. Then, as the bus weaved its way through the traffic, I suddenly realised that I was looking at the ball of flame that would burn the retinas of anyone who stared at it later in the day. Yet it was possible to look directly at it at dawn and dusk. It occurred to me that the Decalogue is a bit like that; the longer you look at it, the brighter it becomes. As if you were looking at the edges of the mind of God in the cool of the day. As the sun rises, the contours of goodness become more precise, and the more aware you are of the gap between desire and reality, or being and becoming.

'There is nothing sunny about the words "Do not murder". But things heat up when you include everything that leads to murder; the slow-burning hatred, the inflamed and irrational imagination that distorts reality, petty acts of revenge and tedious self-justification, gossip and slander and a culture that talks of cancelling another human. I want a society that refuses murder, but the brighter light exposes hidden attitudes that lurk in the shadows of my wounded soul. Harbour murderous thoughts and you will exclude yourself from the circle and remain in the shadows. Destructive attitudes melt like ice in the full glare of the light. It is a choice between trust and freedom or suspicion and chaos. The vision awakens desire and exposes limits at the same time.' He pauses for everyone to catch up with him. 'Maybe the rough edges of the fingers symbolise the unbending aspect of goodness. You can't have a little bit of murder. It cannot change if it is to remain good. The light uncovers the darker intentions of the heart and requires us to leave them behind.'

Silvio sighs. 'They fill me with both longing and fear. I feel like I may enter, but not on my terms. I must want what I find there.'

Ramone has been thinking for a while and speaks up. 'It has occurred to me several times this evening that while each *word* would change a great deal, it is the sum of them that makes a difference, and it is much greater than the parts.'

'I agree,' says Marco. 'Each pillar and gap is unique, but they stem from a common mind. I think that they are a description of other-centred love.'

Marco pauses for us to take hold of what he says. 'Love has two sides; it excludes some acts and includes others. The Ten Words are the measure of love, describing its boundaries; what it includes and excludes. Loving people are generous towards those they love without a second thought and never think of stealing from them. The Ten Words act as guardians to benefit and protect the community and each person in it. The more one moves to the centre of the circle, the greater the love and trust, the more the protective guard can be relaxed. There is freedom to turn to more fruitful preoccupations. The inside is infinitely larger than the outside. Three-dimensional space is much larger than the shadows. What is sad and surprising in moral discussion is how often we want to play at the edge of the circle, to see how much we can get away with.'

'How did they get such a negative reputation?' asks Samat.

Marco thinks for a moment. 'I am not sure; I suppose the view from outside *is* negative, and exclusion often leads to envy, although in this case people exclude themselves by choice. On the other hand, perhaps the vision of the good life became a set of rules. Blind obedience replaced desire and love. It is a bit like having ice cream because you don't want your sister to have it, rather than enjoying it for its own sake. The rules became an end in themselves, no longer pointing to the better country beyond them. We are self-justifying and want to be right. For that reason, people gradually lowered the standard to reach it, but in doing so they lost the wonder. Goodness became a burden and lost its joy.'

The onlookers who have been standing around the sculpture begin to sit down. Some truths can be discovered by thought alone, but others must be experienced before their meaning becomes clear. A waiter turns up the lights a little and relights the candles on the tables, and the shadows fade.

Marco gestures to three musicians – a violinist, a cellist and a guitarist – who come out and play for us. The music concentrates and clears our minds. The music is a selection from the Goldberg Variations by Bach. The rain still runs down the sheets of glass, and the streetlights still shudder in the storm outside. Time for quiet reflection is a rare gift in our times.

As the musicians leave the room, Marco introduces Nadia, who is tall and wears a dark formal dress and will lead us through this part of the evening.

She speaks graciously but with conviction. 'Imagine you were constructing a city in which everyone was committed to seeking the good life. It is a gated city. Before anyone can come in, they must commit to the life you are going to describe tonight.'

Anna-Liisa speaks again. 'Wouldn't that be too judgemental or exclusive?'

'An important observation,' says Nadia. 'When you order tea, you would not expect the waiter to bring you coffee. Yet there are many kinds of tea. The circle that defines tea must have space for everything that is tea. It must not be so tight that there is no freedom, but not everything is tea. The definition must not be so broad as to be meaningless.' She pauses for thought. 'And without judgement, it would be a very unforgiving city; without judgement, there would be nothing to forgive. But we should include ourselves in the circle of judgement.'

'Wouldn't it make us all the same?' asks Ramone.

Nadia pauses and then responds, 'The earth, the sun and rain are necessary to every tree and plant, but each type of seed is unique. Perhaps we should think of our moral choices as the quality of the soil which makes everything else fruitful.' She continues, 'What you are about to describe should come from your desires. Remember, our activity is not about moralism but about the possibilities and failures of loving others.'

She explains the activity. 'On the back of the menu on your table you will find a text.' There is a shuffling of papers, and people look over their neighbours' shoulders to read. Someone drops a pencil on the floor. There is laughter and an apology.

What would change economically, sociologically and psychologically or, more practically, what difference would it make financially, in how we lived together and how we felt about ourselves, if everyone, everywhere agreed to . . . The papers on each table are slightly different and stem from the Decalogue. One table will discuss theft and generosity; another table murder and life-giving actions. Others will think about truth-telling and lying. Each table has a different area of life that spans from negative to positive behaviour.

'Please take notes, and in about forty minutes we will share what we have discovered with other groups,' Nadia adds. 'Of course, at one level it is a ridiculous question. You may find feelings of cynicism stirring in you,' she warns. 'The more you go into the detail, the stronger those feelings might become. We fear disappointment, and imagining something good when you know you cannot achieve it might seem like an exercise in futility. However, a clear vision gives direction.'

She tells us that we must not think narrowly about the question, but widely, imagining and exploring logical connections. 'What would change if we excluded all the attitudes and steps that lead up to the final violation? So not just the act of murder or even the sharpening of the knife –' she stabs the air, smiling with a glint in her eye – 'but the petty acts of hatred, the gossip and slander, that went by, barely noticed for many years before that dark night.' The room becomes thoughtful.

'That is the dark side of the argument. But we must not stop there,' she continues. 'We must explore the light and imagine positive behaviours – if we forbid murder, what are we promoting?'

It takes time for the conversation to get started. The imagination is a rusty tool, not often exercised in this way.

Anna-Liisa has taken charge at table eight. She organises paper and a pen for notes, draws three columns, and writes *Economic*, *Sociological* and *Psychological* in neat handwriting at the top. A man with a bright bow tie asks for a definition. What would the city look like if we all agreed not to steal anything? Would life be better or worse?

Someone pulls keys from his pocket. 'Would we need these?' he asks. Someone else raises the problem of unemployment if we no longer need keys.

The question is more complicated than at first glance. The inventory soon includes keys, locks, safes, window bars, chains, miles of CCTV cable and cameras, the PINs we must remember, passwords, theft insurance, and all the other things that exist for no other reason than because we steal from each other.

Anna-Liisa describes the woes of a recent robbery and how the insurance company suddenly wanted purchase receipts long discarded. She complains about how long the process took and the sense of violation.

The waiters circulate, bringing tea and cakes here, wine and cheese there. Someone asks for water, another for a cognac.

There is a ripple of laughter as table seven begin a discussion about the permanence of relationships. There are no neat lines; the paper starts to look like an untidy field, scribble everywhere. The debate is more spontaneous, passionate and less systematic.

What is love, and what are the benefits of faithful love? Why shouldn't one follow one's heart regardless of the consequences to others?

Someone remembers there is a difference between envy and jealousy, but they cannot remember what. Someone else spills their drink, and a waiter hurries to repair the damage.

The temperature is warming up at table eight, and the discussion is lively; an argument has broken out about the causes of theft. It follows predictable lines: laziness and the benefits of hard work, application, poor education and lack of opportunity. The conversation is abstract, a sign they find imagining the outcomes difficult. Someone in the group calls them to order, and they get back to the task of being practical.

Some people are more interested in technical issues, like the energy used to design keys and locks, mining and smelting the iron. Why not make a list yourself? Is it possible to imagine a society where lock and key would be unnecessary?

Aaron, the architect, wears a black turtleneck jumper and tips back his chair; he has distanced himself slightly from the table and is withdrawing mentally. I have seen that sceptical look many times. He is sceptical of the exercise, unsure of committing himself. Why dream of something impossible? His imagination is practical, and he is afraid of this more hopeful kind; it is a dangerous and unfamiliar tool he abandoned in childhood.

He is wise to question and doubt. We should not be gullible. But what if he is so afraid of disappointment that he has lost the capacity to dream or hope? What if he has become cynical? His friends try to draw him in. He is practical, down to earth, he says. He must deal with realities.

But what if our present idea of reality is the problem? What if we have mistaken *average* and *normal* – the sum of what we can all tolerate in poor behaviour from each other – for a norm that could lead to a better country? 'Normal' has two meanings. It can mean what is average in our behaviour, or a norm that all are measured by – like the weight that you measure your vegetables by, an external measure that should be the same for everyone.

Observe Aaron. In a moment some idea will spark his interest and he will re-engage. He will not be able to stop himself. He will speak and then laugh and then withdraw again for a while. He cares deeply and is intrigued, but life has disappointed him, and he is afraid to dream. Sometimes, when two people like him are at a table, they feed and reinforce each other's prejudices.

Table nine are deep in a discussion about truth-telling and lies. Leia, a doctor, wonders if a social or white lie is a lie at all. 'Do you like my dress?' she asks, tempting anyone to tell her the truth. She seems a little overbearing and might be fishing for a compliment.

Does truth-telling include all truth? Is withholding truth the same as a lie? They have already talked about hiding Jews from Nazis and other, for them, abstract ideas. Someone points out that not even God tells all the truth.

Imagine not needing a passport because everyone told the truth, and you could trust everyone's word. This thought opens Pandora's box. Beata, the group scribe, writes a long list of the documentation needed in modern life to prove the validity of our words.

'Imagine the time we would save and the levels of trust we could have if everyone told the truth,' says Beata.

'An empty word is as useful as an empty glass,' her husband says, signalling to the waiter.

My mind drifts back to another café, somewhere in Eastern Europe, where some politicians were exploring these issues. The party ideologist, a passionate man, suddenly jumped up, slammed his fist on the table and said, 'This could be our manifesto.' He had seen the potential of a trusting community. As the discussion continued, and we turned to ideas about truth-telling, his head fell and he spoke with sadness. 'In our country, not telling lies would be impossible.' He spoke truthfully, and not only for his country.

Who of us has the power to live up to such demanding standards? But without a map, how do you know which direction to take? Don't we all wrestle with the same moral weakness as my politician friends? But the ideals describe loving acts and help us imagine how we want to live.

Listen in on table five. They are talking about being reconciled to historical opponents – always a challenging theme, especially in Central Europe, which has known so much conflict and bears the weight of so much unreconciled history. What would change economically if our armies did not go to war to support the greater powers surrounding us?

Waiters move silently among the tables, fill orders, take away used tableware, and make sure we have what we need. The rain taps on the window, and the streetlights cast strange shadows as they sway in the wind.

Table two, near the window, have the topic of deceptive images. They sit quietly; everyone is deep in their thoughts and feeling a bit lost. You may be too. What would change economically in society if there were no deceptive images? Maria suggests that a forged banknote might be a deceptive image with economic consequences. She means it as a joke, but the ball has begun to roll and is gathering pace.

'What about the images in our minds?' asks Silvio. 'Images interest me. As an artist, the imagination is a tool of my trade. I earn my living by speaking to the pictorial language in people's minds.'

Soon they are talking about the beauty of non-verbal language. The conversation turns to how easily we project fear and prejudices onto one another.

'I want to be taken seriously for who I am and not pre-judged because of how I look,' says Silvio. 'When I came in I did not know what to expect as this is my first event here, and I imagined something quite different.'

'Are you disappointed?' asks Mehran, who often attends these discussion evenings.

'Not at all. I am rather relieved. I thought we might have to listen to a lecture.'

'When you arrived at the café, you didn't know the rest of us. How did you feel?' asks Mehran.

'Apprehensive,' replies Silvio. 'I am often tempted to assume people have feelings based on my experience, which has nothing to do with them.' We all know what he means, though few have previously put it into words.

At table three, they are talking about words and language, and the importance of good communication.

'Do we want to commit to our language in the new city?' asks Samat.

'What do you mean?' asks Tibor.

'Exactly the right question,' replies Samat. 'I want people to ask about meaning and work towards understanding each other.' He is in his last year of school, but is wise for his age.

'You want them to tell the truth?' Marta has been silent, but finally speaks up.

'I do want that, but that is not what I mean here. I want people to know what they mean and mean what they say,' says Samat. 'What would happen if we took our language seriously; if every word was full with meaning?'

'It would be a bit intense,' says Marta.

'Yes, I don't mean that every conversation should be deadly serious or without humour, but that we would think about the meaning of our words,' says Samat. 'I read somewhere that most of our disagreements are merely confusion and misunderstandings, and not disagreements at all. When we speak, we have so many hidden assumptions. In our city, we should commit to working towards a shared understanding of them.'

The conversation is loud, and there is a lot of serious reflection amid the laughter and banter. The lists are growing longer as we write down our thoughts. The room feels full of life. Nadia claps her hands to draw our conversations to a close, and the head waiter, Marco, stands in the centre. A few of us stop talking and look at him; others are too deep in conversation to hear.

Marco rings a small bell that pierces the din, and we give him our attention. 'I hope you are enjoying thinking about your new city,' he says as he invites representatives from each table to share their main ideas. As the evening draws to a close he thanks Nadia for her contribution, and the guests clap to express their appreciation. Waiters appear and begin to refresh drinks.

At the end of every gathering, people ask if the ideas discussed in the café are written down anywhere. This book summarises our guests' reflections and some of my own, and I hope they are a stimulus for yours. You will not agree with all of them, nor should you.

I think this matrix of ten interlocking instructions supplies the scaffolding for freedom and enables trusting relationships. I use it as a starting point to explore our current practices, and a framework to understand where we might improve.[3] I would not claim to have fully answered my questions about a better country. I hope these reflections open a door to a larger vision for the good life, and will help you imagine a better world, an alternative *relational* vision, when so many people feel short-changed by the promises of the modern world.

Beyond the Café

In the next chapter, we will explore themes that often occur in discussions about the search for a better country. They will reappear throughout the book and explain why goodness matters. They include the following:

- The abuse of power – how can we exercise dominion over ourselves without dominating other people?
- The tension between our responsibilities for communal well-being and personal freedoms.
- How to relate to others with meaning and integrity, and reduce loneliness and fragmentation.
- The place of trust and trustworthiness in getting to know other people.

These are large questions and I have used personal experiences to unpack and highlight their importance, so let me tell you a little about my journey…

2

My Search for a Better Country

Curiosity and adventure drew me to Central Europe. The Cold War was in full swing, and the Iron Curtain was just thirty miles from where I lived in Vienna, Austria. I crossed often and became friends with people denied the right to read widely, associate freely or travel where they wanted, and I threw myself into helping them. I was angry at the systemic injustice and the humiliation they endured.

People suspected strangers. Trust was hard work, but it was like gold when found. One way the state abused its power was by tightly controlling the production and distribution of printed material. Part of our work was to find people willing to write, translate and distribute books illegally. When the security forces uncovered one distribution network in the Balkans, people were arrested and imprisoned, at least one died and another was exiled. Our task was to find people willing to take their place – ordinary men and women with courage, determination and a love of words and ideas. Sometimes, like me, they were afraid; courage is an unstable virtue.

Rebuilding the network required many visits to people in the following years, mapping out who knew whom, discerning who could be trusted. It involved lots of listening, observing, building trust, triangulating, hesitation and doubt. Confidence is more appropriate than certainty in human relationships, and mistakes have consequences. We learned that truth and trust are not abstractions.

My questions about a better country often arose when driving for long hours across the dusty plains and gentle hills of Central Europe. In the early evenings, as the sun was setting, I was often overcome by a deep melancholy, which I did not realise was a yearning for home.

The superficial reason for it was simple enough. When I was growing up, my family had moved from England to Malta as the sun was finally setting on the British empire. When we left England I was a child, and the fracture was barely discernible. Returning to the UK years later, it had grown into a gulf of alienation. As a child of empire, I returned as a stranger to a country I did not recognise. The question about a better country and the search for home were two sides of a coin. I spent a year wandering, searching for a self and home I could not find in a country I did not understand.

After a summer in Central Europe, I spent a year on a ship in the Mediterranean. I sat in mosques in Istanbul, listening to men discussing their lives and faith; I enjoyed wine and olives with Ukrainian sailors on their ship in Alexandria while listening to their experience of Soviet life. They said it was best not to overthink, because too much thinking might lead to losing the freedom to travel.

Journalists in the Slovak countryside taught me the cost of freedom of speech. They were courageous men and women forced into common labour because of their involvement in the Prague Spring of 1968.[1]

Volga-Germans from Russia helped heal my cynicism about communal life in their community. They showed me what it means to be conscious as a communal being, and challenged my individualism.

I discovered that simple joys are often the best while eating sunflower seeds and watching the World Cup in Bulgaria with friends I love. Then there were Italian communists preparing for a revolution that never quite came, and Polish priests who were more Buddhist than Catholic.

I learned to hold my categories lightly, listen through the words to the heart, and that if you can laugh at another person's point of view, culture or beliefs, you have probably misunderstood them.

Travel gives insight into life through the experience of others. Empathy with an alien perspective takes time and the examination of personal assumptions. We must step beyond the familiar into strange traditions and alternative views of history and perceptions of reality to listen to people with whom we might otherwise disagree.

The Bible, which I first read on a beach in Sicily, was also a foreign country. Intuition told me it spoke of something true. It described my hunger for something I could not articulate, as Sartre, Camus and Hesse described in their novels how I was feeling. I was a child of my time and read everything through the subjective and existentialist lens common in those days. It was years before I could read it without imposing meanings I needed to hear and attend to whispers from beyond time in its ancient texts.

It is hard work to see beyond the borders of your personal experience or cultural horizons and harder still to forget the call of your mother tongue. The view-from-elsewhere is achievable, but never entirely, and it comes at a costly price. Those who travel never wholly lose their accent, but neither can they fully come home.

If you ask most people what they really want, they may talk first about wealth and success, but they will soon talk about the quality of their relationships, because this is where we find much of our meaning. No one likes being bullied or humiliated, or when power is abused. They want some freedom to be themselves, but will compromise for the sake of love.

Some parts of life are so familiar we take them for granted. The following areas may be familiar to you, although like me you may rarely have had time or reason to ponder them. I have tried to organise them logically, but with limited success. Life is multi-layered and does not always submit easily to linear descriptions. While we live in time and think in sequence, we experience life at many levels simultaneously.

In this section I will raise many questions I hope to address later in the book. I have included panels and extensive endnotes for those interested in thinking further.

Communal or Individual Trust

Teg-Chin Go came from Asia. I first met him while working on a ship in the Mediterranean. When we docked in Malta, we walked across the island I knew so well. As we walked, our conversation turned to women. He asked, 'How do people in the West find a wife?' He was new to our confusing ways, so I explained our dating rituals. He grew pale and was visibly shocked. 'But how do you trust yourself to choose?' he gasped.

Now it was my turn to be confused, so I returned the question. 'How will you find a wife?'

'I won't,' he replied. 'My parents will find me a wife.'

'But how do you trust your parents?' I asked, thinking of the somewhat ambiguous relationship I had with mine.

He said, 'My parents know me better than I do; they will choose a good match, someone suitable from our village. They know the histories of the good families. They love me; they will not choose someone I do not like.'

Here were two worlds colliding. My individualism and his communalism. Who was right? Back then, conditioned by my individualistic tradition, I was completely unaware of a communal consciousness. His family came from a village where people knew one another and each other's history and had a memory that spanned generations. I lived in a Western world that had exchanged such knowledge for progress, mobility and increasing anonymity.[2] It was years before I learned the strengths and weaknesses of both. The conversation exposed assumptions I did not know I had and awakened longings about parental relationships that seemed impossible to reach.

Individualism and Communalism

Historically, humans lived in multi-generational communities that were essential for survival and protection. Communal memory and historical narrative gave a sense of identity. Here everyone knew everyone's history and business. Loyalty tied people to specific locations, habits and traditions. Here they had a sense of belonging and a sense of home, somewhere to be from and a place to return to. One should not romanticise this communal consciousness; life was hard and justice could be rough. The community was usually held together by one powerful and dominant personality. They had to iron out relational differences, or conflict would weaken the community. Conformity was the price of inclusion and came at the cost of personal uniqueness.

Mechanisation and technology have made us less dependent on each other for survival. Mobility has fragmented communal life and loyalties; we live, work and play in separate locations, often with different people. Responsibilities once met less efficiently but more relationally in the local community or by the family are met increasingly by the state, which takes more and more authority over mediating institutions like the family, schools, clubs, churches and charities. The impersonal and anonymous nature of this support, received by right in a society that has become increasingly atomised, does not encourage the rituals of negotiation or gratitude that are important for the development of the local community. It is possibly more efficient, but requires and develops less character.

Modern 'communities' tend to be silos of agreement around promoting and defending specific points of view. They are less relational, though no doubt some also provide meaningful friendship. Some of these new communities react aggressively to dissident opinions. Compliance is essential, but freedom of thought is not, which raises questions about how such groups manage internal differences. Is it possible to question communal assumptions without fear that the community will collapse? Has communion become conformity? It is a dilemma that an appeal to human rights cannot solve. These are now in conflict and have multiplied to the point of meaninglessness.

Pure individualism is the loneliest of ideals and impossible in practice. I work in a study centre where young people from many cultures come to think about life. In recent years I have met people who are no longer individualistic but hyper-individualistic. External connections to family, geographic location and history have become increasingly thin; their reference points come less from the shared reality of the external world and more from their internal experience. Physical intimacy has become a biological need to be satisfied rather than the fruit of a loving relationship. What remains is a crisis of identity, feelings of anonymity, social anxiety and a longing for community. However, after several generations of individualism, we have lost the knowledge of the rules of communal engagement, and few understand the costly price of home and life in long-term community.

Changing Consciousness – Hyper-Individualism

A shift in consciousness is beginning to emerge in a young generation, from individualism to hyper-individualism. My assertions come from observations I have made among the young people with whom I work. The transition is nuanced and uneven. This description is somewhat black and white for clarity.

While individualists distinguish themselves from their original community, a significant connection to the community remains. Even though the individual is highly mobile, the memory of historical, geographical and familial ties is strong enough to give a sense of identity and belonging.

As the gap between the individual and the community widens, these external reference points become increasingly thin. Long-term relationships are less common, there is less self-knowledge and roots are less stable. As life is increasingly mediated through digital technology, they have an increased sense of rootlessness and malleability of identity. Internal reference points of feeling, intuition and imagination take precedence over history, location or biological reality.

John from California is indistinguishable from Harry from London and Anne from Singapore. They are lovely, friendly people from everywhere and nowhere. They will move at the drop of a hat and have the same facade and aspirations. They know one another by first names; their last names carry the baggage of history. For them, the family does not fit the narrative – such relationships are inescapably demanding and even hostile. The hyper-individual is cynical of history and ill-equipped for the complexities of relationship. In their early 20s this feels like freedom, but in the longer term it becomes a prison of subjectivity, isolation and disorientation.

Not questioning the materialistic and naturalist narrative they are taught, the hyper-individualist intuits that life has limited meaning. If they exist through random processes, then history has little value and the future promises cold hope. Their emphasis turns, quite reasonably, to the experience of the present moment. This is something, at least, they can be sure of. Pleasure and pain become the matrix through which they validate their experience and set their moral compass. The technological society can produce distractions and stimuli that simulate the feedback of relationships. It is possible to avoid the pain of dislocation for a long time.

The hyper-individualist has strong moral feelings and passions but no framework of thought, and limited knowledge of the history of ideas or human experience, from which to evaluate solutions. They are suspicious of external authority or truth claims, but know and trust their personal experience because they feel it. Truth is equated to authenticity and defined as faithfulness to those feelings.

Identity is no longer something to be discovered, but something to be created. It is infinitely malleable, but emotionally exhausting to maintain in ways that assure acceptance.

As the logical and relational connections between their internal and external worlds are severed, an increasingly closed and subjective experience of the self replaces the open experience of life beyond the self in the wider world. This prison of subjectivity hinders the discovery of the self, because the question 'Who am I?' is commonly answered partially by the external voices of friends, relations and colleagues, who see and experience the person in ways they themselves cannot.

Pure subjectivity has severe consequences; for example, having replaced the old binary of male and female in order to explain how life feels, the new understanding creates a new binary between biology and psychology, which is like being asked to choose between the H_2 and the O when offered water. Something that should be unified, in this case psychology and physiology, has become fragmented. The rupture is painful and disorienting.

Feeling isolation, people seek narratives, which often mirror the old religions, to explain their feelings. When, out of loneliness, they tire of extreme individualism, they idealise communalism and look to political solutions for what are essentially relational problems.

In its isolation, the new self becomes painfully lonely, unstable and introverted. Questions of belonging and identity remain unanswered, because the necessary external reference points of history and location are missing. If the person is narcissistic, it is the unintentional narcissism of one without help to connect to the external reference points of history and place, or help to develop an interest in the world around them.

In 1989, when the Iron Curtain collapsed, there was little time for reflection in the rush of revolution. Loyalties were tested; friends who previously had time for each other were soon too busy with new challenges.[3] In their haste to join 'the West', I wondered if they were not throwing out the cultural baby of community and relationship with the bathwater of that failed political and economic theory.

The communist period in Central Europe showed that an over-emphasis on the communal could crush the personal. But in the Western world, a growing individualism has led to a crisis of loneliness and identity.[4] Neither provides an adequate framework to describe or answer human needs.

Is there a moral framework in which relationships can be maintained, personal agency exercised and power shared, without one dominant will that crushes all others? How can the communal and personal be held in a healthy tension that benefits both, respecting each person's uniqueness *and* the common good? The question is essential to the search for a better country.

Trust, Meaning and Relationship

Meaningful relationships need a foundation of trust, and trust requires trustworthiness. Whatever goodness is, it must describe the basis of trustworthiness necessary to build and sustain trust. A lack of trust leads to impoverished relationships.

When my mother fell ill in her old age, I was beside her hospital bed. We lived in Central Europe and I had travelled widely that year, so the chances of being with her were slim. However, my wife and I happened to be in town for a wedding. The church car park was packed, so I left my wife there and parked outside my parents' house a few streets away. Just as I pulled up, my father appeared at the front door in great distress. My mother had collapsed, and he was beside himself with worry. So I went in and helped them. It was a gloriously sunny day, perfect for a wedding, but there are no good days to die.

The ambulance took hours to arrive, and after examination the hospital told us she should stay overnight. Then, at 3 a.m., we received a call from the hospital and rushed over. The doctor said they could do nothing, as she would not survive an operation. When I told my mother, she prayed and thanked God for her life and family. Then she spent time alone with my father. Who knows how, in those hurried moments, they drew the curtain on sixty years of friendship and love? She then surprised me by asking for a phone and called as many of her children, grandchildren and other friends as she could reach, and commended them to the God she soon expected to meet. Other people were the focus of her life. It was, to me, a beautiful death, as much as any death can be – not all deaths are. My mother taught me how to die, just as she had shown me how to live. She faced dying with the courage and fierce tenacity with which she had confronted all of life's challenges. Encounters with my mother were always meaningful. She met death knowing her life had a purpose, meaning and, above all, relationships.

Perhaps you see death as biological, reflecting more materialist assumptions – a heart no longer beating or an absence of brainwaves – but these signs merely point to the absence of life. The

31

signs have been confused with what they point to. We are much more than the sum of our physical parts and biological functions. Instead, death is about separation. Someone once present is now absent. The severance of a relationship leads to a loss of meaning, and for this reason grief involves feelings of meaninglessness. Those who knew my mother sensed a loss of meaning in their own lives. Her death went beyond her to something dying in them. Something unique to her was missing in us.

Relationships are essential for our mental health and development. We gain self-knowledge through honest interaction with other people, who help us learn how other people experience us. They draw more out of us than we could on our own. Our personhood is dependent on other people.

Trusting relationships also allow us to test our experience against the reality outside. For example, if Mrs Jones trusts me, she might tell me if Mr Jones is being rude because he dislikes me or because he is just having a bad day.

Trust and Integrating the Fragments

As we wandered through the town on the day after my mother's death, people were out shopping and about their business. Stunned in the suddenness of unfathomable grief, my father wondered why the world went on as if nothing had changed. The cluster of artifacts – her glasses, the crossword unfinished on the arm of her chair, her tube of hand cream, recipes in her handwriting – had been woven together by the common thread of her existence. Now they were fragments without a centre. They had been hers, but now she was absent. There was no one to give them meaning. There was no universal reference point to make sense of the particulars of the objects she had left behind.

Is this, I wondered, the human condition without connection to the source of existence – to the personal and infinite being some people call God?

I cannot know what you believe about absolute reality; if your universe is empty, impersonal and without meaning or not. Mine is not, but coming to believe this has not been easy or automatic. Having tried to live with the belief that the universe is meaningless, I was faced with the need to make sense of a life that includes death. The need for the universe to have an infinite and personal being behind it – one who makes sense of all the particulars and gives them meaning – has been a strong argument, to my mind.

On grey Saturday afternoons in my London childhood, we would visit my parents' friends. Our host would give me an old plastic bag full of dismembered alarm clocks to keep me entertained while the adults discussed politics with one eye on the football scores. The long-unwound springs, brass cogwheels, bells and clock faces were fascinating, but my six-year-old mind could not put the fragments together. I knew they were parts of alarm clocks because I had seen a working one. But where could I find a plan or map that made sense of the parts? My life has sometimes felt like broken clocks, and I see from stories in the media that I am not alone.

Whatever you think of God – a fundamental truth, a useful fiction or a dangerous lie – it's undeniable that the death of belief in a transcendent being at the centre of Western culture has left us with profound fragmentation.

We discover the fragments in our search for authenticity, the sense that we do not measure up to our own standards. They are behind what some people call alienation, that experience that life has no meaning, or when we look for integrity in people to whom we relate.

We experience the fragments in our dysfunctions: in our broken relationships and the struggle between chaos and control, impulse and order, the ideal and the real, and in emotions that loom too large or are frozen shut. They show up in moments of loneliness, envy, misunderstanding, defensiveness and disconnection. We feel their sharp edges when we lose our sense of direction and feel worthless. They appear in the relentless self-justifications of a conscience that allows no peace, or in restless nights and an anxious mind unable to switch off, or in the strange distortions of the imagination. They appear when our biology and psychology feel at odds with each other. They show up in our psychoses, phobias and prejudices, in the terror between shame and exposure, or in the gaps between belief and behaviour.

We numb them with our addictions, be they socially acceptable or not. Think of the wealthy woman whose irrational fear of poverty keeps her working late every night even though she has more than enough money for two lifetimes, or the addict hiding in the alley, trembling for his next hit.

Society searches relentlessly for norms around which to organise the fragments, shuffling the deck time and again, hoping for the golden hand. We know there is something better if only we could see it. Did you ever hear a politician say, 'Vote for me. Things are as good as they can get,' or an advertiser proclaim, 'This product will add no value and do nothing for you'? Though many have promised and tried, no political system left, right, centre or periphery, cosmopolitan or provincial, has ever put the clock back together. And yet we *can* imagine a better life; we long for integration, beauty, meaning and relationships of trust.

Do the fragments point to something that was once whole?[5]

Do the glass shards on the floor point to a window that once kept out the wind?

My desire for home and a better country made me wonder if the fragments of our relationships point to the possibility of meaning, trust and love from which we have departed and to which we might return.

Trust and Personal Knowledge

Students arriving for the first time at the study centre and community in the rambling manor house where I have a study often feel the growl of apprehension in their stomachs as they knock on the old wooden door. *What is this place? How will I be received?*

For my part, on the other side of the door, I do not know them. *Who are they? How will our time together be?*

Three months later, we are saying goodbye like old friends. Something has changed. Knowledge has replaced ignorance and has begun to grow into trust.

I have white hair, carry too much weight and remind some students of their fathers. I see their hesitancy and cautious eyes. We must dance for a while until we find our rhythm, a ritual that may take weeks until they see me for who I am through the fog of their projections. I must also examine my prejudices. I must be respectful and not overwhelm them or make them feel foolish. I must listen and not assume I know their thoughts. Nor must I give my prejudices free rein to impose some judgement on them; each person must be a blank page on which they are free to write their story at their pace. I must offer an unconditional welcome, a hospitality of heart. None of this is easy or automatic.

Trust grows in a virtuous spiral: the door of the heart cracks open; a step forward, a step back; a little faith in the other's good intentions until we learn we can safely reveal thoughts, feelings, emotions, memories, hopes and desires. Revelations of this sort are risky; will we be respected or mocked? The evidence is rarely exhaustive, and vulnerability can feel unpleasant.

Knowledge gained through revelation is more tentative and has different rules from the scientific knowledge modern people prefer, but it is nevertheless real knowledge. Scan my brain with the latest technology and you will learn *about* me, but you will not *know* me. There is no other meaningful way apart from self-revelation for humans to get to know one another. Trust is the oil of good communication, which is the basis of such knowledge. Without it, relationships become polite fiction, the joy runs out of life, and loneliness becomes inevitable with all its psychological disorientation.

I read somewhere the story of a father who, aware of the troubles his son would endure in life, wanted to teach him a lesson in trust and courage. So he took his son into the hallway and placed him on the second step of the staircase. Then he said, 'Jump – I will catch you.' The boy was afraid, but he jumped and his father caught him. 'Well done,' he said, and the boy laughed. So he placed him on the fourth stair and said, 'Trust me. I will catch you.' Now the boy was shaking, but trusted his father, as children naturally do, and he jumped. Then, as his father caught him, he threw his head back and laughed loudly with relief. His father put him on the next step. The boy trembled, then jumped, but this time the father stepped back. The boy screamed and fell. He was shaking, angry and hurt. Then, as he picked himself up, bruised and confused, his father said, 'Let this teach you, my son, trust no one.'[6] History had taught him to be cautious.

When I first heard it, the story made me angry. Later it made me sad. Why should a father have to break the bond that love has woven? Little children lift hands of earnest expectation for others to receive them, until they learn through disappointment that they cannot always trust others. We should weep at this reality. People who cannot discern trustworthiness become isolated and lonely, but too much blind faith leads to sorrow and disappointment. The wise parent must teach their child to appraise and negotiate trustworthiness, although perhaps not as painfully as in the story.

The abuse of power, or betrayal, quickly crushes trust. When trust is broken, we feel the pain of hurt and hate, rage and revenge; we erect protective barriers of prejudice and call for justice. We may blame someone else, society, structures or systems for our moral lapses, but that is rarely the whole picture.

If humans are as good as some traditions would want us to believe, why must we lose our childhood trust? And why must trust be established with every new encounter?[7] Shockingly, we remember the abuse of trust in the Holocaust: 'Take your suitcase. You are going to farm in the east...' Just enough crumbs of hope to leave the door of doubt open until it is shut for ever in the gas shower and the furnace. Humans want to believe the best; we turn from evil in denial, we trust blindly, hoping against hope that our *normal* will be preserved. We should not be naive. Trust without a commonly agreed foundation is dangerous.

Trust matures like a fine wine and is costly to preserve; to drink deeply of it is to taste paradise. A better country must be one where the rivers of trust run deep because people are trustworthy, but the ideal arouses a cynicism that reveals the deep wounds in our fragmented minds.

On what foundation can trust be universally established? What virtues are essential to it? What external code might make trust easier and provide the measure to show when trust is breached?

Trust, Perception and Reality

Whatever moral code we share must help us to better discern the external world we share and put personal subjective experience into a wider context. Relationships become unstable if there is no common ground or shared reality. We use other people for personal benefit in transactional relationships rather than to benefit others in covenantal ones.[8] Is yours an honest revelation or a facade? How do you know I am telling the truth? Is one or are both of us entering an illusion or deception? Is my new work colleague genuine in her welcome, or is she planning to undermine me? In a digitalised world of social media, distorted news and misinformation, we cannot even trust photos. Who checks the fact-checkers? The speed of our new social media communication can overwhelm us. Mistakes can be ruinous.

Our interpersonal and national conflicts arouse anxiety. An undisciplined imagination pours petrol on the fires of fear and anger, feeding untested assumptions, while poorly considered language keeps us awake in the night and further increases our confusion. Sickening feelings of shame or bitterness make reality too painful to acknowledge. We invent narratives to explain and justify disorienting confusion and painful emotions we feel but do not understand.

Our grasp on reality is always partial, because reality is much larger than our ability to engage with it. However, when we speak with integrity the distortions are minimised. Did you ever turn to a friend to ask his or her opinion about something you'd just experienced, because you were unsure if it was real? There was nothing sinister about it. You were merely testing the veracity of the signals coming through your senses to your inner world, and the outer world from which they came. You were wise; you just needed the view from a different angle, another external and perhaps more objective viewpoint, to check your subjective intuitions. We should not despair. Young children learn to make sense of the world, and we can know external reality well enough to land someone on the moon.

Trust and Power

Power is the energy necessary to change from one state of being to another. Everyone uses it every day to get up in the morning, from making a cup of coffee to governing a nation. It is fundamental to human existence; we cannot survive without it.

In a communal setting, power is often in tension with personal freedom, because conformity to norms or laws is either voluntary or must be coerced. In unjust societies, the rules benefit those who hold power. Agreement takes time and patience; it is easier and faster, in the short term, to abuse power, which is why power gets a bad name.

We intuitively think of power negatively because our encounters with it are often harsh or humiliating. Domineering people and systems take away something vital to being human in everyone else. Power that is not tempered by love where possible, and law where love fails, can be corrosive; life becomes cheap, and fear rampant. Those who have been humiliated often humiliate others as a pre-empted defence against future humiliation – yesterday's victim is often tomorrow's tyrant. History shows that the revolutionaries are the next dictators; the people at the barricade are often the elite-in-waiting.

Some see power primarily as the relationship between the oppressor and the oppressed, but that is too narrow a view to encompass the complexity of reality. Power *can* be dangerous and it may be abused, though it does not have to be. For example, love is the power to benefit others and when used wisely can empower the powerless. To walk away from power is to give it to someone else. Learning to use it positively for the good of everyone is essential to a vision of a better country.

A Czech friend[9] told me of a lady he knew in Prague in the turbulent November of 1989. She had a terrible cold. When she went to bed, the communists were firmly in power. She sweated and slept for several days. Eventually, she felt well enough to make some tea. Then, turning on the television, she was shocked to see almost a million people praying the Lord's Prayer, something unthinkable in communist times. She thought she was experiencing the second coming of Christ. The reality was not quite so dramatic. Power had changed hands and a corrupt elite had fallen. People were giving thanks and seeking a vision of a better country. Free elections would be held in June the following year.

After years of oppression the ideal of freedom in that moment was electric. People could taste the potential of liberty and felt relief that they could speak freely without fear of who might be listening. They went back to work with more personal freedom and, as they later discovered, much more responsibility. The ideal was short-lived; before long new forms of corruption appeared. Knowing what you want is harder to describe than what you do not want.

Forty years passed from the communist takeover in 1948 to the Velvet Revolution in 1989. Britain and France's abandonment of Czechoslovakia into the hands of Hitler, the trauma of the Second World War and the presence of the Soviet army made the outcome of communist rule almost inevitable. However, by 1968 a generation exhausted by central control over personal initiative called for 'socialism with a human face' – a request brutally denied by the invasion of Soviet troops in August 1968. The brief interlude of freedom was called 'the Prague Spring'. Another generation passed, and in 1989 people simply wanted their faces back, and the regime fell. People now have more personal freedom and responsibility, but corruption of a different kind remains. Mostly life is better, but some aspects are worse.

In the same period in 1968, but in Paris, students were rioting to overthrow capitalism and traditional institutions – two revolutions going in opposite directions on the same continent at the same time. Power ebbs and flows from left to right, personal to communal, and back again like the tide. Both communism and free enterprise speak to something real in the human condition, and both take something away. Everyone seems to hunger after something better, to resolve the crisis of the moment.

How can power be shared so that it does not dominate or enslave? Power must be focused and guided like a laser if it is to be more than a mere explosion. But who chooses the direction? Where are the boundaries that contain and channel it to fruitful ends, and how is it mitigated and moderated so that everyone is free and empowered?

Why did people in Prague, the most secular nation in Europe, pray the prayer of Jesus, 'Your kingdom come, your will be done, on earth'?[10] On a crowded hillside two millennia earlier, Jesus had urged his followers to desire a better country. 'Hunger and thirst,' he said, 'for righteousness,' but what is that? Many of us think we know, but when we stop to think about it, we find it difficult to describe. What he was describing in his sermon on the mountain was an outline for a better country. The words of his prayer, spoken in expectant hope or mumbled in monotonous repetition, have echoed down the centuries by people hoping for a better country and looking for a way to describe it.

Like a Child – against Idealism and Moralism

In Charlie Mackesy's wonderful book *The Boy, the Mole, the Fox and the Horse*, the mole asks the boy what he would like to be when he grows up. His answer is unexpected to our career-focused ears and yet straightforward: 'Kind,' the boy says. His book is innocent in ways that I wish I could be.

As I wrote earlier, children trust by nature until they discover by painful experience and disappointment that people are not always trustworthy. I wish I could adopt a childlike faith in humanity again, but the world I have lived in has occasionally been dangerous and often dark, and I have become too defended. I spent too many years looking over my shoulder, in mirrors or through shop windows, watching for the watchers. Occasionally I still feel the tug of paranoia of those days. Trust is still challenging. 'Who can I trust?' and 'On what basis can they be trusted?' were existential questions and have kept the search for home and a better country on my mind.

Sadly, we give up our innocence too quickly. Naivete and innocence require an unfamiliarity, even a childlike ignorance of evil that, once lost, is not possible to regain; an image once seen cannot be unseen. Our reasons for street-smart knowledge do not flatter us. But if we cannot be innocent, maybe we can be more trustworthy. For this reason, we need a clear vision of goodness.

But this book is not a call for idealism, nor is it a call for mere moralism. One is high minded and reaches too far too soon and the other is too low and hollow. Rather it is a call to awaken the imagination towards the goodness of other-centred love, to live thoughtfully and not automatically, and to awaken hope that reorients desire in fruitful directions. We need to recognise our true moral condition and yet have a clear vision of what we might become. When we lock our doors, we do it with sorrow at the waste and work towards freedom from keys and all they imply.

What could be more freeing relationally and economically than living in a world where people *can* trust each other, because we are trustworthy? What does it mean to be free within the limitations necessary to hold a community together? This is the subject of the next chapter.

3

Out of the Land of Slavery – The Way of Freedom

Man is born free, and everywhere he is in chains.
(Jean-Jacques Rousseau)

If the Son sets you free, you will be free indeed.
(Jesus of Nazareth)

The story of the exodus from Egypt is one of the foundational stories in Western culture and one root of our love of freedom. Several millennia ago, a nation recently liberated from 400 years of enslavement wandered in the desert. The Israelites had travelled to Egypt in a time of famine. Enslaved by the pharaohs, they had been dramatically led out of slavery by Moses.

But what would come next? What would make them a better country than the one from which they had been delivered? What would keep them from further enslavement? What would bind them as a nation? Would they drift further and further apart until they were no nation at all? Some people might think that would be ideal, but no one is an island. Who would be there to help in times of trouble?

The Decalogue, given to Moses on a mountain in the desert, was a guide to keep the people from future slavery. The preamble to the Decalogue is a declaration of freedom: 'I am the LORD your God, who brought you out of the land of Egypt, out of the house of slavery.'[1] In other words, 'I want you to be free!'

Perhaps freedom is one of the principles by which we may know we have interpreted the Decalogue well; if we are not freer after our reflection on it, then we have probably misunderstood it.

Even though they are ancient, the Decalogue and the exodus story resonate down the centuries because they speak to the perennial tension between chaos and order.

How are we to understand freedom; how does it work? Freedom can be life-giving, but it is also its worst enemy. Too much freedom and things fall apart, the community has no identity or cohesion; too little and people feel trapped and cannot develop their uniqueness. When does one person's freedom become another's oppression? What are the temptations of recently freed slaves? In their search for a better country, they would have to consider these pressures. Resolving the tension between freedom and cohesiveness in society is central to our communal life. These are the puzzling issues we will consider in this chapter.

The Freedom of Kites

Imagine a kite high above the ground, dipping, climbing and trailing its colourful ribbon as the wind pulls it up towards the sky. The wind, the kite, the cord and the kite flyer create the thrust that enables the kite to soar. The freedom of a kite depends on the limits imposed by the string.

Over the fields near our home, a different type of kite soars in the sky: the red kite, an elegant bird distinguished by the red tint on its forked tail feathers. It hangs on the thermal updraughts scanning the earth for prey. The bird of prey is less restrained than the kite with string. It can fly further and untethered. Yet both depend on the upthrust of the air, an external condition through which they find and fulfil their purpose. They are most free when submitting to and co-operating with the appropriate form.

Once, when working on a ship, I made a huge kite. To catch the wind, I climbed onto the roof of the stern deck. It was amazing to watch the kite soar higher and higher as I let out the exceedingly strong fishing line I was using as 'string'. As the kite rose almost out of sight, I wound the line around my hand. It was less amazing to watch the kite hesitate, turn and plunge into the sea, especially as the strong fishing line cut into my numbed hand. My window of freedom narrowed as the kite, dragged by the water, pulled me towards the roof's edge, which had no protective railing, and the sea far below. The fishing line snapped as I grasped the flagpole, but it was touch and go.

Both the kite flyer and the bird engage with the reality around them. We can change some aspects of reality, like the size of the kite or the length of the string. There are other conditions to which we must submit – for example, the wind speed. It is not always clear where the boundary between fixed and flexible lies. The kite flyer is free to make the kite in any shape and size she wants. She is free to wonder, discover and explore. But her freedom is not limitless. To fly the kite, she must co-operate with the external reality of aerodynamics.

Feel the tug of the string; it enables the kite of humanity to fly and creates the necessary conditions for freedom.

The Decalogue provides the conditions because, as we will see in later chapters, it creates the basis for trust and trustworthiness, the mitigation of power and the preservation of a common perception of reality. It is the form in which we can be fully human as unique persons while keeping communion in the community.

Over the years, I have asked hundreds of people what words come into their minds when they hear the word 'law'. Not many said 'freedom'. Their immediate reaction was adverse, until they thought more deeply about it. The modern mind intuitively prefers a kite without a string.

Freedom and Form

On the bank of the Vltava River in Prague, there is a playful postmodern building called the Dancing House.[2] It is as if the architect made the building and squeezed it in the middle with his hand. It stands out against the stiff formalism of the surrounding buildings. An architect is free to create the most experimental structure he likes, but it must conform to laws of gravity and building regulations beyond his control.

True freedom always has an appropriate form, just as unlimited freedom leads to destruction.[3] It is cheaper for the builder to use less cement and more sand, but if he wants the building to remain standing, he is not free to mix the cement and sand in any proportion he wants. Violate the form and lose the freedom. What is true of buildings and cement is true of all human activity.

Conversely, too much form can crush freedom. The wood burning in the stove heats my study. If the wood is packed in too tightly, the fire does not have enough oxygen to burn, and I am cold. If the fire were to spill out from the stove, the room would become fuel for the fire and consume me with it. The appropriate form allows the most freedom.

We often consider form restrictive, like a knife edge on which one must balance precariously. But if we imagine form as the circle of the sculpture in the café I described in Chapter 1, there is space within it to move. The outer limit defines the boundaries of inclusion and exclusion; inside the circle there is freedom for difference, choice and even disagreement.

Think of the circle of eating. The edge of the circle is, by definition, the necessity of eating because, without food, we will die; this is an absolute limit. We do not generally think about eating as a law of life, because it is usually pleasurable and we intuitively associate law with negative limits. However, there is immense freedom within the circle of eating – everything from the most exquisite French or Indian cuisine to America's fast foods. If they fulfil the requirements for health, all choices within the boundary are good. Outside the circle, there is sickness and potentially death.

Think of a glass of water. If I drop the glass and it breaks, it can no longer fulfil the purpose of carrying water, as the glass has turned into shards. A certain beauty may remain, but it has lost the form necessary to fulfil its function. So we must ask: what is the appropriate form to enable us to be fully human, both as unique persons and in community?

It is not always clear where the lines between form and freedom lie. We can change traditional forms that we have socially constructed, like the rules of football, if there is a consensus. There is no reason why the form should be absolutely fixed. Sometimes change is essential, because the reasons for the tradition have disappeared. Changes in the form imposed by nature or divine will are more complex to negotiate. We cannot change the distance of the sun to the earth. So, are the ways we associate – individualism, marriage or gender – social constructions or are they part of a more complex reality? How we answer such questions depends on how we understand reality to function. Over time reality will exert its authority, whatever it turns out to be.

Freedom to Trust

A better country is one where people are free to trust because there is an agreed basis on which people can be trustworthy.

Yesterday I met a friend riding his new electric bicycle. I asked him if it had the range to reach the local shops in a nearby village. He laughed and said it did, but he wondered if the bicycle would still be there when he came out of the shop. This question would not require the slightest consideration in a genuinely free and trusting society.

Once, when walking through the streets of a city in eastern Ukraine, I noticed a man carrying a huge bundle of keys. It seemed strange, but I did not think more about it until we arrived at my friend's apartment block and he took his keys from his bag. He unlocked seven doors between the entrance and his apartment. Over several visits it became clear that the lack of trust and the need for constant vigilance put a significant strain on his life.

People came to our learning community in Slovakia from all over Central and Eastern Europe. We would begin our six-week sessions by giving everyone the key to the house. It was a practical necessity and we did not think much about it until, on the evaluation day, person after person said how meaningful it had been to them to be trusted with the key; that this was a new experience for them.

Trusting others makes human relationships enjoyable, fruitful and free. Well-founded trust frees people from the anxieties of being cheated or harmed. But trust is fragile, easily crushed and, when broken, only restored with much time and effort. Levels of trust vary from country to country; cultures with high levels of trust have tremendous economic and social advantages.[4]

The goodness I am seeking to awaken is the form that enables deep trustworthiness and the trusting relationships that flow from it. In such a society, there would be no need to think about defending life, relationships or property, because there is no fear of domination, deception or theft. Instead, there would be trust, commitment and truth-telling.

The Decalogue is like a guidebook on edible and poisonous mushrooms. It gives a framework to see where trust is justified and where it would be a mistake. To pave the way for freedom, it must expose the poisons in the well of our human spirits so that we may return to trustworthiness.

Freedom requires the courage and honesty to face and confront our lack of trustworthiness. No matter how much we want to resist, the way to freedom is always towards reality and away from illusion. An engagement with reality is the first requirement for change.

Personal Freedom and Life in Community

As I noted in the previous chapter, in the section 'Communal or individual trust', Western society has become more individualistic and less communal over the last 150 years. Understandably, individual freedoms have gradually taken priority over the communal. We have no framework to encompass the unique person and the community – this is one reason for the polarisation of our times and our inability to talk together.

Individualism is such a basic assumption of Western life that I found it hard to conceive or understand what a communal consciousness might be. I learned about it, initially, through Germans returning from Russia, with whom we lived when studying their culture. From them we saw the benefits and challenges of a communal consciousness and identity, and how deeply individualistic assumptions had shaped us.

In the 1970s, ethnic Germans who had lived in Russia for centuries returned to Germany. 'In Russia,' they said, 'we were called Germans, but now in Germany we are called Russians.' In the Soviet Union, their conditions had been demanding and their options limited. As a national minority, they learned solidarity to survive. We grew to appreciate them deeply. Their profound communal spirit was beautiful to observe and awakened my cynical mind to the possibility of community. However, it was not without difficulties. Their deep communal loyalty led them to suppress personal preferences.

They thought of themselves as 'we' before they thought of themselves as 'I'. They took out a single mortgage from the bank for the whole community and bound themselves to each other for twenty years to pay for their homes. They had one architect design a house, which they replicated into thirty-five identical dwellings. They usually had large families of ten or more children and were never short of people to babysit or care for the sick. They were at home with the communal but were unused to the challenges of difference posed by Western life.

As new migrants, they were unfamiliar with how the wide range of choices and options produced differences among people in a more individualistic society. New freedoms require new social skills. As they settled into West German society, they had new and previously unimaginable opportunities. One became a doctor, another a tradesman. This new salary disparity contrasted with the low-income level and approximate equality they experienced in the Soviet Union. Work in the West was more demanding, so they had less time and energy for community relationships. They were no longer so needy financially; buying products was less stressful and saved more time than making them from scratch. They did not need each other in the same way as before. Decisions previously made communally were now made individually. One could now afford a more expensive car or holiday than the other. They had to confront the envy and divided loyalties they had not encountered in their previous life. The community was in tension as it wrestled with its identity. Attempts to keep it together took the form of harsh legalism and manipulation, which crushed creativity and drove away some of their young people. Traditions become oppressive when they descend into meaningless dogma. Freedom was painful to learn to manage.[5]

We should not think that individualism is better. That would be to fall off the horse on the other side. In highly individualistic societies, people suffer from loneliness, a loss of intimacy and identity, and high levels of anxiety, because we have lost the skills necessary for relating well and have no framework for trust except intuition, as naturalism has little basis for a consistent morality.

Morality is relational, and individual actions affect community life for better or for worse. Modern individualists unsurprisingly think of freedom as a personal choice, often in the pursuit of pleasure or avoidance of pain. Such freedom can degrade into a choice between various forms of slavery that are addictive or anaesthetic, avoiding reality rather than responding to it, like looking at the view through an uncalibrated lens that appears natural but is a distortion.

No one is an island, although many would like to be because our relationships are where we experience the most pain in life. The moral consequences of what I do in the privacy of my own home eventually spill into the communal domain and ultimately involve other people. The kite with a broken string eventually crashes to the ground and needs help to fly again.

In a better country the freedom to be unique and yet in deep communion with others should not be an either/or choice. Instead it is both/and, a dynamic tension held together continuously through trust.

Freedom to Say Yes and No

Simone Weil wrote, 'True liberty is not defined by a relationship between desire and its satisfaction, but by a relationship between thought and action.'[6] When I can enact my thoughts, I exercise authority over my life. Jesus himself said something similar: 'Let what you say be simply "Yes" or "No".'[7] 'Yes' and 'no' are the simplest words to say and among the first we learn, but they are among the hardest to implement.

Applying 'no' is as important for freedom as being free to act on 'yes'. Everyone struggles to implement their will on even the most basic level. How quickly my intention to lose weight crumbles in front of the fridge. Enacting these simple words is an exercise of personal dominion in pursuing freedom.[8]

Freedom's greatest enemy is freedom itself. Desire and discipline are uneasy bedfellows; appetite resists the discipline of restraint. Every craftsman knows that mastery requires short-term sacrifice for long-term benefit. Once learned through disciplined practice, the form allows for experimentation, discovery and creativity. The outstanding musician is the one who has mastered their instrument and profoundly understands their art.

Freedom: Responsibility, Courage, Maturity

Freedom presents those who were formerly enslaved with many challenges. The newly liberated nation of Israelites were not yet sure they wanted freedom. On cold desert nights, when thirsty and hungry, they recalled romanticised memories of Egypt and longed to return. They had been enslaved for 400 years. During that time, they developed the habits and mindset of enslavement. Enslaved people are not generally encouraged to take the initiative; they obey orders.

In Soviet culture, people learned that 'the highest corn gets the sickle'. So it took courage to stand out as a unique person. Such people threatened the communal spirit and were forced to conform or face exclusion. It was common in Central Europe for the communists to say, 'He who takes the initiative is worse than the class enemy.'

Václav Havel, the first post-communist president of Czechoslovakia, wrote of his experience under the old communist system, describing the mentality of the directors of a brewery when confronted by the initiative of someone who wanted to be free.[9] In 1974, Havel worked in the brewery with his immediate superior, whom he called 'Š', to protect his identity. Š loved his work and wanted the brewery to brew good beer. He was continually thinking up improvements. Havel wrote, 'In the midst of the slovenly indifference to work that socialism encourages, a more constructive worker would be difficult to imagine.' The manager of the brewery was a politically influential man, who cared little for his work. He was ruining the brewery and became increasingly hostile toward Š, whose initiative showed up his laziness. He tried to thwart Š's efforts to do a good job. Eventually, Š felt compelled to write a lengthy letter to the manager's superior to analyse the brewery's difficulties. Conditions in the brewery might have improved based on Š's suggestions, but unfortunately the opposite occurred. The manager loathed workers and change, and was afraid he might be replaced. He was a politically powerful member of the Communist Party's district committee and given to intrigue, so arranged for his friends in higher places to resolve the situation in his favour. They described Š's analysis as a 'defamatory document', and Š was labelled a 'political saboteur'. He was dismissed from the brewery and given a job requiring no skill. By speaking the truth, Š had stepped out of line and was stigmatised as an enemy. He could now say anything he wanted, but could never expect to be heard. He had become the 'dissident' of the Eastern Bohemian Brewery. In such conditions it is easy to give in to despair. [10]

Formerly enslaved people have thought patterns to unlearn but few models from which to learn. Such work is demanding and it requires courage to step out of an old identity after years of conditioning. It is tempting to avoid the risk and responsibility of the new thought and action needed by freedom, instead reverting to unquestioning obedience in the name of loyalty to culture, politics or religion. Yet to hide behind old ways because of fear is an act of cowardice.

A friend who worked at the refugee camp near our home in Austria told me of a Czechoslovak refugee who had shown extraordinary courage and initiative by flying a hang-glider over the Iron Curtain to escape. He recounted the gunfire as the guards had tried to stop him. At the camp, he asked my friend when he would be told what to do next. My friend asked him what he thought freedom was. He was confused by the question as he was not used to taking the initiative over essential areas of his life. Decision-making had not habitually been his responsibility; he was used to being told what to do to fulfil his part in the plan that came down from the central planners.

A community of liberated people need the courage to grow towards maturity by taking responsibility. They must learn to balance power among themselves or risk new forms of oppression, this time from inside their community. They need to recognise and wrestle with the destructive behaviours developed under oppression. Passive aggression and cynical humour[11] were powerful weapons of resistance against the centralised power behind National Socialism in Germany and communism in Eastern Europe. They are less valuable under conditions of freedom, which require discernment, skilful negotiation and responsibility.

In those two forms of government, we encounter the problem behind *all* bullying: the domination and coercion of one mind over another, allowing no room for discussion or disagreement. Those unwilling to take responsibility for their freedom hand that responsibility to others, who will happily enslave and use them. There is always someone seeking to enrich themselves at the expense of the labour of another. Freedom is bought and kept at a price.

Free to Be Human

What is the goal of freedom? I believe it is to be free to be fully human in a society where trust is normal and possible.

Many people see any limitations as a restraint on free choice, and communal morality as the abdication of individual moral responsibility. But does a perspective from the self give a broad enough perspective for life? The view from 'my perspective' is too limited to develop trust. My desires alone are an unfaithful witness to reality.

In my childhood we had a dog. One day during the Christmas celebrations we went to a church service. For tea my mother had made a tray of twenty-four cream slices, layered with sticky jam and icing. They were my favourite. We returned to discover the dog groaning on the floor, lying in its vomit. It had eaten the entire tray. Our approach to freedom can be similar. Being fully human requires discipline to focus desire on appropriate ends.

Some modern views of freedom aim to be free of external restraint or authority, striving for authenticity that is faithful to desire. Such freedom is only as stable as the desire that drives it, and runs the danger of enslaving the object of desire.

In my early wanderings, I tried to live faithfully in the existentialist authenticity recommended by Sartre and others. The result was existential loneliness and a brush with psychosis that was profoundly dehumanising. It was a relief to read, some years later, what Hans Rookmaaker, a Dutch art historian, wrote:

> Modern art teaches us that the humanistic kind of freedom cannot be realised. Such freedom delivers people into anxiety and desolation and a sense of not being free, as Sartre's work so penetratingly demonstrates; it reduces people to the slavery of the so-called 'absolute' and turns reality into chaos. Christian freedom is entirely different: it is the essential freedom of human beings to develop themselves as human creatures. In Christian freedom, people are saved from the original sin of desiring to be like God.[12]

Rookmaaker calls this 'Christian freedom', which might seem like an oxymoron for those used to viewing religion merely as a mechanism of control and oppression. He was not thinking in those terms. His conversion to Christianity happened in a prisoner-of-war camp in Ukraine during the Second World War, where he had access to a good library and several thoughtful professors. His Jewish fiancée died in Auschwitz, though he was not aware of it until he returned home. His conversion to belief in a transcendent personal being with moral character happened in the face of a dehumanising abuse of power, with humans claiming to have the right to shape reality in their image.

His quote raises the issue of divine authority and what it means to be human. In an age when authority is no longer hierarchical, claims to ultimate and external authority can sound offensive or frightening. After all, who would wield power in the name of the divine? Many terrible historical examples of religious oppression come to mind. However, they are no more tyrannous than an absolute and unrestrained relativism in which the one with the loudest voice or the largest stick has the last word. Both forms are oppressive.

The idea that God, as the originator of life, knows how best to live and desires our freedom should not frighten us, if those who administer law are also fully compliant with it and committed to the other-centred love that the Decalogue requires. It is our self-centred love and lack of respect for one another that we need to examine.

In our attempt to be free of any absolute external authority, we take on the burden of the God-like attributes of omnipresence, omnipotence and omniscience. Someone in society, usually the government but not always, must emulate the all-present, all-powerful and all-knowing capacities necessary to provide justice and security. In the technological age, we do this increasingly through surveillance and data management systems of big data and artificial intelligence (AI). It is a burden for which we are morally unequipped, as present discussions about privacy and ethics show.

Here Rookmaaker is saying that being morally good is the form in which we are most free to be fully human as unique persons in a trusting community.

Freedom from Determinism

It is challenging to write the word 'God' without it filling readers' minds and memories with concepts, mental images and feelings that might be far from mine. Why should the question 'Who is God?' matter if you are not sure God exists? My goal here is not to persuade anyone but to clarify. What we believe about fundamental reality has practical consequences. You are unlikely to go fishing in the pond if you don't believe in fish.

What do you think is the fundamental basis of reality? The prevailing outlook of Western society is materialism, sometimes called naturalism – the idea that our existence is nothing more than the product of time, matter and chance; that biological death closes the book on existence; that nothing is real beyond what is available to our senses. So any meaning exists because we create it. However, this outlook has created widespread feelings of alienation from the world and each other – a 'meaning crisis' as we have struggled to make a meaning structure on the basis of naturalism that is sufficient for us to live in and to build shared life together as communities and culture.

Most people do not come to their beliefs through intensive reading and study but through casual acquaintance with widely acceptable and plausible ideas. These beliefs are accepted, for the most part, because we trust what we're told by authorities in a given field – that is, we believe by faith in knowledge we receive by revelation from these authorities. Many in our culture are 'nominal naturalists' in the same way that many used to believe in Christianity nominally; happy to go along with the consensus opinion picked up by cultural osmosis, beliefs that make few demands and don't rock too many boats. We don't think about the consequences of those beliefs until they affect us unexpectedly. The search for meaning and significance can be a heavy burden. Naturalism diminishes the value of persons and relationships, because they are accidental and not part of the fundamental reality. Many naturalists believe freedom is an illusion; biology, chemistry and factors outside our control drive our choices. The view offered in the Bible is radically different, as we will see.

We rage in vain when we think of the idea of God. Our beliefs do not change reality at this level; either God exists or he doesn't. Either there is something beyond death or there is not. Yet still we rage because we want to be in control and need to make sense of suffering and the futility of life without a beyond. These are real questions – we should not be afraid to face them.

As humans, we experience ourselves as personal and not merely mechanical. The evidence of our desire for love, justice, freedom, understanding, rationality, beauty, direction, progress, meaning, significance and knowledge to satisfy curiosity, the poetic and imaginative, is overwhelming and undeniable. Yet such categories fit uncomfortably in a naturalistic frame because they are often unnecessary for survival and transcend nature. On the other hand, if naturalistic theories do not account for such everyday experiences, they may be a reduction of reality and incomplete.

Notions of spirituality abound in our times. Often as vague as 'the cosmic self' or 'the absolute', they tend towards the communal, experiential and esoteric, possibly in response to the individualism and rationalism of modernity. These spiritualities are a search for something beyond the self and are not wrong for that. But are vague definitions of the esoteric enough to make sense of life?

I have never quite understood what it means to be religious and am not attracted to religious practices that separate the religious from the ordinary. The etymology of the word 'religion' is not clear.[13] One definition suggests that it means 'to reread' (from the Latin *relegere*) or 'to reconnect or bind fast'. If I am religious, it is in this way. Everywhere there is evidence of broken hearts that need rebinding. I do not have the faith to believe these rich fragments of life mean nothing, and cannot believe in a meaningless and random evolutionary existence. There is a need for a rereading of the world beyond naturalism.

Those who believe in transcendence must ask if their idea of transcendence is personal – one that is not only there in the future but also here and now, which a human could relate to in some way – or merely an impersonal power of 'the force'? Christianity claims that God is present, as close to us as our breath.

Believers in such a transcendent reality have another issue to consider. Just look up at the stars on a cloudless night. What does 'freedom' mean in the company of an infinitely powerful being who can speak billions of galaxies into existence? The author of reality, described in the Bible, is infinite in power. Paul, the writer of much of the New Testament, describes it in this way: 'He [God] who is the blessed and only Sovereign, the King of kings and Lord of lords, who alone has immortality, who dwells in unapproachable light, whom no one has ever seen or can see.'[14] The sheer scale is overwhelming. How can we be free in the light of such power?

The God described in the Bible is both infinite and personal, one of many truths that followers of the Christian faith must hold together in tension. Lean too far on the side of the infinite and we experience God as distant and unreachable; lean too far towards the personal and God seems sentimental, like your girlfriend/boyfriend. Our need for security or hunger for love and relationship will likely push us one way or the other.

This God is also moral. The Decalogue is as much an expression of his character as it is a call on our behaviour. It points to goodness that makes absolute power safe because it is not self-absorbed, but intent on the goodness and benefit of the other.

The call to freedom at the beginning of the Decalogue shows that God is neither a divine puppeteer nor a distant clockmaker. He did not rescue people from slavery for them to enslave themselves again to mere passions, projects, programmes, techniques, systems or even ultimately to himself. Instead, he seeks free sons and daughters in loving, other-centred relationships rather than slaves who obey in cowardly and abject fear.

God is free, and humans made to reflect God's image gain freedom within finite limits as sons and daughters of the infinite and personal Creator. Learning to be free in a society of free people requires maturity – it is not easy or automatic.

Our freedom is limited by our finitude and distorted by moral corruption, which confuses our perception of reality and limits our ability to engage with it. What look like reasonable choices are often rationalisations trying to make sense of emotional confusion. Nevertheless, it is meaningful freedom with real consequences.

God, the ultimate reality, invites our participation in creating reality. Our freedom is vastly more than that of the kite with string or the red kite that hangs so beautifully on the edge of the wind. Our choices have consequences, and our language has meaning. We have immense but not limitless freedom within whatever forms are appropriate to build our institutions and make our social constructions with care and wisdom.

The apostle Paul confirmed this desire for freedom when he wrote to his friends in Galatia, '[It is] for freedom Christ has set us free; stand firm therefore, and do not submit again to a yoke of slavery' and later, 'For you were called to freedom, brothers. Only do not use your freedom as an opportunity for the flesh [to serve yourselves], but through love serve one another.[15]

Believing in a morally good, personal and infinite God is a step too far for some readers. I understand that and would not expect it to be otherwise in a society steeped in a century of naturalism. I hope I've given enough reasons to entertain at least the possibility that God, freedom and goodness are not necessarily in opposition but might even be connected. I hope to show that the Decalogue offers ancient wisdom relevant to our cultural challenges, regardless of whether you believe it to be of divine origin. And I invite you to consider the Decalogue as a signpost to a deeper reality and a revelation of God, goodness and love – a framework for a better country and freedom.

4

Word One: An Invitation

How would you describe the God you do or do not believe in? Unsurprisingly, we give the word 'God' meaning from our own positive or negative experiences, whether we believe there is one or not. Our gut responses often stem from childhood exposure to one of the major religions or the naturalism promoted in reaction to them.

Because they are dim childhood memories, often from the anxious pressure of a religiously devout relative, or weddings, burials or religious services we did not understand, they are unarticulated, dimly remembered and associated with emotions like confusion, fear, anger or grief.

We might have ambivalent attachments to the ideas, but a loyalty to the culture and home from which they came. Our intuitions can be influential, but challenging to name and hard to own or change. We often shy away from thinking for ourselves, because we don't feel adequately equipped for the complicated Pandora's box we fear to open.

I discovered this one night when thinking about my views of ultimate reality. I had just read the first line of the Decalogue when the following scene came into my mind. Imagine an actor on a stage. The house lights have dimmed, and an expectant hush has fallen over the audience in the theatre. With what tone should the actor speak the words *You shall have no other Gods before me*?[1] Should the tone be violent or inviting? Is the speaker angry, a cantankerous bully, or benevolent and kind? Should the actor wag a finger or shake a fist. Is he saying, 'Don't you *dare* have any other gods before me'? Should the tone be kind and inviting?

Reason might say one thing; the stomach might feel something entirely different. We have many levels of belief and not all are rational.[2]

A Call to Intimacy with the Infinite

That night, while reflecting on that sentence, I heard my inner voice projecting an angry petulance onto the divine voice and wondered if it was justified and if it was getting in the way. Undoubtedly, the moment in which the Decalogue was given was solemn, even intimidating, but was the harsh voice I was projecting onto it right? What if I was wrong? Could it mean something else? I questioned whether my gut image of a cantankerous God was right and if it might cause me to misunderstand. Later, I wondered where such a view came from.

Perhaps the voice on the mountain was saying, '*Let there be nothing between us*'? Might this be an invitation to know the most generous, hospitable and gracious being in or beyond our universe? A call from the most exceptional intelligence and most profound wisdom, from the source of all that is beautiful, a call from the consuming fire of absolute goodness. Was the first word of the Decalogue an invitation to draw near; an invitation to intimacy with the infinite?

The 'other gods' block the view between the one who calls and those who are called.[3]

Was this a call to realignment with reality, since there is none more real than the source and sustainer of reality itself?

Was my fear of the dark standing in the way?

Who is Calling?

Imagine the instant *before* that first creative act.

God plus nothing. No time or space, no heavens or earth. Just the infinite and personal being whose mind alone knows all things that will exist: earth and heavens, plants, animals, humans male and female.

The biblical narrative presents us with a self-giving being who, as we will see later, does not need to create. This is not a lonely

God looking for someone to love, but one who acts intentionally to share existence with something beyond himself. One who creates from desire in an extraordinary act of hospitality and generosity.

If this is true, we are no accident of time and chance, but we exist because the transcendent God wants us to exist. Unless he is absolute evil, such a being is for us and not against us and is the ultimate source of our meaning and significance.

As the narrative unfolds, it reveals God as Father, Son and Spirit, working as an absolute and infinite intimacy that existed within the divine being before the creation.[4] God is solitary but not alone, trinitarian in nature, one divine being in three persons, whose need for love is satisfied within those persons, and who therefore did not need to create for company or ego.

The idea of trinity is not easy for finite minds to understand using metaphors from within the creation.[5] But it has very practical applications, as we will see in later chapters.

The Father is God, the Son is God and the Spirit is God, yet there is only one God and not a committee or fellowship of three Gods. To be one and yet three requires moral integrity so profound that human language cannot do it justice. Here we see why goodness matters. It is necessary to keep communion, intimacy and distinction.

The gods of Greek mythology fought and tricked each other in epic struggles, but there is no hint or rumour of power struggles within the God of the Bible, never a whisper that the Spirit might envy the Son or gossip to the Father. No hint of suspicion that the Son grumbled when considering the incarnation. The idea sounds foolish. Instead, there are clear statements of love.

Communion and distinction are in tension and, in a self-centred society, work against each other. Other-centred love resolves the tension without loss of the difference. Here we see the archetype for trust and relationship among humans when we reflect the divine image.

The communion of unique people in relationships of trust is the fullest expression of what it means to be alive and free. Goodness is a requirement for communion among diverse people. Without it our communion becomes mere conformity.

When people used to say 'for goodness' sake' they were referring to God, whom they saw as the definition of goodness. This goodness, love and trust precede creation and are foundational to the structure of all reality and communion.

The one who calls is a great mystery to us, yet desires to be known. The veil is thick; we approach cautiously and by invitation. This call is not merely to know *about* a person, but to know a person in relationship. As I wrote in Chapter 2, meaningful knowledge of someone comes as we reveal ourselves to each other, and cannot be discovered through the scientific method or other means. The divine has revealed himself as one would expect persons to do. The basis of revelation is trust in the character of the other person.

The question is not only whether I can trust God, but can God trust me with such knowledge?

The scientific view is the view from within material existence; the more we discover, the greater our wonder at the universe. But science has no tool or perspective from which to discover what might exist beyond it.[6] Nor can it discover the inner life, which as an exercise in trust is moral.

One mystery of the universe is that it *can* be understood rationally. We *can* take a perspective and understand something, albeit imperfectly, outside ourselves. There is no reason why that should be the case. Christians believe that God is the source of rationality in the universe. Do away with God and you must explain how we can explore the universe reasonably at all.[7]

The opposite of reason is not faith, but madness and irrationality. Reasonable faith looks for evidence but does not limit that evidence to what can be perceived by direct sensory experience. Our hunger for love, meaning, beauty, truth, justice, freedom, equality, understanding, rationality, progress, significance, the poetic and imaginative is culturally shaped but undeniable, and evidence points beyond material existence to something only explainable through a transcendent reality.

As in the scientific sphere, reasonable faith considers the uncertainties and limitations in the evidence. It may express doubt where confidence is not called for, but trust where it is.

We often assume that if there is a divine being, he is deaf, dumb or distant. But why should that be true? He reveals himself through the creation, though the creation is ambiguous, multifaceted, complex and yet elegantly simple. It is not clear from looking at it alone what the Creator would be like. We can read of his dealings with people in the Old Testament, though that is also easily misread. Christianity makes the extraordinary claim that God has come in the flesh in the person of Jesus, as an historical event. He is 'the radiance of the glory of God and the exact imprint of his nature',[8] the key that unlocks the door. His character is the standard by which we can judge our reading of nature and the sacred text.

Who Is Called?

The invitation is a call to us as humans. It is a call to regain a humanness that reflects the communion of infinite trust and trustworthiness enjoyed within the Trinity but which is broken among humans and between humans and the Creator.

It is a call for humans who, having lost their home, must carry the burden of creating their identity and belonging, meaning and significance, alone.

Goodness shakes us to our foundations. Its presence is uncomfortable. The moral light of eternity casts a long shadow and illuminates what we prefer to remain hidden. On a spring day, shafts of sunlight warm the living room, but also reveal the dust that has settled on the furniture. Move the oven from the wall, and the light will reveal a different level of grime altogether.

This moral light will eventually uncover the unowned self, which we hide even from ourselves for fear of shame. It is a shame covered by bravado or anger, but who does not fear exposure? Though it might not feel like it, such disclosure liberates us from the exhaustion of self-deceit. An in-depth diagnosis provides the best cure.

I worked for a while with someone from Poland who had grown up in the humanist tradition that says humans are good. She saw so much good in human life. I agreed with her; humans *are* capable of great creativity, personal sacrifice, love and kindness. Then I wondered aloud if Polish history justified the idea that we are as good as she thought. In the Second World War about 20% of the population of Poland were killed. Two warring ideologies – National Socialism in Germany, and communism in the Soviet Union, both believing they were morally right and wanting the best for their own – carved up the country and destroyed its cities. They had prepared lists of intellectuals to execute in advance so that after the invasion they could eradicate potential resistance leaders. These facts of history puncture a purely optimistic humanism.

Our goodness is real but limited; it is a remnant of a former glory, infiltrated, corrupted and hollowed out by the virus of self-centred defensiveness. As the moral imagination comes into focus, we become aware that our moral palaces are illusions of grandeur. Our noble house has seen better days and needs repair.

Called Together – as One and Many

The invitation is to come close to God *and* each other; love God and love our neighbour.[9] Morality concerns the quality and depth of our relationships. It is among family, neighbours and associates at work that we experience our moral inadequacy. Deep relationships are hard to maintain; it is far easier to cut off difficult people than to confront and heal the wound. Developing good relationships always involves confronting ourselves.

The Trinitarian idea of being one and more-than-one reflects our human condition, but this is often forgotten by practising Christians. Ask Christians if they believe in the Trinity, and most will say yes. Ask if they are practising Trinitarians, and they will not understand the question. It is worthwhile explaining what this means, as the concept offers answers to many puzzles of human life.

God is simultaneously three and one. We reflect God's image in being in communion with each other while simultaneously being unique. The invitation to intimacy is to a communion of unique persons; to each and to all. Both the communion and the unique persons are important.

Under the influence of Western individualism, Westerners struggle to grasp or reflect the communal aspect of the divine image, while those under a more Eastern influence neglect the uniqueness of persons.[10] The Trinitarian model offers a basis for balancing and integrating unity and diversity in our relationships.

My use of 'unique person' is not synonymous with 'individual'. Individualism is the idea that a person cannot be divided into anything smaller. But to be an individual is already a division too far. Personhood always means to be in relationship with other persons. Each person draws something unique from others. The interaction is where identity is discovered. Without someone to engage with me, I cannot fully know or understand myself. Without relationships to other people, I cannot get out of my own head. Their observations give me alternative perspectives on reality.

Both individualism and communalism are inadequate frameworks for life. An individualist society tends to loneliness and loss of identity, and communal societies tend to suffocate personal uniqueness. Neither is notably better or worse; both are incomplete.

I described previously how my German/Russian friends were conscious of themselves in a communal way, whereas I was aware of myself as an individual. In their community, someone exercising too much personal freedom would cause unrest, because their community depended on uniformity of customs and culture. In our eighteen-hour drive from Vienna to their community in north Germany, we had forgotten these very conservative people did not let their women wear jeans. On the day we arrived, my wife was wearing jeans. The father of the family, fearing how this would look in his community, drew me aside and asked if my wife would wear men's clothing while staying with them. Even though we disagreed with this, we were not there to judge but to study their culture, so we had decided that we would submit to their ways while we were with them. Our submission opened the door of trust within their community and its many other beautiful attributes.

Once, after speaking on Trinity as a model of culture with a group of businesspeople in Kyiv, Ukraine, a lady from Georgia approached me.

'I became a Christian in 400,' she said.

At first, I had no clue what she meant, until I realised there was no distinction in her mind between *I* and *we* in her national identity. Her identity and the history of her country were seamless in a way I had never previously encountered. It was like the solidity of people I met in Austria and Slovakia who had lived in the same town for many generations. I had no experience of their sense of place and rootedness. They, on the other hand, were sometimes confused by the mobility of modern people and occasionally resented the intrusion of the modern world.

Submission to God as supreme authority enables each person to stand with equal dignity beside all others. When we bow to worship together we rise as equals, no longer merely bowing to the will of the most assertive or most persuasive person in the community – we may even have to resist them. By worship I do not mean something that happens in a religious institution, but a recognition of the worth of the infinite and personal Creator.

In receiving this Trinitarian vision, each submits with humility to the one who is wiser than all. A sign of this happening is the creation of space for the weak to grow in confidence and maturity rather than be dominated by others.

The oil of union in communion is humble love; humble because it values the other as much as itself, and love as the energy needed to sustain action towards the other's good, despite inevitable feelings to the contrary. This love is not the self-centred sentimentalism of ego attraction that is often confused for love, but an other-centred commitment for everyone's good. As bearers of the divine image, we learn to love who and what God loves in the way he loves.

A Trinitarian consciousness involves agreement around the purposes of God and his virtues. Paul, an early follower of Jesus, called this having the mind of Christ,[11] a mind committed to a society based on other-centred love and trust. Having such a mind makes our communion safe and fruitful. It means, among other things, that I will respect your calling and gifts just as you respect mine.

Our aim should be to regain the consciousness of union or being of one mind while simultaneously respecting and honouring differences: communion, not conformity or uniformity. It is a challenging exercise for people trained to think sequentially and dialectically to think of both/and, in ways that are not mutually exclusive, without losing both categories. It might take many generations to recover a sense of consciousness both as unique people and as communal people simultaneously, but it is our task to work towards it.

In looking to maintain the appropriate tension and arrive at a more profound union, our self-centredness and moral weakness become more evident. Humility is the way of freedom. We learn through the pathway of forgiveness to grow to a maturity in which we confront and overcome the impediments that keep us from loving one another.[12]

This is perhaps the heart of the matter in the search for a better country. Much abuse of power comes from the attempt to force others to conform to our ways and desires.

The Invitation to Reality

The encounter with infinite goodness is first painful and humbling before it is restorative and healing. Suffering Job (from an ancient story about suffering in the Old Testament) listened with patience to his well-meaning but unhelpful comforters, but he trembled when God himself appeared.[13] Although he was suffering, he discovered joy and was awed by God's goodness. Something about the quality of God's presence satisfied his need to make sense of his suffering, like a woman rejoicing in her child after the pain of childbirth. He had known *about* God as a theory, but now: 'I had heard of you by the hearing of the ear, but now my eye sees you; therefore, I despise myself and repent in dust and ashes.'[14] In knowing God, he discovered himself and his real condition. It gave him the perspective necessary to step towards reality.

When we approach God, we move into the circle of truth as a description of reality. Every step towards reality is a step towards God, who is the ultimate reality. When the illusions and delusions fall away, we become more real and substantial as human beings.

Admission of any truth is the first step of drawing near to God, just as any untrue confession is to step away. A young man once came into my study to talk. He was, he said, a Christian but had some questions. As we spoke, it became clear to me that he was not a Christian by conviction, but had grown up in a Christian family. His doubts about Christianity conflicted with his loyalty and genuine love for his family. When he left my study, he knew that he was not a Christian. I realised, somewhat painfully, that this was progress. Now he lived in truth and not in an illusion. Some years later, he returned and wanted to talk again. 'I have become a Christian,' he said, then told me the story of his journey; of how leaving the boyhood illusion had allowed him to find real and reasoned faith as a man.

We should never be afraid of the truth; even unpleasant truth will eventually set us free.

Who or What Are the Other Gods?

To respond to the divine invitation, we must see the inadequacy of the other gods. In ancient times, idols were physical representations made of wood or gold, but they had a potency in the mind of the worshipper. Our modern idols are often idealisations of people or objects, to which we ascribe God-like attributes. We give them ultimate meaning, and place on them ultimate expectations. Because they cannot deliver on their promises, they are not up to the tasks we assign them.

Humans are meaning-makers; we need narratives to navigate life, to make sense of events, to soothe our anxieties, justify anger or explain other emotional states of mind. If none is obvious, we will invent one. Inasmuch as it is incorrect, the new story distorts the associations between the symbols we use and what they represent.

Having been liberated from slavery in Egypt, the people were waiting for God to give them instructions about what to do next.

While Moses was up the mountain receiving the new narrative for the nation of Israel, the people waited for him at the base. They became uneasy. They wondered if he would return. Had he abandoned them in the desert? Their catastrophising imagination went into overdrive. Who would lead them? Where should they make their new home? Eventually, they made a golden calf from the wealth given to them as they left Egypt.[15] This creative activity absorbed their anxious energies. But it was all unreal; they ascribed attributes to their golden calf that it did not have. It met their immediate needs but blinded them to the greater reality of the burning mountain and the presence of God. The eye is quickly drawn from the beauty of the Creator to the more accessible wonders of the creation.

Suppose I want to own a fast, bright red sports car. There is nothing necessarily wrong with wanting a fast, well-designed, beautiful car (maybe it is less suitable for the environment, but this is a simple illustration). It has a brilliant design, good speed and excellent engineering. So far so good. But the moment I look to the car for status, it becomes an idol. I ascribe to it an attribute it cannot fulfil. It might raise my status in the eyes of some for a while, but an expensive car is not suitable for real status, because every car gets scratched or rusts with age; its value declines and my status with it. God does not want my value reduced by objects that are not up to the task.

God alone has the eternal and absolute attributes we mistakenly ascribe to our idols. In trusting the car for status, I reveal a lack of trust in God and the value he confers on me as one made in his likeness. I create a false hierarchy of values by which I measure myself against others. I lower the status of others who, also made in God's image, have equal value to me. This hierarchy of values eventually distorts every value. I become protective of the car. It holds me captive, and I am no longer free either to worship God in his fullness or to enjoy the car for its own sake.

An object is free of idolatry when we associate with it only those attributes it actually has, no more and no less. In the case of the car, these might be the speed, fine engineering and design. The divine qualities the mind might project onto it, including its ability to give enduring status, are unreal, and to trust them is to step towards unreality.

Our idols overwhelm our senses and distort our mental abilities. Their sensual immediacy is addictive and instantly available; they feel close when God seems distant. They comfort us in our anxieties, but their comfort is unsustainable. We trust them, but it is a trust in something unreal.

The skylines of our cities reflect our aspirations and what we value. They have changed over the centuries, from church spires and factory chimneys to industrial silos, banks, investment firms, universities, shopping malls, entertainment centres and sports stadiums. Our towers of Babel are never far from us.[16] But their foundations are deceptive and parasitic: the gods of power, work, success, fashion and image, consumerism, nationalism, scientism, technology, historicism, progress, equality, politics, economics, management and business; the great gods of state and bureaucracy; the gods of entertainment and religion. We control them for a time until, eventually, they own and enslave us.

The gods we bow to dictate the kind of kingdom we live in. They rise only to choke us again. Each might be good in its proper place when seen through an eternal lens, but as masters they reduce reality and become tyrants.

The idols speak nothing enduring into being. Theirs is the mimicry of the puppet. If there is speech at all, it reflects human desire or more sinister forces. Their 'priests' make claims to power they do not have and knowledge they cannot possess. Their economy is inflationary and addictive; they own us and then dispossess us, inhabiting heart and mind until the self, distorted and bent, is hollowed out.

Over-promising and under-delivering, they hide in systems and techniques. Fashion and great design can be delightful, but a facade does little to cover secret shame. The false prophets say, 'Everything is OK, and we can fix what is not.' They ignore or explain away the underlying problem: that every human cut off from the source of life lives in the shadow of death.

It can be a temptation to idolise places or practices that have been helpful in the past. There is a powerful desire to preserve and repeat experiences precisely because they have been so profound. It is easy to associate intense or even pleasant experiences with people and objects present at the time and put misplaced trust in them. Notice what happened on the Mountain of Transfiguration when Jesus pulled back the veil and showed his followers his glory. Somehow two Old Testament characters, Moses and Elijah, were present in the time warp between time and eternity. The moment was glorious, but Peter (Jesus' follower and apprentice) was concerned about preserving the experience rather than living in the encounter: 'Master, it is good that we are here. Let us make three tents, one for you and one for Moses and one for Elijah.'[17] Attention shifted, changing subtly from object to subject, from God himself to Peter's experience of God. The experience is not wrong, but it should not take centre stage. To attempt to hold on for ever to experiences given for a moment is a return to slavery. In seeking to preserve the experience, Peter sought in it what God wanted Peter to find in God himself.

Idols can even be worthy in themselves. My wife is an amazing woman – she is a constant source of love, she reassures me in moments of failure and frustration – but she cannot fulfil my heart's eternal longings, nor can I fulfil hers. The burden would crush us. Thus, in the strange story of Abraham and Isaac,[18] God commands ancient Abraham to sacrifice his only son and the future of his line. Abraham must be prepared to sacrifice his son Isaac, for if Abraham trusts his future to Isaac rather than God, then Isaac is dead already, for who among us can survive the burden of being God to another human being?

The idols were faithful in their time, they worked for a while, but now they must go. There will be grief. It will be a sad parting, and we will miss them – though it is wise to remember they were killing us. They must die as idols if we are to receive back those who are in other ways legitimate. It is a delicate operation because the false gods might be gifts from God that have grown too large in our minds and hearts. It is not my wife I must banish, but my idolatrous idealisation of her. We have trusted the gift rather than the giver. Patriotism and loyalty to one's country are honourable, but not at the price of despising the image of God in other nations and people. As the idols fall and the debris is cleared from the heart, we draw closer to God and one another. As we die to our illusions of each other, we can rise to meet face to face as real people.

It is a mistake to seek in creation what is beyond it. It is short-sighted to look in the temporal for what time will take away.

Trust and Attachment – Faith in the Dark

Reorientation of trust, from the idols to God, is not instantaneous or automatic. God's invitation will continue to raise a fundamental question: should I trust God or my experience?

Humans survive long early years of dependency through trusting attachments formed with parents and other caregivers. But when those early attachments break, through tragedy or carelessness, trusting anyone, even God, can become anxiety-ridden. Once broken, attachments do not renew quickly; it takes time and practice to relearn how to trust. Anxiety and doubts can drown out reason or positive encouragements. It is helpful to realise, amid doubt caused by unruly feelings, that my mechanisms of perception are broken and in need of repair. I wear glasses to correct my sight and hearing aids to hear more clearly, and I must make allowances for faculties of the mind and memory that are less than perfect. The truth is real, whatever my mood. I can trust God whether I am experiencing him or not, just as I trust that the sun is still there on a cloudy day.

As a chronic insomniac, I often struggle through the night and it feels that trust and reason have gone to sleep, leaving the imagination to play. In the fatigue of my more depressive mornings, I wake feeling numb to the reality of God, the love of my wife or the affection of friends. I must choose: will I trust in my direct experience or in the revelation of God and friends?

In those grey mornings, I sit on the side of the bed and remind myself of the truths I have come to believe and, just as important, the reasons and evidence that led me to consider them in the first place. Existence is not random; the beginning of life was personal and not impersonal. There is a transcendent being. This being is good and not against me. He communicates and is not silent, and wants my participation in life. I remind myself that I am a human, not a machine or an animal. I live in the company of other humans, some of whom love me. Usually, the darkness lifts as I get into the day; occasionally it does not. But the absolute existential blackness of earlier years has long gone, and I have discovered the reality of God's presence, not usually in the extraordinary and spectacular but in the ordinary: the relationships, events and interruptions of everyday life.

Drawing Near

In accepting the invitation to draw near to God, we welcome the process of restoration to true humanity. It is a difficult road; the idols must be exposed and stripped of their magical power. Trust, once invested in them, must be reoriented towards God. As the distortions of the idols diminish, the roar that once sounded like distant thunder becomes clearer; it is the liberating voice of God himself, not a mere idea but a living reality – personal as well as infinite.

The Creator invites us to draw near. He offers himself; we should not settle for anything less. In orientating ourselves towards the infinite goodness of the Creator, we can enjoy the finite goodness of creation as a gift from him. He is willing to lift the veil and let us know the goodness of his being. He will enable those who desire it to reconnect to himself as the life source who alone makes sense of existence and gives life its ultimate meaning.

The first word is an invitation from the source of life to enter reality: draw near, allow no substitute.

Coffee Break – Transitions

 Welcome back to the café. What would you like – coffee for the morning, tea for the afternoon, something more substantial as the sun goes down?

We have been busy while you have been reading. How are you getting on? Complicated ideas can't be rushed. Do not worry – the mind has a curious ability to work on them even when you are not aware of it. I often wake in the morning with a clarity of thought so rich I wish it would last for ever, but it fades at my first encounter with the newspapers. A boy from the paper shop near the market delivers us the full range of political opinions by early morning and I can't resist a glance. How does one hold the tension between important questions and daily life? Immediate concerns make little sense without a longer-term perspective.

The atmosphere in the café changes through the day, the phases merging into one another with a slight lull just before and after lunch and late in the evening. Early risers rush in for a quick espresso on their way elsewhere. The breakfast crowd talk business or read the papers they pick up from the table by the door. The leisurely morning coffee people, usually in pairs and threes, begin to arrive around 10 a.m. and merge with the 'let's do lunch' types too busy selling their ideas to taste their food. The 2 p.m. lull is a relaxing moment before afternoon coffee and cake, mostly groups of older ladies accompanied by a few men and endless memories of how much better things once were. They thin out around 5:30, by which time the early supper people are arriving. Many regulars know the menu inside out, and we know what they want. Familiarity can be a great advantage, but some prefer anonymity and being alone. By late evening lonely insomniacs and harried students sit and stare over their coffee or wine, deep in their studies or writing poems. The arc of life bends towards our longings.

5

Word Two: What Do You See? Image and Imagination

You shall not make for yourself a carved image, or any likeness of anything that is in heaven above, or that is in the earth beneath, or that is in the water under the earth. You shall not bow down to them or serve them.
(Exodus 20:4–5)

Humans have a formidable inventive ability to visualise possibilities that do not yet exist. We create magnificent art that can help us see reality in a new light. We imagine and design new buildings and bridges. The imagination enables us to empathise with those who are hurting, yet the landscapes of our world are scarred with the battles of prejudice. It is not for nothing that the second instruction of the Decalogue addresses how we use the imagination and the images that proceed from it.

In the search for a better country, we need a creative imagination to think of how things could be. But an imagination unhinged from love and driven by fear leads to destructive speculation and accusation.

We experience reality through images that arouse strong emotions of wonder, joy, love, fear, anxiety, anger and envy. The emotions supply the impulse and energy to engage in life. Without them we would be passive and passionless, but our emotions should be appropriate to the task at hand if they are not to be out of control. We assign value to what we see and imagine through the filters of our experience, desire and hope.

Imagine various workers entering a tall office tower by the

river in your capital city. Each one has different assumptions and expectations because they see the building with different eyes.

The receptionist sees clients needing direction to the correct location, while the security guards scan for potential threats to a building they must protect.

Mid-level workers come expecting hours of creativity or tedium.

The chairman of the board arrives in his chauffeur-driven car and ascends in his private elevator to his penthouse suite, the pinnacle of his power and the source of his prestige.

The street cleaner outside sees the cigarette butts and detritus of last night's festivities.

They all experience the same building but with different meanings and associations. Each person experiences a fragment of the whole from his or her perspective, but reality is greater than the sum of personal perception.

When combined with good relationships the imagination opens our windows of perception by enabling us to live in the experience of others and connect our islands of reality.

This inventive ability is full of potential, but becomes a wilderness of speculation if left to grow untended. It will summon up demons and dragons when none exists, while overlooking the ones that do. It will ascribe attributes and abilities to objects that they do not have and cannot sustain, leading to disappointment and cynicism. Under pressure and left to its own devices, the imagination will try to create reality rather than enable us to participate in a shared reality with other people.

Modern people see more images in a week than the average person did in their lifetime just a century ago. Advertisers spend billions to stimulate our imagination, to gain and keep our attention and arouse our desires. They set standards of success and behaviour that slip past our critical faculties.[1] However, you may have noticed how every invention that promises to revolutionise our lives eventually reveals its downside. The motor car freed us from the horse and cart but caused air pollution and urban sprawl. Atomic energy was supposed to supply unlimited free electrical power but produced atomic waste. Social media was going to connect everyone, but its algorithms feed our prejudices and consume our data and attention. Every human invention mirrors our moral capacity for good and for evil.

The second word of the Decalogue points to both the potential and the danger of this powerful capacity. It warns against assigning divine qualities or powers to objects in the world and against overvaluing the potential of our creations. The boundary frees us from slavery, superstition and romantic idealisation, to allow for creative engagement with objects as they are.

Capacities of the Imagination

Our two physical eyes are a window between the external world and the inner world of the mind. They give depth of field and perspective. We also have four *inner* eyes, which allow a more profound view of reality:

1 The *eye of memory*, which recalls to mind experience and associated emotions from the past.[2]
2 The *eye of the heart*, which concerns our relational link to the external world through a web of attachments and loyalties.
3 The *eye of the imagination* through which we visualise potential and possibility, and make poetic and provisional associations.
4 The *eye of perception and reason*, which sorts and orders information and experience into meaningful patterns, before giving language to describe and communicate.

Children use the imagination when playing, as a safe place to experiment with life. They learn over time to differentiate between reality and illusion. Adults use it to practise difficult conversations and plan future scenarios. It can also be a place to hide or a means of filling a painful void, a place for daydreams and fantasies to soothe a deflated ego, or a way to provide comfort in loneliness.

The mind uses the imagination to innovate and find solutions to problems, creating the potential for change. The engineer imagines a bridge and the architect a building. Scientists construct mental models to explore phenomena that are hard to understand and harder to explain. Poets and painters use it to explore the familiar and show alternative perspectives.

Images awaken emotions and desires that provide the energy to connect to other people and objects, liberating us from mindless conformity. Desire is a powerful stimulus for change, but it must be shaped and directed to be effective. Leaders use images to rouse their followers to action with stirring visions for better or worse.

The images can be a welcome guest or an uninvited intruder, raising the heart rate and inflaming anxiety or filling the mind with wonder and anticipation. A corrupt imagination will read a threat from a neighbour's frown. In one callous moment it will plot murder and destruction, and dream of dinner the next.

Our imagination allows us to walk in another person's shoes, to see their point of view, to feel their feelings; to empathise, commiserate and give comfort and courage. It helps us see the potential in other people, to understand who they are and might become. But the imaginative mind is finite, and who has time to process all the thoughts and emotions it throws up? We must make do with a few selected impressions and choose where to place our attention. Unchecked and untested, it will be the source of prejudice, feeding on fears and projecting judgement onto a person before they have time, space and feel safe to reveal themselves.

Imagination and the Subjective Perspective

The imagination arouses emotions that facilitate *participation in life*, while reason and revelation provide *an understanding of life*. The first is the view of experience, sometimes called the subjective view, and the second provides the view from elsewhere and is potentially more objective, though not automatically so. Both are important and require a measure of alignment if we are to share experiences and participate in life with other people.

Imagine that I invite a group of new friends home for dinner. As we stand in the living room, a few guests are talking to each other. They are looking at an ugly painting hanging on the wall in a discreet corner of the room. They exchange puzzled glances with each other. Without additional information to challenge their perspective, the ugly picture represents the taste of their host. It is out of keeping with the room, and people are making judgements. A slight but discernible distance grows between us. One of the guests cannot resist a glance at me.

I walk over to them. They are embarrassed.

'I see you are looking at the picture,' I declare with a smile. 'It is ugly, isn't it?'

They look at me with great relief, and the distance between us melts in the light of honesty.

'Let me tell you about the picture,' I continue. 'I have a good friend who died last year and left me this picture. I dislike the picture, but I loved my friend and it reminds me of him, and strangely it comforts me.'

The room is the same for each of us; we see the same objects, but we see them through different lenses. Our associations with them are as unique as we are, so their meaning and value are distinct. As I reveal my history, associations and meanings to my new friends, they enter my world of meaning and, as the conversation continues, I enter theirs. We are all enriched, and our worlds of perception have expanded because of the encounter. The perspective from experience is personal but is as much a part of reality as the *fact* that the picture hangs on the wall. Experts have standards for evaluating art, and with further education I might appreciate it more. But my association with my friend is real and must not be discounted.

The imagination can help or hinder the process of trust. Judgements that come from the imagination, as in the example above, or my friends' opinion about my taste, must be tested to see if they are correct. This is only possible through my act of revelation. Those who suspend judgement create the potential for discovery and revelation that deepens friendship.

All humans are prejudiced![3] Pre-judgement is how humans manage risk in a world that overwhelms us with information and difference. We dislike the unknown and unfamiliar. An undisciplined imagination inflates danger, while evaluation involves hard work mentally. Quick judgements made based on external markers never present the full picture. Trust requires knowledge, which takes time to gather. Generalisations need to be tested and grounded. The mature mind is aware that personal experience is not the sum of all experiences and thus holds those judgements lightly and tests them in the light of specific encounters.

The Schism within the Western Mind

Why does the Decalogue place images and imagination before the names and language we discuss in the next chapter? Perhaps because children first learn to see and feel before they learn to reason and speak.[4] It is not different in adults, but having learned to analyse, some adults mistake understanding for participation. The imagination generates ideas and hypotheses to explore and test. Naming the attributes of objects enables articulation and dialogue. Images and words are an interwoven symbol system through which we communicate and engage in life with others.

The twenty-first-century mind intuitively divides the imaginative from the rational. It is as if we eat from two tables. One table exclusively uses knives, while the other table uses forks. The knives dissect and analyse, while the forks eat and participate. A dimly remembered rule says that those who use knives should never be seen to use forks and vice versa. On one side stands the scientific mind, with its bias towards fact and objectivity; on the other is the creative, imaginative mind and subjectivity.

The schism developed in the European Enlightenment of the late-seventeenth and eighteenth centuries, which sought certainty through analysis, rationality and abstraction. Over time a subtle cultural authoritarianism has reinforced the one-sided view that rationalism is the de facto authority.

Reason and rationality are essential to human understanding, but rationalism stakes a claim to being *the ultimate authority* – although, by its own rules, it cannot justify its claim.[5]

Objects can and often must be described with accuracy and precision. Objectivity is important where possible, necessary and appropriate. Ungrounded subjectivism can impede scientific discovery. However, the dichotomy is false, as every young Einstein knows.

What is necessary for science can be problematic for interpersonal relationships. Relational knowledge belongs to a different category of *knowing through participation* rather than *knowing by observation*. It is necessarily approximate and ambiguous. Involvement in the lives of others includes but goes beyond an objective understanding of how human beings function generically. The imagination enables empathy and emotion to enter the other person's experience. A closed rationalistic mind sees only the logic of its case and is in danger of prejudice. It is as if the heart were trying to work without the lungs.

In reaction the postmodern mind, which developed in the aftermath of the industrial-scale atrocities of the twentieth century, is suspicious of all claims to authority. It is trained to understand through subjective participation and experience. This view continues in the tradition of the schism, but leans to the opposite side.

When reason is the exclusive guide of reality, the result is a materialistic and mechanistic universe devoid of meaning. When imagination is the primary guide, the result is a life of speculation and irrational power. It is a mistake to absolutise the relative or create tension where there should be integration. The imagination frees the mind to explore possibilities and to move beyond personal experience. The wise person uses both but trusts neither as ultimate.

While substantial and objective knowledge of the external world is possible, the healthy mind accepts and lives with probabilities and uncertainty in areas of personal knowledge. A mature mind maintains a healthy scepticism without cynicism, and optimism towards truth without naivety or romantic sentimentalism.

Yesterday evening I listened to a friend playing Brahms on the piano – the room filled with the sounds that mediated the tones of the musical notation. My mind wandered to the piano, and I felt the vibrations made by the hammering of felt on strings placed near the soundboard. Frequencies, decibels and units of time are all understandable through mathematics and the laws of physics. But if the analysis is left there, where is Brahms, the pianist or the piano maker's contribution? The composer's creativity connects the frequencies and wavelengths to the flow of history and the perspective of a specific period of Western music. My pianist friend relates the decibels and timing to his personal choice and interpretation of the piece. As the music fills the room, all these aspects combine to make the experience possible, and I, the listener, enter the music, and the music enters me. I inhabit the music for a moment and find myself in a greater place. As the music resolves, I enter a resolution deeper than the music itself and am richer for it. The calculus of my personal experience of the piece is beyond mathematical calculation. Reality is more than its visible and measurable parts.

The imagination creates space for new perspectives that are not immediately easy to articulate. The poet understands these intuitive expressions of truth. Through them we comprehend at first by direct access what may be accessed later by reason. A healthy imagination describes the glories of life in ways that reason can only grasp and articulate with time.

I discovered the depth of my captivity to the hyper-rationalistic separation of experience and reason through a visit to a large Picasso exhibition in Vienna. I went with a Slovak friend who is an accomplished artist and photographer. We first wandered around, getting the layout of the collection, and then went our separate ways. I saw a huge picture that confused me. Not only did I not understand it, I also did not have the first clue how to approach it. After some time, my friend came up behind me and said, 'You are asking all the wrong questions,' and then he walked away. How did he know what I was thinking? I caught up with him and asked what he meant. What he said opened a door into a new world of experience and understanding. 'You have to experience some things before you can understand them,' he said, then walked away again.

I did not understand what he meant, but returned to the painting. Rather than asking questions, I stood before the painting and allowed it to touch me. My eye caught a single continuous brushstroke, about six inches wide, that went in an arc from the bottom of the painting to the top. I felt the energy needed to bend and stretch to paint it and the violence of the brushstroke. In that moment the picture made sense, though I could not immediately articulate why. An excess of rationality had been keeping me from a deeper cognition. Academic distance kept me from participating, which kept me from understanding.

It would have been legitimate to analyse the picture through many lenses – the history of the period, the genre, the artist's biographical details and his technical skills would have added much to an understanding of the painting. But putting aside the questions for a moment, being present to the picture itself, and allowing it to have its effect, gave knowledge that could not be found in any other way. Gradually, more profound thoughts and new relationships emerged.

With practice, the inner eye of the imagination learns to respond. Reason can then explore this new perspective. But if the rational is prioritised at the expense of the experiential, such perception is blocked.

When thinking about an object or event, we become observers rather than participants. Being time-bound, we necessarily think systematically in sequence and divide life into categories. But we *experience* life as a whole. Who has not felt the enjoyment drain from a meal as a participant discussed the benefits of its vitamins or the dangers of its carbohydrates?

Integration is essential for sound reasoning and healthy imagining. An integrated mind receives energy from emotion, direction and meaning from reasonable thought. The key to integration is humility, recognising the limits of the human mind while remaining free to probe possibility.

Imagination and Religion

The schism between reason and imagination infiltrates the way we think about religion, and religious life itself. I am thinking primarily of Christians, but the division is found in many other belief systems, religious or otherwise. It affects religious thinking from within, and also thinking about religion from outside.

One side of the schism subtly prioritises rationality and ignores or even suppresses the imagination, *abstracting* truth from the revealed text and thinking only in propositions. The subtle message is that we can trust in reason, but emotion (often conflated with feeling) is unreliable. This severs truth from lived experience and the energy required for change. The congregation listen to sermons on serious and majestic issues, sit and nod, stand to exchange pleasantries, and depart with little discernible response and without the sustained emotional energy necessary for action. Propositions and abstract thought are useful, even necessary, as a step towards understanding, but they are a description of reality, not reality itself. It is as if we go to the restaurant and examine the menu, discuss it with the waiter and fellow diners, ponder the labels and pictures, but are then satisfied by dissecting and eating the menu rather than the meal.

The other side, often in reaction to an excess of dry rationality, allows the imagination free rein without restraint, leaving the imagination ungrounded by reason. It bursts out in uncontained, often magical, thinking. This stimulates powerful emotions, which give the appearance of validation. Here faith is founded solely on personal experience or wishful thinking rather than objective realities. It gives rise to an optimism based on sentiment, which feeds a sense of unreality. Leaps of faith and superstitious practices grow in intensity and feed the addiction to the spectacular, which has been substituted for evidence. Unnecessary doubts plague participants when the powerful experiences prove unsustainable.

The crisis of meaning many are experiencing in Western culture is a symptom of the lack of integration of reason and imagination.[6] Even readers who do not consider themselves to be religious usually have a desire for meaningful beliefs that are satisfying both to reason (and thus plausible not delusional) and to the imagination, enabling participation.

I describe two caricatures for the sake of clarity and brevity. Many people straddle the divide or swing from one to the other. Neither the first group with its abstractions nor the second with its unrestrained imagination reflects the richness of reasonable faith in ordinary life.

Envision a community that integrates imagination and reason. Could the imagination provide a more vibrant experience of thought, wonder, humility and empathy, or the freedom to question tired religious categories and refill them with meaning to enter more fully into its story? Might those who tested their speculative assumptions about each other become more honest about their speculation and enjoy more courageous and profound communion? Stronger empathy leads to a greater understanding of alternative positions, and a less fearful imagination leads to richer hospitality and openness to others. Such a community, creating its culture rather than adopting the culture of the surrounding society, will be more relational, spontaneous and creative, and less formulaic and programmatic.

The Problem with the Tooth Fairy

When I was a young child and my milk teeth fell out, I would put them under my pillow. In great excitement I would wake the next morning to find a shiny coin. Magically, a being I never saw or knew would visit in the night. I cannot remember now how often the tooth fairy came but I remember the excitement of the first visit, and how the next loose tooth seemed less frightening than the first.

The tooth fairy has a bad reputation, and is an object of scorn among those who do not believe in her, or him. Insightful rationalists quickly claim that tooth fairies do not exist. But I contend that tooth fairies *do* exist. After all, I have the evidence of the coin left beside my bed. Belief in the tooth fairy was justified. That the tooth fairy turned out to be different from my childlike imagination is a reality I must accept. What was not justified was rejection of that belief in defence of a worldview that turned out to be a failure to understand the proper function of the imagination.

My mother was not lying. There really was a tooth fairy, and she should know. Just as it turned out that there really was a Father Christmas. It is true that, in the case of Father Christmas, my imagination had been badly misled and confused for commercial reasons by a society held captive to consumerism and a desire for distractions on dark winter nights. Father Christmas, it turned out, was real – I had the presents to prove it – and he was closer than I ever imagined. He was present every day, but at Christmas he stayed up late to prepare a magical surprise.

Jesus asked a tax collector[7] and a prosperous young man[8] to leave their wealth and follow him. The first left his lucrative but despised wealth-creation system and followed, while the other hesitated, thought about his wealth and walked away from the offer. Both saw the same man, but they did not see with the same eyes – not all seeing is perceiving. Was it their need or social conditioning that shaped what they saw? Possibly pride controlled the eyes of the young man, and need the tax collector. The accounts are not specific. The prosperous young man saw a good teacher. But it seems the tax collector saw something more: a teacher to whom he could commit his life – and whom the Gospels soon identified as the Son of God, the Maker of all the gold in the universe. In this light, which of the two men made the better investment?

When we lived in Central Europe, I was involved in researching people's beliefs about ultimate reality. We asked people to describe the God in whom they did or did not believe (as I asked you at the beginning of Chapter 4). It was interesting to discover how the culture we grow up in informs our imagination about ultimate reality. The results showed, quite understandably, that our assumptions stem not so much from considered thought as from something intuited and ambivalent from childhood. To touch on these memories is to connect with something deeply personal and often unarticulated, either positively or negatively. Interestingly, even people who did not believe in transcendence had an intuitive idea that was informing their understanding about the character of God. Our enquiries showed that many people living in Northern Europe believed in or rejected a distant but nevertheless personal deity, while in the Balkans, people thought of mother earth. The imagination informs how we believe. The violence of European history influences the imagination still further, but the imagination should not have the last word.

We have evidence that humans are more than matter. Our need to establish truth, our longing for goodness and justice (however we define them), our moral outrage at wrongs done (real or imaginary), our hunger for meaning and significance, our love of beauty (however we define it), our sense of wonder, our gratitude, our capacity for music and other forms of creativity that are not necessary for survival – all are evidence of something more. They point to something beyond nature. It is not unreasonable to think that whatever the *something* is, it might be moral and we might be accountable to it and responsible for our moral choices.

As adults we must put childish ideas behind us and grow towards maturity. But it is worth asking how, and on whose terms, we might get to know a being who is capable of bringing a universe into existence. Personal knowledge comes through revelation, and faith is not blind but undergirded by reasonable evidence, but it would be wise to remember who has the last word.

The Imagination Adds Substance to Abstraction

Modern people tend to formulate truth as abstraction, which might be helpful for understanding but is less helpful for motivating change. The imagination puts the meat back on the bones of abstraction. It is difficult to read the narrative sections of the Bible without imagining the events described, nor should we. As with any work of art, we are supposed to take part through the imagination, to empathise with the participants and see the events from various points of view, to understand them.

In the book of Luke in the New Testament, there is a beautiful story of courage, gratitude and self-control.[9] In it a woman, probably a prostitute, entered the house of a judgemental Pharisee who had invited Jesus to dinner. Imagine her emotional state as she stood ready to knock on the door of the Pharisee's house and gain entrance. Imagine the courage it must have taken her to walk through the door and face the scorn of the host. The woman wanted to anoint the feet of Jesus with oil as an act of gratitude and worship. Smell the costly oil with the senses of the imagination, enter the sensuality of the moment. What trust did it take to kneel and touch Jesus' feet? How would an average man respond to such a sensual act? Do I take the self-discipline of Christ for granted? Am I in awe of his self-control?

This is a master class in storytelling. The extraction of truth into abstract and passionless statements would not do the story justice. Truth is contained within the story, and we can test against wild speculative interpretation by reading the story in the context of the surrounding accounts. We should not isolate the truth from its context, nor strip it of its drama. It should not surprise us to discover the result of such abstraction is emotional starvation and a loss of energy for change.

Cultivating a Hopeful Imagination

Companies worldwide spend billions to stimulate our hunger and thirst to consume things that are momentary and transient. How much more necessary is it to awaken our hunger for goodness and stimulate an appetite for the eternal?

Once, on a hot, dusty summer afternoon in a suburb of St Petersburg in Russia, I walked past a casino located, oddly, in the basement of a tall apartment block. The entrance glared with brightly coloured flashing lights that enticed my eye. The stimulation fired my imagination, and I could visualise the cool interior as I felt the pull of the music emanating from speakers fixed to the windows. I stepped back off the pavement to get a view of the doorway in its context. Putting the impulse in a larger context is always a good way to test the pull of the imagination. Large, crumbling grey apartment blocks towered around it. What, at first glance, appeared attractive now seemed gaudy and worn. It struck me that the casino was a symbol of short-term hope and excitement.

Idols – images elevated to godlike status – appeal to our imagination. Our vision of success, pleasure or nationalism stimulates the imagination to excite our desires but offers what turns out to be an endless treadmill of addictions, delivering momentary relief from the alienation of an empty human existence. You can tell they are idols because they leave someone enslaved or diminished.

Our desires are not wrong, just seriously misdirected and incomplete. Their vision is not big enough. Nationhood, for example, is a common good until my nation becomes more important than yours, or national paranoia is fed by irrational fears that fuel an aggressive posture. It is more effective to work for peace and heal the alienation.

One might say the same for the family, wealth or power. All are good when held in their appropriate place, but when they become dominant at the expense of other people, they are the pathway to tyranny.

Our present alienation fuels the hunger behind our search for the better country, but we do not have to experience the fake to recognise the real thing. For many years my wife and I lived in cities where the streetlights, while sometimes useful, blinded us to the wonder of the night sky. After a while, we forgot that the more excellent glory was there at all. Then we moved to the countryside, served by a road without streetlights. It was surprising and joyful to rediscover the intensity of the stars on a moonless night. It was symbolic that the man-made light had hidden the light of a greater glory from us. Not having the streetlights made our world larger and richer. A nightly reminder of the greater context in which we live.

When we awaken the desire for good, the gaudy and temporary will be put in perspective, no longer as real as we imagined but pointing to something more substantial beyond themselves. Centuries after the Decalogue was given to Moses, Paul the apostle and Jewish scholar prayed for the church of his day, that their desires would be awakened, 'having the eyes of your hearts enlightened, that you may know what is the hope to which he has called you, what are the riches of his glorious inheritance'.[10] For him the eternal was not a length of time but a quality of life, and of being in relationships of love.

Jesus told his followers to 'hunger and thirst for righteousness'.[11] He encouraged them to think of their longing and desire for goodness with the same urgency that they felt for food and water. Hunger and thirst are painful, but powerful drives. He was encouraging his followers to awaken their moral imagination and make the desire for right relationships their guiding principle in life. God's moral character is the road map to a rich moral landscape. We can open the map by imagining the results of obedience to the moral code.

The second word of the Decalogue reminds us that 'I the LORD your God am a jealous God'.[12] In English, we commonly use the word 'jealous' when we mean envious. The two terms describe the positive and negative sides of the same impulse. Envy is the drive to possess, and we will look at it more closely in Chapter 12. Jealousy is protective; threaten my family and jealousy will motivate me to protect them. God is protective of his commandments because they point the way to human flourishing.

From False Images to the True Image

There is one more level yet to explore. In Genesis, the first book of the Bible, we learn that humans reflect the image of their Creator. We need to know the Creator to know and understand ourselves. A tragedy of the false image and the idol is that our view of humanness gets distorted and, with it, our capacity to establish the relative worth of all other objects. We begin to underestimate the value of humans and lose the sense of wonder and glory when in the presence of other people.

How can we know who God is if we can't see the infinite being? Creation in all its magnificent diversity is one sign of God's generosity and joyful but risky creativity. However, the book of nature is not enough to know God fully. We can read it through many lenses. Through one lens it looks beautiful; through another chaotic and violent. It is endlessly fascinating but not a definitive description of the character of its originator. From within space and time we do not have the perspective to understand it. For a fuller understanding we need revelation from beyond our horizon.

Followers of Jesus believe that he, the second person of the Trinity, came into the world for this purpose. He is the ultimate medium through which God reveals himself. Paul, one of his early followers, wrote, 'He [Jesus] is the image of the invisible God',[13] the God who became a man and lived among us, and as John, the writer of the fourth Gospel, wrote, was 'full of grace and truth'.[14] This man, claimed the apostles who knew him, was the Word become flesh; image and Word combined in the perfect man, the complete representation of God. Jesus said of himself, 'Whoever has seen me has seen the Father.'[15]

Jesus is the model of what it means to be properly human. The four Gospels, which describe him from different perspectives with different emphases, show a man who embodies other-centred love. A man willing to give up his life for his friends. He is the fullest expression of the Decalogue, a genuinely free man in control of himself, someone people trusted and loved and more than a few hated because his goodness exposed their deceptions.

In Jesus, the uncreated has reached into the creation, committing to it and to us for ever. For this reason, God is jealous of his image in the world. Christ, the second person of the Trinity, is the ultimate icon – the window onto the reality of the infinite three-person God. God makes himself known through him, and in knowing him we come to know ourselves, and the fragments in us and among us begin to heal. In him we see the source and sustainer of all reality. If there is a better country, the best image of how we should relate in that country is seen in him.

6

Word Three: What Is Your Name?

You shall not take the name of the Lord your God in vain. (Exodus 20:7)

Vanity of vanities, says the Preacher,
vanity of vanities! All is vanity.
What does man gain by all the toil
at which he toils under the sun?
(Ecclesiastes 1:2–3)

What could be more important in a better country than good, clear communication? How full life is when the language we use is rich and full of meaning. How much joy have you experienced through deep, trusting communication? How quickly life becomes dull when language is used to manipulate through propaganda or hollow clichés.

The third word of the Decalogue begins with the name of God. This, if you will, is the first word in the universe, the source of all other words and from which all other words derive their meaning and, by extension, it covers all names and language.[1]

In the Café Now and Not Yet, people often puzzle to understand the third word of the Decalogue, partly because the name of the Lord slips rather more often from their mouths in moments of stress than they care to admit.

It helps to understand that the vanity referred to by the Preacher of Ecclesiastes means 'empty'. We should not think here so much about rude words as empty, hollowed out or meaningless ones. It might be better to think of swearing as the thoughtless use of *any* word. To get the idea, just listen to the pious platitudes of religious gatherings, marketing clichés or political rhetoric. What would it mean for communication in a better country if we knew what we meant and meant what we said?

Imagine arriving at an airport to take a trip. You look up at the departures board to check your flight, and in place of the name of the city you intend to fly to, the board simply says *CITY*. In fact, every destination is listed as *CITY* because the casual use of their names has erased the uniqueness of their names from memory. You go to the desk for help, but words literally fail you. The generic term *CITY* is not enough to distinguish among the cities. Pilots do not have enough information to plot their course, and, naturally, your luggage could end up anywhere.

I find it helpful to think of a name like an old cupboard in which we store all the attributes, associations, meanings, assumptions and expectations of the object the name represents. When I think of the word 'London' I retrieve childhood memories of the city in which I grew up from that cupboard. I think of Nelson's Column or Big Ben, I feel the heat and vibrations of the big, red, double-decker buses and I smell the diesel of old black taxis and the pungent dung of the horses on Horse Guards Parade or the coal of fires that used to smother the London of my childhood in thick fog. People who have never been to London will have images and information from websites, travel guides or encyclopaedias. The meanings and associations are as deep as our curiosity. Residents need a larger cupboard than others, yet no two cupboards are quite the same, and no one knows all the attributes, associations and meanings. Times change, too, and I cannot assume my old associations are still valid or my assumptions are still correct, nor should I think I know all there is to know, just as I cannot escape attributes and associations I do not like or make up meanings to suit myself.

When I travel to London, I follow the signs for London and they lead me to the real place. I do not mistake the sign for the city. To take a name in vain is to empty the cupboard of all the attributes, associations and meanings, or mistake the sign for what it signifies.

Instead, we should fill the cupboard, and thus use language that is rich and meaningful.

In recent times we have been pulled in two directions. The first says that truth is to be found only in the data or the objective facts that are common to all of us. The second says that what matters is my personal associations, and the facts are not important or relevant. The tension can be useful because it makes us thoughtful about language, but both are important, and the fight is itself unnecessary and leads nowhere but to unnecessary polarisation.

The gift of language is so important that two words of the Decalogue govern its use. This one is about the meaning of words, and the ninth, which we will come to later, deals with telling truth, and protects against those who would distort another person's perception of reality.

The Gift of a Name

I have known my wife Tuula for over forty-five years. I probably know her better than anyone alive, yet she still surprises me. As a quiet adventurer, she has travelled all over the globe yet loves her garden with equal wonder. Her idea of happiness is three days among the beautiful ceramics on the top floor of the Victoria and Albert Museum in London, but she explores and knows the history of our old pots and bric-a-brac. She gives her heart wisely but with generosity. I have often watched her love a stranger with fierce concentration and compassion. She has immense empathy; she mourned the passing of our old dog for several years. She comes from one of the most advanced countries in the world and yet did not have electricity in her house until she was seven; such is the technological journey of her lifetime. The clean Finnish air and the quiet, gentle landscape of lakes, granite and trees have shaped her soul, but its climate requires tenacity, and when we fight she holds her ground.

Her name is the storehouse for her attributes and reputation, the summary of who she is. A few letters conferred by her mother soon after birth is the short form for all this and much more. The storehouse has filled with more meaning as we have shared life, but even she does not know its full depth or potential. Some people know her well; others hardly know her at all and do not know what they are missing. It would be a great mistake to treat her name as if it were empty when it is full but unknown. It would be a more significant mistake to think that it can contain whatever I imagine or want. Tuula is her own person and not mine to make up.

Most of the time, we honour and respect each other's names. I wish I could say that our communication is flawless, but even though we can draw on several languages, we stumble over our words, miscommunicate and say things we do not mean and hear things that were not meant. Occasionally, we throw words at each other in exasperation, like the builder who smashes his thumb with a hammer. In those moments, our words are empty and become weapons or shields. When we are angry, we exaggerate and generalise, and our words take on meanings that are unique to our struggles and you would not find in a dictionary. When sanity returns, we rediscover the meaning we lost in the madness, we feel sorrow at the failure of our love and express it when we say sorry. How rich we are when we have good, clear, true and meaningful communication.

Name and Identity

Now I know in part; then I shall know fully, even as I have been fully known.
(1 Corinthians 13:12)

When Eastern Europe was under communism I used another name, for security reasons. After the Iron Curtain fell, I had to tell some friends that the name they had known me by was not the name my family used. It was a strange moment because they had attached my attributes and associations to a name that was real for them. The death of that name was real death; my friends had to move the characteristics from the old name to the new one and learn to trust the new name to renew their gift of friendship.

Children receive their name as a gift – they are usually named by someone else. In later life some people find this painful because they are ashamed of the identity that comes with it. I have had more than one friend tell me they changed their name to escape their past. One friend told me he reclaimed his name when he resolved the shame of the association with his father.

Little children call out in a thousand ways: *see me, hear me, look at me, notice me.* Their call is not to just any mother or father, but to a specific mother or father whose voice they recognise. Sometimes the child wanders away but does not go far before looking back to see if Mother is watching. When Mother returns the call, she calls to the child by a specific name like John or Jane. The child is reassured and freed to wander further, to explore and encounter new challenges and their identity in relationship to them. In being noticed, the child knows the world is safe. The bond of trust is built first between unique people before it can extend to others. But imagine if all names were generic, everyone was called Child, and all people were unnamed.

Identity is formed primarily by association and exploration. Little children spend hours watching those around them, learning by imitation. They take on the habits and attitudes of those they have learned to trust.

Once, while visiting some friends, my wife and I went out while our then four-year-old son remained to help with the washing up. On our return, our hostess recounted their conversation with some amusement.

'Oh, shit!' our son had said suddenly.

Being a wise woman with children of her own, she asked, 'What does that word mean?'

With the innocence of doves, he replied, 'It's what grown-ups say when something goes wrong.'

Children trustingly reflect the image of the ones closest to them and on whom they depend for their very lives. It is how they learn, for better or worse. It is a beautiful device and gets to the heart of the meaning of worship; to organise our reality around the value and worth of the one who is honoured or worshipped. Children order their reality to conform to those they honour, modelling their lives around the example given to them.

The Loneliness of Vanity

This is, of course, in contrast to how modern people build and maintain their identity, at great psychological cost (I refer you to the sidebar on hyper-individualism in Chapter 2). Modern people bear the burden of discovering and describing their identity. At first, it feels like freedom, but the pressure to create and maintain a persona to the world is exhausting.

God is the source from which all other names flow, whatever we think *God* might be. Our understanding of everything else in the world will flow from and reflect what we have enthroned as ultimate reality. Many people do not believe in the transcendent personal and infinite being described in the Bible. But everyone has an ultimate authority through which they understand reality, even if it is just their rationality. For the rationalist, reason is God. In that sense I am not sure I have ever met an atheist.

Why would the infinite and personal God care what we think about his name? After all, abuse of his name does not change or diminish God. But it reduces our understanding of God. We are poorer for the misperception, deliberate or otherwise. The Bible describes humans as made in God's image, the idea being that when we look at him and see his face in our mind's eye and trust it, we become like him just as every child reflects their parents. If there is no face of God, we turn to other faces to gain a sense of identity.

Perhaps hell is the state of being unnamed and having no image to reflect; of being trapped in a hall of mirrors where the self is the only object. If God is the ultimate external reference point for what it means to be human and how we should be human, repudiation or distortion of his image will leave us eventually with nothing but subjectivity. This is lonely and perhaps accounts for the extreme anxiety that disturbs so many modern people.

If we let it, modern society will un-name us but then brand us as we take on the identities of the consumer culture. Our value comes from a brand of sportswear or i-gadgets, and familiarity comes from fast-food outlets rather than home cooking.

After generations of modernity, people feel alienation and depersonalisation. The benefit and convenience of the modern age have been bought at the price of loose relational ties, transience and the loss of a common narrative to hold society together. This results in alienated communities and distant relationships, raising the issues of polarisation and cohesion in society that are just starting to surface in both our public and private discourse.

The modern age offers us the robotic, mechanical, transactional and functional, and efficiency. When society, business or government reduces humanity to the sum of its data sets, unique persons become lost in the generalisations.

Personifying machines by naming them is one of the significant reductions in our times. Alexa, Siri and the like are a convenient interface with the machine sphere but have the unintended consequence of conditioning a generation of children into thinking that the machine has consciousness. First, we imagine ourselves as machines, the brain as hardware and thought as software, until we come to see a reflection of ourselves in the machine. In attempting to humanise the machine, we are dehumanised.

With the proliferation of new kinds of machine language and the vast quantities of data that enable artificial intelligence, the danger of dehumanisation is growing.[2] Big data, so helpful at many levels, turn out to be the largest selfie of them all.

We are right to rebel and be offended when a number replaces a name, be it tattooed on the arm or a barcode in a file; a person is stripped of their uniqueness and dehumanised by removing their name and all it signifies. Recently, while sitting in a hospital waiting room, I overheard an administrator explaining on the phone to a client why she could not correct their misspelled name on the computer system. She explained that she was powerless to make the simple change because the system was centralised and she did not have the authority. The client protested, and the administrator empathised, but there was nothing she could do. The waiting room filled with cynical laughter at the system and sympathy for the administrator as she apologised for a system that disempowered and humiliated her in the name of data standardisation.

In the Western world we have a first name, which is a unique identifier, and a last name (or family name), which binds us to a group of people. Through our names, the community acknowledges us as unique persons in community. But while we belong to a family, tribe or nation with specific identification of language, culture or colour, we are also human among all other humans, the primary marker to which all other identities are subordinate. Those who follow Christ believe that we live before the face of God, who loves each person with equal passion, which is the foundation of equality among humans.

The image of God is the basis for human identity and personhood. To be made in God's image means to reflect his personal attributes and virtues: his relationality, creativity, hospitality, generosity, beauty, humility, justice, wisdom, trust and freedom, among many others. Our calling is to be fully human, an expression of all these attributes, and we should not be reduced to mere religious categories.

God is the source and sustainer of life, the ultimate location of our belonging, the core of our identity. God is our home country and culture; it is from God we learn our mother tongue. Turn on the lights at home, and the lights will go on in the universe.

Shared Authority to Name and Order Reality

The extraordinary story in the ancient book of Genesis describes God as creating the earth without form; some translations talk of chaos.[3] It is interesting to wonder why God would create a chaos. In the account, form or order emerges from the disorder through naming the parts; the lights in the sky, the earth and seas, and man – male and female.

Having brought order to the greater reality, God called on Adam to name the animals. The symbolism is profound. 'And whatever the man called every living creature, that was its name.'[4] In giving Adam this task, God was sharing authorship with him. This is real authority. Adam's authority was on a lesser scale than his Creator's

– he could never change the earth's distance to the sun – but it was nevertheless real and significant. He was free to name and adapt those parts over which he would govern. The boundary between God's sphere and Adam's was not always straightforward, nor was it clear where they overlapped. The tension was positive and allowed for dialogue and participation between the man, the woman and their maker.

There is something final about the clause 'that was its name'. Those who define language exercise both authority and power over others through the way they shape perception. How I describe reality may not be how it really is, but it is how it will be to me. We live with the consequences of the descriptions we use.

Thus, the authority to describe reality is a gift and also a responsibility. Adam's act of naming had the potential to change perception. How an object is understood to be determines, to a great degree, how we experience it and what we expect of it. How we describe reality affects what we can do. Proper naming enables a fruitful relationship between subject and object. Incorrect or incomplete descriptions hinder effective action. To see an object from a limited point of view might be a distortion. A correct diagnosis is essential to find the appropriate solution. Before certainty is fully justified, it is a hindrance; intellectual humility allows for the continued pursuit of clarity.

A man's behaviour might tempt me to call him a fool, and he might even be a fool, but my attitude towards his foolishness might blind me to all his other attributes, which are now as good as dead to me. Jesus said that to call someone a fool, I have murdered him.[5] In doing so, I have reduced all those glorious attributes solely to my experience of him. Our experience is essential, but it is not the final authority when describing reality. The subjective point of view is likely to be a distortion if it is incomplete. Poor use of language excludes attributes, while rich language identifies characteristics truthfully, regardless of my relationship to them.

The power to name reality has very real practical benefits. Just as God, in the first chapter of Genesis, brought order to the formless earth by naming the parts, so wise people use the principle of naming to sort through their personal chaos as they sit with a friend and name the various components of the chaos until clarity emerges. A wrong or incomplete description can hinder the process. As reality is named with increasing precision, order emerges, and with it the power to act and implement effective change.

Young people come to my study in search of wisdom. They are wrestling with some confusion and are seeking clarity. They want me to be honest with them. My task is to help them name their concerns. They may have described their issue inaccurately or incompletely. As they describe reality with increasing precision, they see the contours of order and direction emerge, and they gain hope. My work is to listen for the hesitation in their voice and help them uncover what is hidden or avoided; to listen for self-deception, fear or anxieties they have found too painful to face. In their desire to avoid suffering they may have misnamed and reinterpreted reality as an escape route from their pain.

Clarity comes as they become aware of and then evaluate their hidden assumptions. The process is rarely pain free. First, they must clear out the debris of illusion and longings they are afraid to name. I must help them explore the experiences and associations behind their words until reality resonates and they have clarity and understanding. It is an act of love to ask someone what they mean; to take their words seriously.

Doctors ask their patients to describe their symptoms, to facilitate diagnosis. Clarification of the description, a new viewpoint, a slight change in perspective, gives further clarity and leads to more effective action. If a problem appears unsolvable, it may be because it has been misnamed, and incorrectly named problems lead to ineffective or even destructive solutions. We should not take the names we use lightly or for granted.

Language and Power

Authority is the power to describe reality: this is how things are and what they mean. Where no ultimate authority is acknowledged, the relative powers will fight among themselves to claim that space. It is wise to ask what assumptions each claimant is making and consider their impact. For example, the reductions of scientific naturalism can lead to a reductionistic and deterministic view of humanness, but there are many other views of reality that depersonalise humans.

Thoughtful language matters because language shapes perception. A slight modification can hide emotional impact and moral resonance. Soldiers become 'assets', and 'collateral damage' is a by-product of war. We call the product of sexual activity a baby if it is wanted and a foetus if it is not.

While culture and language change over time, fundamental reality does not. Reality can be painful, and our hidden agendas, aimed at protecting against shame or concealing envy, are dangerous. We play language games in our attempt to control others and protect ourselves. We deceive ourselves (a spectacular moral feat in itself!), tricking the mind into thinking reality is different from how it is. When a grasp of truth is unavailable because one or more people want to hide it, confusion abounds and the search for solutions becomes harder.

Some people view life, almost exclusively, through the lens of a power imbalance between oppressor and oppressed, and want to expose binary opposites of economics, gender, race and sexuality. But are all binaries in opposition, or are some complementary? Identity is far more profound than skin colour or sexual preference, so should we really reduce people to such? This is also a reduction of personhood. Power is necessary for change, but is it always oppressive? Other-centred love is a manifestation of power. The exercise of personal dominion does not have to mean the domination of others, but one needs to work for the conditions of trust and empathy that make co-operation possible.

In resisting the dominant idea of individualism, some social theorists struggle to find language for unique persons. The project exchanges one prison of pain for another. Abstract collective nouns and sweeping generalisations depersonalise everyone and are an injustice that sets up strawmen in the place of real persons. It is a reduction of persons to objects and, as Martin Buber reminds us, reduces a *you* to an *it*.[6] Once a person or community is objectified, they become a tool in the service of others. Trinitarians would agree with the need to critique individualism, but to see people as the sum of their social grievances makes no pathway to forgiveness, reconciliation or freedom and dignity for anyone. This is important because these are all universal needs.

A more helpful question in the search for a better country would be: what are the moral conditions that make power safe for everyone?

The Gift of Language, Speech and Communication

Words are signs or symbols that enable thought, articulation and communication. The use of language goes beyond the need for survival. As I write this I am listening to music, itself a form of non-essential communication. Through language, we move beyond reaction and instinct. We reach beyond ourselves with intentionality to exchange understanding and meaning. We use language to touch our neighbours and, in turn, receive from them.

Not using a name vainly will result in using words with substance, rich, deep and full of meaning; signs true to their signifiers that resonate truth and describe reality. We might think of swearing as the use of language without substance, a signifier with nothing to signify, a sign that points nowhere, mere noise that masks reality more than revealing it.

The mind has an astonishing ability to work on problems unconsciously and without words. However, clarity comes as reality is named, and this enables sharing of specific issues and concerns. Shakespeare wrote, 'A rose by any other name would smell as sweet,'[7] but it is easier to talk about roses using words with commonly shared meaning. A name enables communion among and the distinction between. 'Rose' includes anything that is a rose and contains all possible differences among roses. It excludes, however, anything that is not one.

Human communication is imperfect, rarely exhaustive, yet substantial enough for mutual understanding. Language allows the exchange of meaning, validation and verification of experience. It is not difficult to verify if it is raining or not; I can check the weather forecast and look out of the window. It is harder to discern whether someone is just an angry person or specifically mad at me, until we talk meaningfully. Shared meaning increases the possibility of trust and frees us from the prison of pure subjectivity. The capacity for reasonable dialogue is essential because, without an external perspective, the conscious mind cannot locate itself among other objects and descends into irrationality or psychosis.

If the imagination of the previous chapter speaks to the subjective, the interior and the creative, *language* speaks to the rational, the external and in some measure the objective.

Speech and language are key to rationality and help us make sense of the world and communicate what we discover. By examining and testing assumptions – evaluating, sifting, weighing evidence and probabilities, reinterpreting findings in the light of new information or the challenges and revelation of others – we learn to describe objects and the relationships between them. If our analysis does not match the reality, we feel the dissonance. Our speech will be characterised by hollow language and unsound logic.

Without prior evaluation of assumptions, the rules of logic, which are so important to clear thought, are just as likely to lead us astray as lead us towards clarity. It is perhaps for this reason that some rationalists sound so unreasonable. Rationality and reason are not the same as rationalism. The temptation to rationalism, which would reduce reality to what we can think clearly about, is as deceptive as it is reductive.

The opposite of reason is not faith but irrationality or madness. Faith should not be blind; it should be tested against history and reality. It is right to ask for evidence. When doubting Thomas needed evidence of the resurrection, Jesus showed him his wounds.

The Grammar of Love

I tell you, on the day of judgement people will give account for every careless word they speak, for by your words you will be justified, and by your words you will be condemned.
(Matthew 12:36–37)

Words used well deepen trust and bring the fresh air of reality to bear, freeing us from our illusions. In my search for a better country, I have wondered about the impact of my emotional life on my relationships and their meaning.

In using language, we attempt to describe reality meaningfully. 'I love' feels incomplete, but 'I love you' is a commitment that we might observe and verify. It is an injustice of grammar if the subject becomes separated from the object; how much more when this happens in practice.

In what we might call the grammar of love, the subject and object must be related.[8] 'I am angry' may be accurate, but it is more specific to say, 'I am angry with Mr Andrews because he cheated me.' If Mr Andrews is the boss and I might lose my job as a result of expressing my anger, it is tempting to take the anger home and take it out on my wife, who might, in turn, give it to our child, who then kicks the dog. It is unjust to misdirect the energy of an emotion from its real object to a different object. Emotion untethered from its real object and directed towards any other object might also point destructively back towards the subject in self-hate.

A young child rages in silence, powerless to stand up to her brutal and abusive father. Later in life, now grown, she burns with anger, but the object of her rage is unnamed because pain and fear have fragmented her memory. She creates a narrative to explain her emotional confusion by blaming other people for how she feels, but it is not real and distorts her perception in every area of life, which is a toxic burden to carry. When the object and cause are named, there is at least the possibility of realignment, resolution or even reconciliation.

A young man comes into my study. His anger is burning just below the surface. Occasionally it spills over without any specific direction. People feel unsafe in his presence; the anger is getting in the way of his relationships. As we reflect on his life, he becomes aware of previously hidden patterns of destructive behaviour that stem from specific complicated relationships. He begins to own responsibility for his speech and action. He realises the stories he has told himself are incomplete. He thinks about the necessity of forgiveness and wonders aloud if reconciliation might be possible, but he is not sure. As he unties the knots by naming the emotions and their sources, he discovers new freedom to express himself. He also reports a new sense of awareness of his surroundings, and people say he is more present to them. He becomes aware that the turmoil of his emotional life has caused distortions in his perception. Now he is more aware of the real world around him and has the potential for freedom to trust and participate.

The grammar of love requires the strength of the emotion to be proportionate to the situation. Emotional energy from prior unresolved relationships is a heavy burden to lay on present ones. It is vital to find resolution, because unresolved grammatical errors of this kind will reoccur, festering destructively in many relationships, until it is.

In Central Europe, under the absolute power of the Communist Party, it was dangerous to speak out about the inefficiencies and petty injustices inflicted by bureaucrats empowered by their positions. People suffered silently from shame and humiliation, unconsciously developing passive–aggressive habits that redirected their anger to safer objects or addictions. In the new reality of post-communist society these patterns were difficult to change. Western companies that bought the large, state-owned factories discovered attitudes with which they were unfamiliar – a generation, primarily of men, who had never been allowed to take the initiative but had had to fulfil the state-mandated five-year plan. The resentments that had shaped their former lives now hindered them in the post-communist era. If they understood the vision and goal of the new company, they would disrupt it in acts of petty revenge that were perhaps appropriate to the heavy-handedness of the previous regime, but which now blocked progress.

We can clarify our most deep-seated prejudices by asking simple questions about the justice of our grammar. What prejudgements am I making to defend myself? Are they justified? Who am I afraid of, or who is the object of my anger, and why?

The penetrating words of Christ call for recognition of the profound grammatical errors of human existence, the greatest of which is the misdirection of anger towards God, whom we blame for our human mistakes.

Language – Lost and Regained

How do we rediscover language that has lost its meaning? I remember going to a Greek restaurant in a small town in the Midwest of the United States. The people who took me did not need a menu. They ordered the meatloaf and potatoes they habitually ordered. I like Greek food and have been to Greece many times. I saw some Greek food on the menu that I had enjoyed in Thessaloniki and ordered it. The waiter had trouble with my pronunciation, which I began to suspect was more accurate than his. He then spoke to the chef and asked if they did that dish. Clearly, it had been a long time since anyone had ordered it. I should have taken the hint and asked for something more Midwestern, but I nursed fond memories of Greece. I am not sure what I ate, but it was nothing I recognised, and my neighbour's meatloaf looked better with each bite. Reality, our experience of reality and our descriptions of it are often at odds.

The purpose of human language is to share meaning. Years ago, a storm blew down the sign outside a seventeenth-century country pub near where I live. The story goes that the locals liked the fact that this meant fewer non-locals stopped by, and asked the landlord not to replace it, and the pub became known locally as the Pub with No Name. For many years I did not realise that it was officially called the White Horse. The No Name became its name and added a little mystery to its many other worthy attributes. It does not matter much what we call it if we all know what we are referring to.

There are many reasons why labels lose their power to signify. Overused or archaic labels change with time and lose their clarity and authority. It is easy to forget the ideas behind them and take them for granted or use them for other purposes. Cultural minorities, often communities in exile, use language as a social marker to distinguish between those who can be trusted and those to be suspicious of. Language becomes as much a code of belonging as a means of communication. The meaning of the words becomes less important than their power to identify insiders. Political or religious groups often use theological or political code language for the same reason. The words themselves can come to contain little significance and have little power to provoke meaningful action.

The meaning of words changes over time, and their attributes may be forgotten and might need to be rediscovered or reclaimed. When the substance of a word is lost, it loses resonance with experience and no longer makes sense or rings true and thus loses its dynamism. It no longer raises awareness of the reality to which it points and must be reimagined or discarded.

In my youth, the dominant idea for the word 'love' came from Hollywood and popular music. I struggled to understand what the apostle John meant when he said that God is love. Both popular culture and the apostle claimed to describe reality, but the infatuation, sentimentality and romance of Hollywood seemed very different from the love of Christ shown in his crucifixion. It led to serious confusion. My search for the older meaning of the word 'love' required me to acknowledge that my existing intuitions were at best incomplete, and at worst misleading. I had to explore the historical implications and it took many years during which the word 'love', which held out so much promise and which was referred to so often, was painfully meaningless and unusable. I had to find substitutes for the attributes of the older meaning of the word until I formed new associations that I could indwell in thought and experience.

The exploration of the ideas opened many doors of understanding along the way. It became clear that when God is reduced to a distant and impersonal power, or when people abuse power in the name of

God, the very idea of a loving God is abandoned as a reference point. What remains for us humans is a sentimentality that describes a felt human reality without the depth of commitment and personal discipline necessary to sustain it. Without a greater glory to attract it, the human mind attends to itself, and self-centred love replaces other-centred love.

The process of reimagining is not without its dangers and anxieties. However, such a process can reinvigorate the community that, through a patient re-examination of its historical, philosophical, theological and sociological roots, can rediscover the lessons of history and old or forgotten truths. It is a search not only into ancient meanings but also into the reasons for the transition to the new meaning. The work is objective (what does the word mean historically and publicly?), but it is also subjective (what are my associations with it?), raising questions for me: what am I missing? What have I misunderstood? Where are my prejudices?

A New Name

There is a story in Luke's writings in which Jesus confronted a wild and naked man who had made his home in a cemetery.[9] His family had chained him up, but he had broken the chains. He was running at Jesus and screaming. Then Jesus asked him a profoundly personal question that would not even remotely have come to my mind in such circumstances: 'What is your name?'

'Legion,' he replied, 'for we are many.' But Legion was not the name his mother had given him. His mind was occupied territory; it no longer reflected the image of his Creator, but the fragmenting malevolent spirit that robbed him of his humanity. We can only imagine the names the people from the surrounding villages gave him. When Christ came, these dark forces had to go. The distortions of his madness went with them. Submission to Christ freed him to become himself, to take on human attributes that reflect the image of his Creator.

Later, when his family arrived, they found him clothed, in his right mind and sitting at Jesus' feet. But 'they were afraid', as they should have been, for who among us has ever fully seen or known what a right mind is? We have all been renamed in some way or other through the distortions of our journey through life. No one fully reflects the divine image, even though the residue of the image is seen in people everywhere.

Name Bearers and the Family Likeness

Many people have a first name and a second name. The first name identifies each as unique, while the second name has traditionally identified the extended network of relationships to which we owe familial loyalty. This is an insight into one God in three persons.

Historically, in some Christian traditions, a 'Christian name' is added to the family name at baptism as the name of the Father, Son and Holy Spirit is pronounced over the one being baptised. They are adopted into the family of God. The symbolism is important. The apostle John wrote, 'But to all…who believed in his name, he gave the right to become children of God',[10] and again in the book of Revelation: 'the one who conquers… I will write on him the name of my God'.[11] As we discussed earlier, a name is not a label but a cupboard full of meanings. We do not need a better old name but a new name; not just a slight moral improvement but resurrection from the dead and a new name for the new life we receive.

The invitation to bear the name of God is an honour in which God entrusts his followers with his reputation. For generations, Europeans have cursed the name of Christ because of an institutional Church that lost sight of the goodness of God and thus its humility. It sacrificed its prophetic role in search of short-term political power. Its scandals are well known: persecution, commitment to unreasonable dogma, arrogance, abuse of power, greed and sexual abuse. Such criticisms overlook the good done by the Church, but good works do not simply right the wrongs. Those of us who claim to be Christian must own our history, even where we are not directly culpable, and turn from what is wrong.

The messages of society are everywhere and impossible to avoid. The anxious pull of success, affluence, influence, power and control conflicts with the eternal call to fruitfulness, faithfulness, thankfulness, contentment and trust in the originator of life.

We stand in the relentless flow of data, impressions and thousands of messages that no one can process. They will shape the mind unless actively resisted. Resistance to their pull is an act of worship, and of course by worship I do not mean attendance at some religious service, but honouring the attributes of the fullest name in or beyond the universe.

Here are some questions that might help:

- Who do I allow to name me?
- Who is my ultimate authority?
- Who describes success and failure and what is valuable?
- Do I reflect the image of God, or the image of the society around me?

Worship, which means 'to assign worth to something, or ultimate value when thinking about God', is the way we regain an eternal perspective. This requires the hard work of sorting out what we value and why. Meditation on the infinite and personal attributes of the Creator will show up the inadequacy of what is offered in time alone.

Fear the Name

Ancient Jews rightly feared mispronouncing the name of God, and some still do. To invoke the absolute and eternal name behind reality is awesome. For this reason, public prayer can be intimidating. We speak with fear and trembling at all the name contains. We speak with fear and trembling, and yet with joy, because that name symbolises the attributes and actions that give meaning to our existence. God calls himself the 'I am', a name that summarises his being, and the answer to that sum is both infinite and personal.

An awareness of that name should be with us throughout the day, and we should be awestruck by its meaning, for the divine being is for us and not against us. The sum of his attributes is love, but not the modern sentimental reduction that takes the word 'love' in vain. It is love that desires our best good.

Fear has a bad reputation. Our experience of it is often humiliating and shameful, and associated with cowardice and intimidation. But fear also reflects respect and honour where they are due. Fear summons our attention to moral danger. Tremble at the name of God with absolute dread, then all other fears – the abuse of power by peers, governments, employers and the neighbourhood bully – will be relativised. True worship of the kind and merciful Creator gives the courage to confront brokenness and evil. Proper perspective returns when we see that God is great and we are small. We gain the courage to face evil, even if the result means the sacrifice of our lives. We fear the eternal over those who exercise power in time.

Hallowed Be Your Name

Whoever has seen me has seen the Father.
(John 14:9)

When the name of God is genuinely honoured among us, all names will be honoured, and until all names are hallowed, we have not understood what it means to hallow the name of God.

The honouring of names means the honouring of language, truth and knowledge. Knowledge is never exhaustive because there is always more to know, and more questions than answers. Continual discovery is one of the joys of life and not to be feared. Signs and symbols are *necessary* reductions because we cannot reduce the complexities of reality to language. The meanings of words will necessarily have a fuzzy edge, because there is more to any object or situation than our ability to describe it. Nevertheless, language can be sufficient for honest and substantial communication. We must accept our limits and continue to deepen the wells of knowledge and wisdom, recognising that it is in the act of wrestling to express ourselves that we grow in understanding.

It is not fanciful to imagine a country with clear communication, where energy is not wasted on misunderstanding, where the grammar of love is strong and no word is spoken with regret – every name bearing the full weight of its meaning. So we should be thoughtful about what we mean and mean what we say.

Among all the signs we use to communicate, one sign alone is irreducible. Christ is the sign and signified, the message and meaning. The incarnation is the breath-taking claim that in Christ, God has taken human form. God himself came to live among us so we can know him not merely by speculations of the imagination, or logic alone, but by revelation as is befitting of all personal knowledge.

His word and act are the same; the description is the reality. His word brought reality into existence. His word sustains it. He still speaks and what he says happens – a pillar of trust that makes a country of trust possible and desirable.

Coffee Break – Reality

 Welcome back to the café. Take a break; you deserve it. We have some excellent carrot cake and shortbread with or without chocolate. I particularly recommend the Danish pastries; they are my favourite.

Maybe your imagination is already working. You will be disappointed if I bring you something less than you imagine. How can I exceed your expectations?

When you order a coffee, you expect me to bring you coffee, not tea. You have high expectations of your coffee – criteria by which you measure whether it is good: hot or cold, strong or weak. Your preferences are neither good nor bad, merely different from mine. Bitter or mild, French or Italian, espresso or flat white: categories used to communicate and evaluate. Carrot cake is not a ham sandwich. We trust our shared categories. If I don't serve what you asked for, you ask why.

We see what we know through our assumptions. Seeing what is there is an altogether trickier proposition. Cynics favour the dark side and screen out the good, while romantics avert their gaze from all that is ugly. Freedom requires that we see life as it is, not just through the lens of our judgements. The emotions we bring into the room influence how we respond and how well we listen.

Something about a café like ours creates an instant intimacy of sorts. One hears customers complain about friends and enemies, not to mention politics or religion. When anger is boiling hotter than the tea kettle, arguments become furiously one-sided, self-justifying, or worse. Humility is rarely the principal virtue. As a waiter, I listen and nod but rarely take sides, though occasionally I put in a balancing word. Customers speculate with a vivid imagination but scant evidence about the motives of their enemies.

Isn't it strange that we see our side with such clarity? It's hard to see another point of view when looking in the mirror. In their anger, they struggle with their choice of words; finding common ground is wearing. Language is imperfect – not exhaustive, but sufficient.

I can tell the anxious people as they order coffee, by their sudden eye movements. Anxiety and anger storm against the shoreline of the soul, ruining a good night's sleep and sense of reality. How do we resist them?

Take your time. There is no need to rush.

7

Word Four: What Disturbs You? Finding Sabbath

Remember the Sabbath day, to keep it holy. Six days you shall labour, and do all your work, but the seventh day is a Sabbath to the Lord your God. On it you shall not do any work, you, or your son, or your daughter, your male servant, or your female servant, or your livestock, or the sojourner who is within your gates. For in six days the Lord made heaven and earth, the sea, and all that is in them, and rested on the seventh day. Therefore the Lord blessed the Sabbath day and made it holy.
(Exodus 20:8–11)

You shall remember that you were a slave in the land of Egypt, and the Lord your God brought you out from there with a mighty hand and an outstretched arm.
(Deuteronomy 5:15)

Come to me, all who labour and are heavy laden, and I will give you rest.
(Matthew 11:28)

Lost in Time

What disturbs you or steals your sleep? Was there ever an age like ours, so driven by anxiety? Life can be very stressful. Some stresses are self-inflicted, others are inflicted by society. We dash the children to school, go on to work and then go to the shops and gym. Finding time is not easy in the rush to pay bills, put food on the table and chauffeur the family on a merry-go-round of engagements. We rush through life as if there were no tomorrow. We crave rest from the demand to beat targets, to produce, to grow, to be competitive. Yet empty time fills us with dread, exposing the emptiness within.

In the communist era in Central Europe people had time, because however much or little they worked they were paid the same. This came home to me when visiting a friend in the Balkans who translated books for us. He was an electrician by trade and maintained electrical substations. I asked him once how he could take time off work to talk with me. He was a prolific translator and it had not occurred to me until then where he found time for it. How did he manage it? He told me about the state holidays, and that he took several sick days each month, whatever his health. He would take a day to get to and from the substation, even if it was just around the corner. When we added it all up, he was only working about six full weeks a year!

I asked many people in that country after that, and their answers were similar. Everyone knew that to survive you had to have relationships, contacts and something to trade on the side. I came to understand the common saying at that time: *you pretend to pay us and we pretend to work*. Hunting for provisions for daily survival took time. But my translator friend also had time for relationships and for his family. It sounds ideal, but the system fell apart because, among other reasons, it was unsustainable economically.

In the aftermath of communism in Central and Eastern Europe, several friends jumped at the chance of employment with international companies that paid many times the average salary. They benefited from training and travel. At age twenty-five, this was a dream come true – flying around the world was exciting. For some, the price was high. One friend told of a staff meeting in a major accounting firm, where the manager said, 'If you are not willing to sacrifice your family for this company, you should leave now.' She decided to leave, but most did not. By the time they were thirty-five, leaving the warmth of family for a lonely hotel room was less attractive. They felt trapped. Thirty more years on an ever narrower and increasingly precarious ladder seemed like drudgery, but if they stepped off the treadmill, the loss of income and prestige would also be painful.

We are in a perpetual race against time, hurrying in the panic of success and its trappings.[1] Relationships have become secondary; time is scarce. What if I don't make it? What if I fall off the ladder – a ladder easily shaken by a pandemic, an economic crisis or international conflicts?

But everyone falls off the ladder of life eventually. We work hard to survive and prosper, only to discover that old age and death set their own agenda. This is the tension that mocks the Western world. If time is a limited resource, why are we in such a hurry to use it up? But if death is our destination, we have no time to lose.

A doctor friend in Budapest told of the middle-aged men recovering from heart attacks at his hospital. What struck him as odd was not the heart attacks, which were common enough, but the lack of visitors. On further investigation, he heard a familiar story. At the fall of the Iron Curtain, these men seized the opportunity to be entrepreneurs and make money to give their children the life communism had denied them. In the process, their work so absorbed them that they had no time for their families. Success led to broken relationships and divorce, and consequentially no one to visit them in the hospital. How easy it is to become so absorbed by the means that we lose sight of the ends.

How do we decide what is important? Especially when our restlessness is driven, in part, by the need for work to create a sense of identity, secure our status and find significance and meaning in our lives. Busyness is exhausting. We need regular time to reorient ourselves to the purpose of life in an age where everyone and everything competes for our attention.

What might a better country look like if we had nothing to prove? What if we had a larger story that gave the sense of meaning, significance and identity we crave, without the need for hustle, exhaustion and burnout? In a better country we would work from a state of rest rather than a state of stress and anxiety.

How Do We Experience Each Moment?

Every experience happens in the present moment. Each moment flutters like a butterfly between the past and the future, between memories and hope. The clock ticks, time passes, light pours in from the universe from stars that have moved on. To experience the moment, we must be present to it and not absent while consumed in anger or anxiety.

When I was twenty, someone pointed out to me that if I lived to be seventy I had only 600 months left to live. While seventy seemed an eternity away, I was already experiencing how short a month could be. I was not thankful for the observation – it haunted me for several years. There never seemed to be enough time to make sense of life, which seemed like a moving target. How could I be present in it?

At the same time, the heady existentialist novels of Sartre and Camus touched me profoundly and described my experience of time. Living in the shadow of the Second World War, their experience of senseless brutality made life feel absurd. Their history was without meaning and as impersonal as their universe, and their future was pregnant with limitless but empty possibilities that they must seize responsibly and with courage. Their morality consisted of living authentically with the pain of life's meaninglessness. Their *moments* were disconnected, and consisted of immediate experience with little historical context. I later discovered that I had deeply internalised their ideas. They had filtered widely into our cultural life through their novels and plays, which found resonance in a generation wrestling with the absence of meaning caused by the pain of war and the loss of a transcendent reference point to orient ourselves. Those ideas had a profoundly disruptive effect on my experience of time, and a restless and oppressive black depression, born of anxiety at the passing of days, lingered long after I became a follower of Christ.

My deeply subjective experience was in stark contrast to that of a friend of a more scientific bent. She sought meaning in the discovery of objective understanding. Her moments were filled with a universe to explore, through which she filled the void created by her commitment to naturalism. Her history was formed by chance and cause and effect, her future determined by chemistry. She knew her will was an illusion through which she satisfied the requirements of morality necessary for living with others. She had no framework to deal with the inevitable collision of subjective personalities.

Other friends went to work every morning: to an office, a bank, a building site. They did not think, from one moment to the next, about any of their moments, until some crisis arose and the questions poured in – a single moment wiping away their illusions of comfort.

I do not want to create strawmen. All of us enjoy the world as it is, we know pleasure and pain, and have relationships that are meaningful and sometimes hurt. But without an eternal reference point, the meaning is local and temporary. Our experience of a wider narrative – and its influence on the way we experience the present moment – is at odds with the cultural assumption that the present moment is where we find meaning.

Reality is demanding. Questions of time intrude on even the most settled of minds and challenge our basic assumptions, whether we like it or not. What we believe about reality determines how we experience each moment of time and reminds us that we are finite. The questions are not always clearly articulated but are merely felt or intuited.

Questions from Beyond Time – What Disturbs Me?

The following are some existential questions buried in the questions asked by young Western individualists who come to our community, but the perplexity and disturbance are common to all ages and cultures.

- *Being and existence*: How will I support myself? How can I get ahead? Who describes the limits of possibility? Am I in danger? Do I exist, or is this illusion? Does anyone see me?
- *Belonging*: Where is home? Who can I trust, and on what basis? Can I trust anyone at all? To whom should I be loyal – who is

my tribe? What is our territory? Where are the borders? What are my responsibilities to my history and family? With whom can I form alliances? On which relationships can I lean? Am I alone?

- *Identity*: Who am I? Who am I to you? What is my real name? Can I trust your observation about me? Which mask should I wear today? Can you see through me? Why does my identity feel so relative? Am I merely the sum of my oppressions? Can I really be anything I want? Why do I hate who I am? Can anyone see my shame? Is anyone real here? Is life a performance?
- *Meaning*: Why are we here? What are the essential connections in life? Does anyone love me? Is death the end of all meaning? Is this all there is? If I died tonight, would I be content?
- *Significance*: Am I visible? What am I worth? With whom should I compare myself? Who must approve of me, and to whom must I prove myself? Am I successful? What is my status among my peers and in society? What is 'enough'? What am I for, and to whom should I look for endorsement? What do I do with envy?
- *Morality*: Am I acceptable? Am I good enough? Is my conscience a reliable guide to what is right? Is there a 'right'? What should I do? What can I get away with? Who am I performing for? What is the best course of action? Where do I get the courage to act?

These existential questions press painfully on the mind. To create and curate an identity or try to find meaning is the daily burden of millions of people. Millions more capitulate to the fashion and flow of the times.

The questions require answers to settle the anxiety they arouse. Some need answering through relationships with other people. Some need a voice from beyond time, but the materialist/naturalist perspective is impersonal. Nature alone has no voice, just silence.

Without the eternal, time seems incomplete, and these questions become a burden; flour and water without a baker.

Recovering Eternity

Humans are time-bound. We live in sequence, we cannot be in more than one place at a time, we do not know what the future holds, and yet we know all humans die. Is it possible to make sense of time, or find rest in it, without reference to something beyond it?

Death is an undeniable reality for everyone; it is not only the fear of death but the loss of meaning at death that haunts us in life. If life ends at death, if there is no way of transcending it, then all of life – our meaning, significance and morality – is subjective.

Sabbath is where perceptions of reality diverge, and for some what follows might seem unfathomable or absurd, but reason is only as good as the assumptions it is based on. The naturalist/materialistic view has little time for a personal and eternal source of life, though it is useful to remember that the scientific method of knowing, important for understanding material objects, is not equipped to answer questions beyond material boundaries.

If there is a benevolent source of life beyond time or space from whose eternal perspective we are known and valued, independent of our work or productivity, then we can be free from the prison of subjectivity and impermanence.

As we noted in Chapter 2, persons know each other through revelation, through the giving and receiving of knowledge freely exchanged. If God is personal, might he not do the same? I raise this question to invite you to consider what comes next, though this is not the place to explore how revelation might take place or be understood.

The book of Genesis describes our contemporary problem of anxiety and identity through the story of Cain. He had murdered his brother in a fit of envy over the question of what formed acceptable worship. Murder is not a solution acceptable to God, so Cain was sent away from his presence.

Cain understood what being separated from God would mean for him: 'Cain said to the LORD, "My punishment is greater than I can bear. Behold, you have driven me today away from the ground, and from your face I shall be hidden. I shall be a fugitive and a wanderer on the earth and whoever finds me will kill me.'"[2] Cain became a restless wanderer far from the Sabbath rest enjoyed by God on completing his creation.[3]

Cain was alone and in competition for power with all the other wanderers. He feared for his life. If you are alone in the universe, you can't afford to rest. There is little forgiveness, mostly suspicion, revenge; the world soon becomes your enemy. The consequences of what Christians call the Fall – the radical breach of trust by the creature towards the Creator – are revealed in Cain's dilemma. In breaking faith with the Creator he lost the centre that holds everything together and plunged into a sea of self-referential isolation and despair. Cain must create his identity, work for his significance and discover what is good and evil for himself by trial and error. From now on his life would be hard work. Some might see him as heroic, but it is the heroism of a thirsty person convinced they can draw water from a dry well.

God is personal and not an abstract idea or mindless force. Augustine saw the issue when he wrote of God, 'You stir man to take pleasure in praising you, because you have made us for yourself, and our heart is restless until it rests in you.'[4] Knowing the Creator gives us a place to call home. It is the source of our identity, equality, meaning, significance and morality; a reference point for knowing ourselves and others.

The eternal should be understood neither as infinite time nor as life after death. Rather, it is the quality of the life of God; the sum of his attributes and intentions. All that is good and true and beautiful, and which may be enjoyed in the universe, is bound up in the presence of the personal and infinite God who gives it meaning and completion.

We live in time, but God is eternal and present to every moment, yet without taking our freedom from us. This idea liberated me from the existentialist moment, which was often despairing. The biblical moment is the meeting place between time and eternity, which opened the door of meaning to history and future hope.

It allowed me to put my personal history in the context of all of history and understand my hope in the context of God's intention. In each moment, immediate experience does not stand alone but in the presence of God. History has meaning, and the future is open to possibility and an infinitely deeper knowledge of the eternal and his purpose. His world is understandable and open to reason because God is rational. Each moment has the potential for relationship because God is an infinite intimacy of three persons, which we reflect in our restored relationships.

The Two Tellings of the Sabbath Law

This word of the Decalogue says simply to take one day in seven to rest and remember. Remember your Creator; that you are not alone – you have a partner who has invited you on the journey of freedom. Remember you were a slave, how you bowed under the burden of another master. Remember *often* because if you forget you will begin to think you are on your own. You will forget the rules of freedom, and in your loneliness you will be consumed by anxiety, and work yourself to death. Sabbath is a call to dwell in time, with eternity firmly in mind.

Remember the Creator

How do we regain a sense of eternity when we have soaked in the waters of naturalism since childhood? The hearers of the Sabbath law were told to remember. Memory is the ability to reach back in time. They were told to remember events beyond their personal experience. This was not the individualist's memory but multi-generational memory of events that happened before any of them existed; memory handed down from one generation to another and ultimately from God to a community in which they belonged. As Goethe reminds us, a person cut off from generations of memory lives from hand to mouth.[5]

The Decalogue was declared twice. First by God to Moses and then second when Moses repeated them forty years later as the people were about to enter the land promised by God to Abraham, Isaac and Jacob.

The first telling of the Sabbath law reminds us to remember the Creator.[6] It would have called to mind the ancient story from the beginning of time when only God was present. There God created a formless chaos, and like a master craftsman forged *order* out of the chaos. When the chaos was ordered enough to please him and fulfil his purposes, he rested, not because he was exhausted but because he had accomplished his purpose. Now the creation was ready for living. The peace of God reigned over it. He had built the house; now he could enjoy it. Job, recounting the act of creation, said that 'all the sons of God sang for joy'.[7] God, who lacks nothing and did not need to create, freely created from desire, a manifestation of his love because he chose to share existence with something outside of himself. The dark and hostile view of God that many of us carry in our gut, or mind, is far from the generous hospitality the Bible describes.

We are to remember that our existence is God's choice. We are his guests; he is the host. We receive the creation as a gift. In our Sabbath, we remember the giver.

We are to remember the eternal God, who exists beyond time and created time, and as Alpha and Omega knows the beginning from the end.

It is a reminder to remember that we are finite and have no source of life within ourselves; that any claim to eternal life comes only through relationship to the infinite God who is life. We receive life from the eternal source: not mere existence as the product of a mindless impersonal process, but all that life is supposed to be – the richness of the life of God. Relationships of trust and the joy of creativity, discovery and of being present to every moment in its fullness.

His followers claim that Jesus is the second person of the Trinity, the embodiment of the eternal in time. The Gospels describe his extraordinary character – not just his extraordinary abilities but his self-control and presence of mind. A study of his life will make abstract ideas about goodness visible.

To find rest, time must be reconciled to eternity. To remember the creation is to recall the tear in the universe, told in the story of

Genesis. The strange delusion of a man who wanted to be like God and demanded the last word. It is the tale of how a simple act of disobedience could separate eternity from time. The tiniest of acts, a bite from a small piece of fruit, released suspicion into the world and caused a breach of trust so deep that it could not be repaired without immense sacrifice.

In bowing to worship as created beings, we rise to receive eternal life in time, growing into a trusting relationship of obedience freely and lovingly given, even as we recover from the damage of separation.

So Paul the apostle to the early Church wrote to the churches, telling them to redeem the time.[8] In other words: do not live any longer as if there were no eternal dimension. Let Christ's rule of life, described by the Ten Words, be the organising principle in your life, following the maker's instructions, not out of fear of judgement and punishment, but because you have learned to love what is good.

Remember You Were Slaves

The second telling of the Sabbath law occurred just before the people crossed into the promised land. This time they were told: 'You shall remember that you were a slave.'[9] Between the first and second telling of the law, Israel wandered in the wilderness for forty years. Out of fear they had refused God's invitation to take the land he offered them. When the going was tough, Israel remembered the delicacies of Egypt but forgot the slavery that went with them and from which God had freed them. Immediate sensory experience distorts our memory. Freedom requires that we take up responsibility, which is hard work of a different kind from slavery, and they were not yet sure they wanted it. They were in two minds – to go forward or to go back. It took only one night to get Israel out of Egypt, but it took forty years to get the desire for Egypt out of Israel.[10] Now forty years later they were ready to move forward to take up their freedom as a people.

This reminder balances the first. In meeting God as Creator, they might have come to the wrong conclusion that they were mere puppets in a predetermined existence. Only the free can lay their work down voluntarily and enjoy Sabbath. Slaves do not get to choose. God wills our freedom; he is not against it. It is not a freedom that is independent of God but in relationship with him, a freedom that is impossible without him. Paul the apostle reminded his friends after the resurrection of Jesus, 'So you are no longer a slave, but a son, and if a son, then an heir through God.'[11] Many of them were slaves to other people and had to learn that this temporary evil was not their primary identity. We choose to live out our freedom by daily taking up responsibility for our lives and relationships. Forgetfulness opens the door for a return to the slavery of chasing time as if there were no tomorrow.

As we saw in the discussion on freedom in Chapter 3, the newly liberated young nation had to confront issues that as slaves they did not have to consider. *Who is responsible for what? How do we live together and organise our community? How do we share power so that everyone prospers? How do we govern ourselves?* Such questions disturb our rest. In seeking the eternal, we find the source from which to address these questions.

Recovering Sabbath – Learning to Abide

> Consider the lilies, how they grow: they neither toil nor spin, yet I tell you, even Solomon in all his glory was not arrayed like one of these. But if God so clothes the grass, which is alive in the field today, and tomorrow is thrown into the oven, how much more will he clothe you, O you of little faith!
> (Luke 12:27–28)

How should we seek the eternal being behind all of existence? The very idea seems intimidating, and it should fill us with awe. To worship simply means to ascribe worth or value to something, as we began to explore in Chapter 6. We should not limit this to the sometimes inexplicable activities that happen in religious buildings on special days. The habit of worship focuses the mind on what is most valuable and reorders the value of everything else.[12] We do it all the time, whenever we decide to attend to one thing over another.

Contemplating the Creator gives a wider context in which to understand immediate pressures, and provides perspective and proportion to the mountains and valleys of daily life.

The world is full of wonders that reveal the mind of the Creator, from the night sky and the mountains to the humans who inhabit the earth. But the creation is hard to read; it is also violent and cruel.

Other factors get in the way of knowing the God who invites us to 'come into his presence with thanksgiving'.[13] God is always present, but I am not. When I sit in God's presence, at work, in my study or in communal worship, a thousand lesser thoughts steal my attention as I wander back and forth across the landscape of my anxieties. The thoughts are habitual and invasive. I grasp for the fading vision of God on which I have been reflecting, as it withdraws into the distance like some word on the tip of my tongue. I am afraid and aware of vague feelings of guilt. Is there some hidden sin, or is this my overwrought and misinformed conscience? Leonard Cohen once wrote that when feelings of holiness betray you, loneliness says you've sinned.[14] Solitude and communion become loneliness and isolation. Perfectionism is soon at war with righteousness. This is not the sort of *experiential* loneliness cured by company, but an *existential* loneliness felt among friends when your heart is telling you lies.

In biblical language, the opposite of simplicity is not complexity; it is duplicity. A *simple* heart goes in one direction, but divided desires and loyalties pull a duplicitous heart between competing paths. Like the ex-slaves in the wilderness of old, my heart is often divided. I long to be present to the one who is always present and in whom 'we live and move and have our being'.[15] Yet I am not entirely sure I do. I am afraid of God's judgement and his holiness; I see how far I am from the ideals I am talking about and I am tempted by the vain hope that I can justify myself. I look back with some forgetfulness to the patterns of thought and action to which I have been enslaved in the past.

Recovering the capacity to experience the eternal in the moment – to be aware of God and his eternal concerns in time – involves a process of healing. To be present to the moment, to feel, experience and participate, is not automatic but contingent on becoming whole as a person. I discovered this when I was young and travelling with friends across Europe. As we looked up at the Swiss Alps, everyone was amazed at the beauty. I was surprised that my friends were awestruck and breathless. They were experiencing beauty in a way I could not. Intellectually I knew the sight was amazing, but earlier negative experience had left me cynical, and I was suspicious of their joy. I was a slave to my own unresolved pain. Thankfully, I dimly understood there was something wrong with me and not with my friends. Fifteen years later, as I was walking through the Vienna Woods, I was suddenly stunned by the breath-taking beauty of a deep blue sky, emerald-green grass, and two trees with bright yellow and red leaves. As I caught my breath, I knew I had just encountered and experienced beauty. It was a sign of healing. Unbeknown to me, my capacity to feel and be vulnerable had grown in the intervening years.

Some Western Christians, caught in the tension of analysis (through reason and language) and participation (through the imagination and emotion), mistake abstract ideas *about* God for God himself. As important as beautifully formulated theological propositions are to the Christian faith, they are no substitute for learning to live in the presence of God, who is present in all times and places. In communion with the Spirit, we receive the capacity to heal the fragments and enter life.

'Abide' is a word that has fallen out of use except in poetry or law. It means 'to live or remain somewhere'. To abide in Christ is to discover and enter rest amid the tensions and temptations of daily life. Christ is the source of Sabbath rest. He says: 'Come to me, all who labour and are heavy laden, and I will give you rest. Take my yoke upon you, and learn from me, for I am gentle and lowly in heart, and you will find rest for your souls. For my yoke is easy, and my burden is light.'[16] Christ invites us to join him in pulling the plough of life. The yoke is easy because Christ is pulling alongside in active friendship.

Learning to abide in every moment is, ironically, a struggle. 'Let us therefore strive to enter that rest,' said the writer to the Hebrews.[17] We are used to struggling alone. Old habits are hard to break, and only fools trust blindly. Trust grows with experience, in small steps at first, especially where the capacity to trust has been severely damaged. It is never instant or automatic, because it is relational. Some will say, 'I tried to trust God, so why do my questions and struggles remain?' This question has plagued many sincere Christians who struggle to find rest or a sense of God's presence. The concept of a personal loving God can be hard to grasp by damaged souls in a world of suffering, especially in an age when the idea of love is misunderstood.

A Special Day?

Therefore let no one pass judgement on you in questions of food and drink, or with regard to a festival or a new moon or a Sabbath. These are a shadow of the things to come, but the substance belongs to Christ.
(Colossians 2:16–17)

The Old Testament Sabbath was commonly associated with one day in the week. A day once a week is useful, but I think it is scaffolding for a much larger building: training for a more profound rest seven days a week, twenty-four hours a day. I ask myself, 'Am I at rest and present to each moment of the day, trusting the Creator for wisdom and answers from his eternal perspective, for all the questions raised by my being, belonging, identity, meaning, significance and morality?' You will not be surprised when I confess that I have not reached that high ideal. Perhaps it is not such a bad idea to begin practising one day a week and working up from there.

Sabbath is a place in time to practise resting in God's eternal life – not primarily as an infinite length of time but as the quality of relational life. I ask myself, 'Am I living in time with eternity in mind, or have I slipped back to living in time alone?' A weekly Sabbath is a moment to process the activities, attitudes and emotions of the week and allow the soul to reflect on them. As our community meets to worship together, we refocus from the distractions and pressures of daily life to remind ourselves of our ultimate purpose and to ask God for help to regain perspective and proportion.

Sabbath is an invitation to learn to separate the means and the ends, because we often confuse them; the means is the work necessary for living, but life is more than labour. Here we set the means aside for a while and concentrate on the ends. It is a day in which to delight in God, his work and his world, to spend time with God and friends and enjoy the life for which we have worked.[18]

Sabbath is a time to remember; to call to mind our liberation from slavery to the fragmented life. It is both joyful and sad. Joyful because it is hopeful and spent with friends we love. But also sad, as it is a moment to grieve my personal contribution to the chaos and disorder of self-centred love, and a time to remember how all creation groans and waits for God's redemption.

Sabbath is for everyone: me, my family, the animals and the stranger in our midst – we are invited to be at rest together. Work is sometimes a place to hide from painful conversations or the emptiness left by conflict. When we stop working for a few hours, we discover the cracks in our relationships. The cup of communion we drink together reminds us that communion with God and our neighbour is at the heart of what we mean by life. Sabbath is a place to confront the reality of our broken and fragmented selves, to bring order to the chaos of our hearts and return to joy.

Some find the thought of a weekly Sabbath a burden. This is understandable, if being with others is difficult or if there is little honest communion in the community. But would we find it a burden to spend time mending the fences of our souls? It is not legalistic to separate time for remembering, reflection and drawing near to God and friends. This is unless we have forgotten why or how to be together, or if community life has become stale and functional, or if the means have become more important than the ends, and too full of impersonal meetings or programmes that keep us from Sabbath's real purpose.

Sabbath is liberation. In an age of hyperactivity and the over-stimulation that comes with our electronic devices, we need time to slow down. Jesus said, 'The Sabbath was made for man, not man for the Sabbath.'[19]

Rest as Active Passivity

Sabbath is tested between impulse and action. In that moment we discover our object of trust. Is there a God who is active and present? Am I in a trusting community or am I on my own? Impatient for resolution, we are often driven to impose control through power, technique or dehumanising systems.

The commitment to trust God involves *active passivity*;[20] an act of discernment in which we learn to participate with God in ordinary life. We *actively* resist the pull to be in control or act on impulse as we listen for the voice of God in the noise of life. Our *passivity* is an open-handed waiting, which expects God to speak wisdom and act in ways that our techniques and systems could never lead us to expect. It is never completely passive, because we must act responsibly in step with his Spirit.[21]

There are, however, at least four kinds of false rest. First, there is a 'passive' passivity, doing nothing for fear of risk, change or rocking the boat, or for fear of evaluation, a deceptive loyalty to tradition, or a lack of courage. This person puts conformity over creativity, is busy with excuses for their inactivity and too fearful of the opinion of others.

Second, there is the false rest of the one who thinks he has done well. He has ample goods laid up for many years, so thinks he can relax, eat, drink and be merry. This person has mistaken the true meaning of wealth as a restored relationship with God and neighbour, and has been fooled into thinking a financial buffer is a substitute. Seek relative wealth, and you will never have enough. Seek the absolute wealth of the goodness of the infinite God, and you will find it. This person has a modern cousin who hides in the passivity of consuming, who lives to shop or escape in front of the screen.

Third, there is the conscience that seeks relief in obsessive and compulsive rituals. It feels its guilt too keenly, never resting in the mercy of God. This person is driven to incessant activity to avoid some psychological pressure. A restless hyper-rationalising mind or an imagination aflame with hypothetical scenarios and an irrational craving for control keeps them far from peace. This kind of perfectionism *rests* on the dysfunction of its damaged conscience rather than in God's loving standards of goodness.

Fourth, there is the false rest of the one who has abandoned personal responsibility for society and life, who sits back and expects God (or someone else) to fill every need directly or to do the work for them, not understanding that God has extended to us the honour of responsible participation in his creation. This kind of person does not need a call but rather a kick to take up responsibility to work.[22]

Those who can pause and trust God between impulse and action, who can watch and wait for wisdom, will discover that he is present and active.

Recovering Tension

Participants in the café often wonder whether a world characterised by Sabbath might be boring. After all, there would be no murder mysteries. Would high levels of trust and the absence of evil make life uninteresting or even dull? Do we not grow through wrestling with problems and difficulties? What would we do without the cultural artifacts that spring from evil – the paintings, poetry and music that arise from suffering and add drama to life? Does Sabbath deprive us of creative tension? On the contrary, evil casts such a terrible shadow and takes away much more than it gives. Creativity is often restrained or hidden by a fear of criticism, envy and disappointment. Just occasionally a Mozart or a Van Gogh rises above its burden to create or discover something magnificent, but multitudes remain lost in its grey shadows.

Good and evil are only one source of tension. A knowledge of evil is not necessary for a knowledge of the good. They are not opposites in a kind of dualism. Rather, evil is a parasite of the good; goodness subverted and used inappropriately. Goodness stands on its own. Stimulus and satisfaction in life come from the resolution of any tension, and many fruitful tensions exist. We sometimes take them for granted – for example, the gap between better and best, easy and difficult, or finite and infinite. Imagine the satisfaction of having longings deeper than you ever thought could possibly be fulfilled. Imagine waking every morning ready to satisfy curiosity, to explore, discover and understand something new. Sabbath rest is not about peace and quiet, nor the absence of tension, but a return to fruitful tension, and the celebration, joy and trust that flow from it.

Recently I was invited for coffee in a garden in the English countryside. The coffee and conversation were rich. The Italian–Austrian architecture of the house was magnificent, and it was a beautiful late spring day. The garden had been planned and planted years ago by someone who knew their business. A stream with several waterfalls ran through it. Plants, exotic and unique to the area, had been expertly planted to complement each other and every view was a feast to the eyes. As I lay in bed that evening, I could not put the wonder of the garden out of my mind, because the beauty had imprinted itself so deeply. When I woke in the middle of the night, often a time when anxieties storm the bastions of my soul, the beauty was present to banish those dark thoughts.

Was this, I wondered, how God would heal the wounds of time? Could I imagine the encounter with an infinite beauty, forever able to take my breath away?

Between Time and Eternity

What does all this mean for a better country? Whatever you believe about ultimate reality, whether or not you accept the idea that there's a spiritual reality, I hope you can see the wisdom of Sabbath rest for human flourishing. Implementing most of the ideas discussed in this book would make a difference to the levels of trust and enjoyment of relationships in any community, regardless of your beliefs, even if you do not accept my belief that a weekly Sabbath is more than just a good idea for a well-balanced life. But I believe Sabbath is a present reality of those who trust God and a signpost to a time of future restoration when God brings Sabbath rest to all creation. I have come to believe that our natural home is in the eternal – not as opposed to time, but in God's active presence at all times. Fullness of rest comes not just in a balanced life, but in being at peace with our Creator.

The question of death hangs over us all, and each of us must settle it for ourselves. One in every one person dies; it is the ultimate statistic. There is simply no fence to sit on.

The poet John Donne wrote, 'One short sleep past, we wake eternally, and death shall be no more; Death, thou shalt die.'[23] Death is not the end of life; merely the end of what is temporary. Entrance into the final Sabbath of God lies through the humbling gate of death, partly because our bodies need renewal to bear the weight of the goodness to come. The resurrection, the promise that God will raise the dead to new life, is a new beginning with renewed relationships. For if death is about separation from all that is dear, then life is about reconnection. The final Sabbath is the beginning of life.

Much of this is a mystery. Who can understand the interface between time and eternity? Our present Sabbath brings joy in anticipation.

In one sense, time is running out, but it is also just beginning. Time in the eternal presence strangely gives all the time in the world. Practising Sabbath is preparing for the restoration to come.

8

Word Five: A Reckoning with History

Honour your father and your mother, that your days may be long in the land that the LORD your God is giving you. (Exodus 20:12)

I and the Father are one. (John 10:30)

In the search for a better country, how we live together, arrange our family and community affairs and reconcile our differences is important if we are to enjoy one another and be free from the burdens of unresolved conflict. Because it is through the family that our loyalties are first formed and our judgements are shaped, we will start by exploring the parent-and-child relationship and then, by extension, the relationship to the wider community and history in general.

Some of what I write here will feel like a detour to a better country. It is because I have realised that unless honour can be restored, the search for a better country remains an ideal rather than a reality we begin to inhabit. I would also not want to leave the impression that the better country is only a heaven to go to when we die rather than a life that grows within and among us now.

There is no small irony that this instruction follows the one on Sabbath rest. Family relationships challenge our rest because they are among the most intimate and demanding of all relationships. How do you get on with your parents? Psychologists repeat what the ancient Greeks told us in their plays: that this relationship, a source of joy and fraught with tension, sets the tone for all other relationships and has the potential to shape the rest of our lives.

I am not sure of the reasons, but honour has not been a deeply held value in Western life for some time. This is possibly because of our emphasis on individualism, the search for equality, or because we travel more widely and have fewer roots. Or perhaps it is because the rule of law has replaced communal justice. We see honour most commonly in loyalty to our sports clubs, but less so in our towns, villages or families. Interestingly, though many of them do not realise it, friends in Poland greet each other with the word *cześć,* which, apart from being difficult for foreigners to pronounce, means 'honour'. This has always struck me as a rather beautiful way of saying hello and goodbye.

Honourable Parents – the Ideal and the Reality

'To honour' means 'to revere or respect, to esteem or value'. The opposite is to hold in contempt or despise. The character traits necessary for honour are the foundation and lifeblood of a long-lasting community. Honouring of parents, and by extension their community, ensures 'that your days may be long in the land that the LORD your God is giving you'. Division surely hastens decline.

Parents are gods in the eyes of their young children. They receive life through their parents, which, you might think, would be grounds enough for honour and gratitude. Honourable parents give more than life and breath; they give provision and protection, a name, identity and a place to belong. Through their nurture, the child will survive and thrive; without it the child will starve emotionally and be stunted psychologically and socially.

Children develop as they interact with their parents or care givers. Children learn to focus their eyes by looking towards the face from which sound comes. They learn to speak through hearing and repeating other voices. They respond in mind and body to touch. Trust, respect, dignity and self-control grow through consistent, respectful examples. In relationship they discover themselves. As they grow to maturity, they learn to differentiate and associate. I am me, and you are you. This is mine, and that is yours. These are the bonds that bind us, and those are the boundaries between us.

Good parents see and hear, know and affirm their children. The time they invest imparts a sense of value and significance. The child's sense of worth is gained from acknowledgement. 'Look at me,' she laughs when learning some new skill. Parents help their children name, contain and channel stormy emotions and impulses.

Parents or primary care givers set the expectations and assumptions of their children. They are the gateway into wider society. What is not transmitted through the genetic code is learned through nurture, teaching and tradition. Children look and listen; they learn far more by observation than they are explicitly taught. Sons and daughters mirror their fathers and mothers for good or evil; reflecting the image of their maker is what humans do.

Parents act as regent, exercising absolute power and authority, and must navigate some rocky rapids as authority is handed over gradually as the child matures. In a mature relationship, the parental bond stays and grown children know their parents not just as parents, but appreciate other aspects of their character and roles in respectful relationships of free people.

The fifth word of the Decalogue is commonly understood to refer to a child's loyalty and obedience to his or her parents, for the unity and strength of the community and the handing down of memory and tradition. However, to honour cannot mean blind obedience to parental authority, because some parents are profoundly dishonourable. The ambiguity between the role and the person inhabiting it is complex and sometimes it can be difficult to negotiate the difference.

Honour Broken: Dishonourable Parents

Good parenting requires love, maturity and self-sacrifice, but sadly not all parents are loving, not all loving parents are mature, and no parent is perfect. Parents fail and children can respond in destructive ways. Thankfully children can survive a great deal of inexperience and imperfection in their parents. But some parents, carrying their own wounds forward from earlier generations, are not merely inexperienced but irresponsible, manipulative or even abusive. To free themselves some children must break violently with parental authority, but they go into the world suspicious, vengeful, contemptuous and hungry for love.

Conflicted feelings tempt us to deride those we should honour. We expect children to be childish, but to see childishness in parents is distressing. But who has not seen it, even in themselves?

Honour cannot mean merely blind obedience. Should a son obey a drunken father who demands he steal, or a daughter submit to her father's sexual advances? For such children obedience is a meaningless pathway to dishonour. These are extreme examples, but there are plenty of grey areas that are less clear.

Violations of love have consequences. The abuse of parental authority ruptures trust and leaves scars of suspicion and contempt, until some stormy night something snaps, a door slams, a heart is closed, there is an absent place at the table and a vacant stare in the room.

The child who is regularly ignored when she stretches up her arms for love will still long for it years later. A craving for validation, recognition or affection may draw her as an adult blindly towards anyone who remotely feeds the hunger, regardless of other character deficits, trapping her in cycles of attraction and disappointment. A daughter who was violently abused by her father may shudder, stutter or shut down completely in the company of her lovers. A son whose father shames him may go into the world deprived of confidence and full of anger. The mother who never allows her daughter a different opinion is raising a child whose adult life may be marked by a rage she cannot name and does not understand. Children who are critically corrected but rarely affirmed may fear that voice in their head long after the parent is dead.

Dishonourable Children

Children are not neutral actors. As with every action there is a counter-reaction. As adults they bring a history and assumptions to their relationship with their parents. Judgements made in childhood and in ignorance may be disproportionate and harsh when carried into adulthood. Disappointments may have been caused by events outside the control of the parent. Parents are also not responsible for every wayward decision of their children. Those who judge their fathers and mothers, or sons and daughters, too severely should watch for the speck in their own eye.[1]

What does it mean to live with a child who is dishonourable, who brings shame on the family name? There are examples in the Bible. King David shed tears for his wayward son Absalom,[2] though he was not completely innocent in his son's rebellion. Distorted and bitter judgements often pass from generation to generation. The story shows how complicated and intertwined our narratives can be.

Emotions are conflicted between a desire for vengeance and a longing for reconciliation. Contempt wars with a longing for love. Suspicion distorts reality and bitterness clouds judgement. Maturity requires acknowledgement that life in its present form is grey, and that no one is perfect. Black and white thinking results in cynical demonising and sentimental idealisation, neither of which is helpful.

Childish or Childlike?

The apostle Paul wrote a letter to friends in Corinth who were quarrelling among themselves and behaving in dishonourable ways – there was even a son who was sleeping with his father's wife.[3] 'Love,' he said, is patient and kind ... it is not arrogant or rude.'[4] If they wanted to love well, he wrote, they must put away their childish behaviour and attitudes. 'When I was a child, I spoke like a child, I thought like a child, I reasoned like a child. When I became a man, I gave up childish ways.'[5] Paul was calling out their childish, dishonourable behaviours; acts of resentment, of exaggeration and manipulation, of judgement and contempt for each other. To love well and be honourable they needed to grow towards maturity.

Contrast their childishness with the childlikeness Jesus said is essential for life in the kingdom of heaven.[6] The difference is important because we should not lose those childlike characteristics that make life rich. Children wonder at the world around them. They are curious and ask questions, they trust and are disappointed by untrustworthiness, they are shocked and saddened by evil and intolerant of hypocrisy. They are happy and spontaneously joyful, they are unaware of themselves and are naturally empathetic. Such attributes are lost far too soon.

A friend recently sent me a short clip of his two-year-old son who, overflowing with joy and bursting in delight, had discovered a large jar of hand cream. He glowed as he smeared a thick layer of it over the entire dining room table. How easy to correct such behaviour with the blunt instrument of anger, and crush the spirit of exploration; how hard to celebrate and channel the wonder wisely. It was a joy to see how my friend celebrated his child's sense of adventure while helping him see that they needed to clean up his 'art' together.

Honour Restored

The nurturing environment shapes children for better or worse. The ease with which children negotiate the transition to maturity is perhaps proportional to the maturity of those who nurture them.

If honour does not mean blind obedience, what does it mean to honour parents who are profoundly dishonourable or, at best, show well-meaning but imperfect love? In its mature form, honouring means acknowledging our parents and their history as those who have given life and shaped us, while living with their failings and limitations as mature adults.

The now-adult 'children' honour their parents by making difficult choices to become honourable and mature despite childhood setbacks. They choose the difficult and courageous path to resist and overcome the destructive hurt of the pain. In learning to become honourable, children discover and regain their own dignity and freedom.

How does the adult overcome childhood scars? It would be naive and simplistic to attempt to cover in a few paragraphs what would take thousands of volumes, but it might be helpful to point in the right direction.

The way of healing starts by awakening to and naming wrongs done and the source of the hurt that is felt. This is not easy, because children are intuitively faithful to their parents and loyal to their tribe. They do not want to believe their parent was wrong. They might even be unaware that the behaviour was wrong, accepting it for want of a better example. Children cling to a secret longing for love that is sacred to every human heart.

Awakening to the reality that something is not right is painful. I might be aware of it without knowing the source. A false and misplaced loyalty blinds a son to the obvious manipulations of his mother. Having blocked out the horror, a daughter says she comes from a loving family, only to realise years later in tears that her father raped her. She must recognise wrongs that are painful to acknowledge. At first, she resists making the judgement and may even blame herself – she will be tempted to excuse the behaviour somehow – but she must judge that this happened and was wrong. The move towards truth is the first step towards maturity and freedom. Honour must be aligned with the truth if love is to be real.

The alternative is to withdraw, hide or kill a part of oneself. That is not to say that temporary or even longer-term withdrawal from the relationship might not be a necessary and painful part of the process as new boundaries are drawn, new attitudes are learned and new rules of engagement are negotiated.

The move from denial to recognition awakens powerful and disorienting emotions of anger, rage, revenge, bitterness or hatred, which must be processed. Anger might be justified and needs to be accepted and harnessed to give energy for the next steps; other feelings need to be acknowledged as present but possibly unhelpful.

Encouragement from friends and mentors is helpful, as the road ahead is unfamiliar. They can help contain disorientation and give permission to feel intense feelings. The powerful negative emotions will subside with time, but the process takes time and should not be hurried. Even the most self-aware and mature people will wrestle with inner resistance and anxiety. It is a move towards reality, self-awareness and humility.

Idealisation

The adult has clung, possibly for years, to childish ideals in the empty hope that he or she might yet receive the acknowledgement, affirmation or some other neglected parental responsibility. In refusing to acknowledge the parents' inability to fulfil their obligation, the now-adult child is guilty of a profound, if somewhat complex, idolatry – the parents are still on the pedestal of childhood idealisation. The now-grown child demands payment for what was, at one time, properly owed them. Childhood deification of the parental ideal traps the child in the past, keeping them from becoming mature, and can continue into adulthood, even after a parent's death.

The painful step of recognising parental failure and moving them from the pedestal is another step towards reality. Neither a parent's nor a nation's historical or cultural identity can give ultimate meaning and significance.

Forgiveness – Releasing the Debt

Change can happen only as the child releases the parent from the debt they owe. Relinquishment is painful. The now-adult child must grieve deeply held hopes and longings, and free the parent from the demand to complete their role. Those childhood needs were real, God-created needs – as fundamental as air for breathing – and should have been met. This lack has led to a distortion just as damaging as suffocation. The soul's lungs still scream for the air of affirmation and acknowledgement. It will take courage to see our mother or father as a human, with their own weaknesses and failings. It will be painful to recognise they will never meet the need, as the window of childhood development has now closed.

In what can feel like a breach of loyalty, the wrong must be correctly named. Without judgement, there is nothing to forgive. We bear the painful and distorting consequences, but now we choose to release our parents from their debt. In releasing them, we will be released. We will not allow our just demand for payment to hold back our growth towards maturity. We will not hold their debt against them, but will transfer it to God and trust him to make up for what was lost. God may do it directly, he may use other mature people to help us receive love and wisdom from older, wiser friends, or we might learn to live with unmet needs.

It takes time to name the debts, but it is essential to be thorough. Unnamed debts can haunt the one who forgives. For survival, we might have numbed the pain. As memories reawaken, and the old emotions return, the emotional pain we feel is a healthy sign of growth. The temptation to avoid or medicate them will be strong. Our judgements may be distorted. Our parents fail us in specific ways but rarely in every way. It is helpful to recognise the difference. The truth of events is rarely straightforward. Memory is selective and from personal experience. It never gives both sides or all perspectives. Imagination and speculation may be unhelpful; we must learn to restrain them. At each step, mature friends can help with perspective and proportion.

At its heart, forgiveness is about who pays, rather than feeling differently. Who will bear the burden of this debt? Something is owed, and justice requires that the books be balanced. Forgiveness takes time and cannot be hurried. It is a process. Not an event accomplished in a single moment, but something repeated until the debt is fully released. The temptation is to cling to it as a justification for pain or poor behaviour.

It is sometimes possible, having processed the pain and worked through forgiveness, for mature adults to reconnect with their parents, because even parents can grow up and learn lessons. It might be wise to remember a humorous remark questionably attributed to Mark Twain: 'When I was a boy of fourteen, my father was so ignorant I could hardly stand to have the old man around.

But when I got to be twenty-one, I was astonished at how much he had learned in seven years.'

In the same way, the mature parent expresses maturity by loving the dishonourable son or daughter rather than abandoning them. However, complete restoration may not be possible; it does not depend on one side alone. Time will show what the situation and circumstances allow. Some parents are committed to their childish ways and refuse to confront their immaturity, repent of past wrongs or change, possibly because they have never faced their own intergenerational pain. One cannot demand change; the choice must be free. In such a case, it will be necessary to breach familial loyalty, step out of the game and refuse to play by their old rules. This might feel wrong, but it is not. The parent will be honoured by the mature behaviour of their adult children who say, 'You no longer owe me what you failed to give me.' In doing this, they learn to love the unlovely and take responsibility for the personal brokenness resulting from parental failure. In the process, they learn to love – not necessarily with joy, but with a rugged and determined commitment to the betterment of the other.

How do we know when this is beginning to bear fruit? This is a process that happens gradually, almost imperceptibly. We will start to see the role and behaviour of our parents in their wider lives; that they are parents to us, but they have other relationships. We will feel less belittled in their presence and more in control of ourselves. Our judgements will be more nuanced and realistic and our perception of the past will become less idealised and more real. We will realise that personal experience is not the sum of all experience. We will be more present to the reality of each moment. Our character will become kinder, where it was once angry; more gracious, where it was once bitter. The childlike characteristics of maturity will reawaken a gradual and growing trust in others, the joy of discovery and the adventure of living. Add to this humility, perseverance, the courage to face and live in truth and speak it kindly, and the oil of forgiveness, and you have the honourable character traits that keep a community together in ways that are life-affirming and not destructive.

The way of honour is the foundation of a better country. Mature people are committed to a world where everyone is treated with respect and dignity, but it remains a struggle. It takes courage to show love to those who are not lovely, whose attitudes and actions have been hurtful and might remain dangerous. One needs a mind secure enough in its own worth not to feel diminished by dishonour.

When reconciled to our history, we are shaped less negatively by it. Rabbi Zusya, who lived in the eighteenth century in Hannopil, now in Ukraine, was in tears before he died. His students tried to comfort him by saying he was almost as wise as Moses. He responded, 'In the coming world, they will not ask me: "Why were you not Moses?" They will ask me, "Why were you not Zusya?"'[7] When freed from the distorting urge to please or perform, our fragmented selves become more integrated. We begin to see each other as we are; the real me can meet the real you and this is the foundation of love.

Loyalty and obedience are not difficult in a community that is honourable and makes space for the gifts and freedom of its members and is reflective about its traditions. Honour gives history a faithful hearing, and though the search for truth can be painful, it can be liberating. History records many sons and daughters who have handed down family traditions from generation to generation meaningfully and with great reward.

History Broken

Tradition is a helpful servant but a poor master. Honouring someone's existence does not mean agreeing with all they do. History also records those who have carried the burden of hollow traditions until they rebelled against them. History and tradition are often misread and unappreciated. The current narrative of progressive individualism might subtly lead to chronological snobbery and the wrong assumption that we can learn little from the past. We tend to assume that today's values are better than yesterday's and that traditions are chains we should unshackle. But there is no inherent reason why, for example, technological or medical progress should not go hand in hand with moral or relational regress.

The ghosts of unreconciled history are not limited to the closest family but haunt the communal mind of communities and nations. History is a storehouse of the memories of injustice passed down through the generations, obligations stored against days of revenge and carried forward painfully, unforgiven and unreconciled. This history is alive and present, informing and inflaming suspicion, assumptions and actions in a cycle that destroys trust and repeats itself until resolution.

In our individualistic culture, we overlook the communal element in human society. In communal cultures, memory is multi-generational, which can be challenging to understand fully. At present, people with cosmopolitan attitudes (individualistic, global, ahistorical) tend to look down on more communal attitudes as provincial (co-operative, local, with a stronger sense of history) and undervalue the positive social and economic benefits of communal responsibility.

We are connected to location, nation, tribe and neighbour through the family. We reflect our parents' loyalties; their nation is our nation, their tribe our tribe. Their culture, habits, judgements and values have become ours. A breach of familial loyalty is a breach of historical continuity and a threat to the coherence of the community. A refusal to repeat destructive patterns may require a violation of loyalty, but loyalty itself is not wrong.

The misunderstanding between individualist and communal cultures explains much of the tension between Eastern and Western Europeans, and the West's interaction with the Arab world and some parts of Asia. At least to some level, it is observable in the unresolved racial tensions in the United States.

Communal cultures have long memories. Communal hurts linger in communal cultures long after the reasons for them have faded. It is possible to remember experiences we have not personally encountered; insults and humiliations are as real to the descendants as to those who were present. Honour killings, common when people had to take the law into their own hands during a time when state law enforcement and the rule of law were limited, persist.[8] A deep offence to one family is made right in their eyes only by killing a member of the offending family. The offence is then reversed until one line is extinguished or honour is satisfied in some other way.[9] It may appear in such cases that an individualist society would be better than a communal one, but good judges and just laws can provide solutions without losing the many benefits of communal life.

I was once asked to help two young men in the Balkans reconcile their differences. I walked up and down the beach for two days, first with one and then the other. I listened as they peeled back the layers of offence. Each layer felt incomplete and superficial. Gradually, it emerged that their great-grandfathers had been in a feud over some land. The family narrative had carried the insult unreconciled through the generations. The young men liked each other, but family loyalty was also strong. Unconsciously they were making up reasons to justify their feelings of estrangement.

The cycle of hatred and revenge will continue until there is forgiveness and reconciliation. A failure to acknowledge and reconcile with history remains until people dare to seek peace. Breaking the cycle requires a breach of loyalty to the past without discounting its meaning or importance.

Examples of unreconciled shame, dishonour and revenge on society are not hard to find. One only need study the sectarian conflict in Northern Ireland to discover the pain of unreconciled history. Germans, humiliated after the First World War, accepted National Socialism to recover from the shame of defeat and re-establish a sense of honour. Russia attempted to humiliate Ukraine, just as Russia felt humiliated after the collapse of the Soviet Union in the 1990s. Examples exist on every continent.

Shame is a powerful emotion that energises fear and hatred when injustice feels fresh and unresolved. Suspicion and vengeance are handed down from generation to generation. The humiliated often humiliate as a means of keeping themselves from being humiliated again.

In individualistic cultures, where the chain of memory has been broken by mobility and distance, the fabric of old structures has been torn, and old loyalties ruptured. But forgetfulness is not the same as reconciliation; forgotten wounds stay unhealed. Forgotten experiences are no less potent in shaping us, though the reasons might be hidden and hard to uncover.

I once talked with someone who had translated for the Truth and Reconciliation process in South Africa. 'How much truth and how much reconciliation did you get?' I asked him.

'I don't think we got too much reconciliation,' he said. 'But we got a lot of truth, and without truth, you lose identity.'

I contrasted that with the post-communist period, in which few were called to account, and many hid their shame. The hiddenness caused many to struggle with issues of identity and the need to assert themselves in ways that were destructive to others.

Christians believe that Christ is the great equaliser, though, through the centuries, many have not behaved as if it were true. Our primary identity and the basis for equality – before nationality, sex, religion or any other identifier – is as humans of equal value made in God's image. Historical continuity, tradition and geography often add an important sense of belonging, structure and stability to communities. They are good as a secondary identity but tyrannous when they become primary.

History Reconciled

I was born in a town near London. When I was seven my parents decided to move to Malta. The reason was empire, or at least its dying gasp. My father got a job teaching in a school for military children. Our small and local decisions are often influenced by a history that is much larger than ourselves. The promise of that sunny Mediterranean island was attractive in the gloom of 1960s England. I did not want to go but was overruled. In leaving, a part of my childhood died; something was broken. Eighteen years later I was living in Vienna and happened to be in England to visit family. For some forgotten reason, I was driving near the town of my birth with time on my hands. On a whim, I decided to find the house where I was born. I drove through the town, found the street, and as I pulled up outside the house, I was flooded by a completely unexpected but overwhelming sense of returning home. An empty hole was filled momentarily, and I experienced something being mended.

We all have a personal history accumulated over time and a narrative passed down through the generations, unique wounds that fragment the mind and dislocate the heart, experiences that have set our expectations and assumptions, and trained our habits and reactions for protection and defence. We must relearn habits of courageous reconciliation necessary to open hearts and restore relationships.

When believers pray the Lord's Prayer, 'your will be done',[10] they are returning home. We seek the restoration of relationship with God and everyone else, because it is God's will that we reflect his Trinitarian image, the three that are always and simultaneously one, a demonstration of the love among the persons of the Godhead. Having been reconciled to God we must be reconciled to lesser enemies. Our protective walls must be pulled down and reordered to reflect the reign of God and his culture of grace. The demolition of those walls is dangerous, dusty work best done with care and patience.

God alone has a complete record of history back to the beginning. He did not write it off as irrelevant. All our sins are first against God, because we have broken the peace and joy of his creation, and second towards others we have wronged. Only God can make a complete judgement and knows what is on each account. God alone has the knowledge and moral character necessary for true vengeance. Therefore, he reserves it for himself: 'Vengeance is mine, I will repay, says the Lord.'[11] He alone knows, while we do not, all the reasons for every act. He knows who is truly guilty and why. In entering the world through his Son, God joined our history to reconcile it to himself and us to each other. He has completed the judgement and wants to release us from the debt we owe each other individually and communally. But first we must own the debt. This is not cheap love that says the debt is irrelevant.

Reconciliation and restoration is demanding, emotionally consuming work, but more possible than we might think, and not just with parents. We should strive for them, knowing that our eternal Father is able to give wisdom and courage in this arduous process. Ultimately, it is God who pays to equalise all debt, and he is honoured when we choose, against difficult odds, to walk the path to maturity.

Imagine a world where each generation is well connected to the next; where shame and humiliation are not accumulated from one generation to another, where a seamless virtue runs through the generations uninterrupted by envy or hate. Love builds a house that none can threaten. God's rule is a kingdom of uninterrupted trust and trustworthiness.

Trinitarian Communion

The Trinity shows the answer to a tension, often felt but rarely articulated, between fathers and sons, mothers and daughters, the community and the people within it. How is it possible to be both in communion with each other and yet unique?

Difference raises the fear of fraying the bond that binds the communion, but the anxiety can be oppressive. A father demands unquestioning submission to lifeless traditions. A daughter, under threat of separation, submits with resentment to her mother's requirement to dress in a particular way. Oppressive power spoils the delight of communion. Domination of one over another eventually leads to rebellion.

Within the Trinity the Father is perfect, the Son is perfect, and so the difference is perfect.[12] What is true of God can be true of those made in his image. I can be myself and you can be yourself and we can still be one. The love and humility at the heart of our communion allows for the appreciation of difference, for various gifts and culture. Think, for example, of the artist and accountant: one paints outside the box, the other needs everything to fit perfectly into the box (or spreadsheet). They make sense of the world in diverse ways, but they need each other to go beyond their own limitations. This takes courage and grace and the ability to negotiate. To reflect the image of God we must aim for communion, not conformity; union, not uniformity.

Adoption

The Christian faith teaches that we enter the family of God through adoption. No earthly parent, however good, is good enough to produce offspring worthy of this inheritance or capable of its virtues because we inherit death from even the best of earthly parents. Those who want life must turn to its source: to God whose life is potent, giving power to reconcile and restore trust. The life of God is both the model and standard for the communion we have failed to achieve but must regain if we are to enjoy real life. 'I and the Father are one,' said the Son.[13] 'This is my beloved Son, with whom I am well pleased,'[14] said the Father.

Through adoption, we gain a new name as sons and daughters of God. The shame of history, with its shattered fragments and open wounds, can be bound up and the wounds begin to heal.

The Father sends the Son and *trusts* him to remain free from the temptations of evil as a human. The Son commits himself into the hands of his Father, *trusting* him with resurrection. The basis of this trust is the moral commitment of love shared before the foundation of the world. Real freedom is grounded in trust and other-centred love. Therefore, the Father can say, 'This is my Son, my Chosen One; listen to him.'[15]

Coffee Break – Power

Welcome again. We are rushed off our feet. We always are in times of crisis. People want to talk, and where better to meet friends than your local café? The sun is shining, and we have tables outside, but we are disturbed by news from the east. War has broken out, and it is too close for comfort. There are rumours everywhere, and not about a better country, but about unimaginable cruelty.

Why do countries go to war? What do people take so seriously that they will fight and die for it?

People are anxious and angry. We do not like our peace to be disturbed. And why should we? You can tell when customers are mad; they eat without thinking or pleasure. They are hungry for sugar. They feel depleted and need food to power their anger and calm their nerves.

We had a customer the other day who ate two cakes almost without breathing. I was polishing the counter when he walked in. He snapped at me in his demand. 'How is your day going?' I smiled in reply. He just growled and pointed to the cake, which he rudely breathed into his mouth, then demanded a coffee and another cake. Then he turned and walked out without a word. At least he paid. Later in the day, he came back and, much to my surprise, apologised, telling the sad story that lay behind his gruff behaviour. I won't retell it here. Sometimes the café is like a confessional.

There is a buzz in the room, a hubbub of rumours and what they might mean for us. The war is unjustified, although I'm sure the enemy has its justifications. Everyone justifies themselves in their own eyes. If you sit in the café and listen long enough, you will overhear people building narratives to justify their hurts. Some narratives are true, but we shoehorn our 'evidence', however flimsy, into the story, then repeat it to ourselves and anyone who will listen to our obsessive rhythms until they harden into 'fact', and we feel justified in our actions. We feel the necessity for justification, and it says something about us as humans, but I am not quite sure what.

Occasionally, when opinions clash, someone's inner violence overspills into the café. They rage and burn hot, disturbing everyone's peace. It is embarrassing and we must ask them to leave, although if we know them well, we will let them cool off in one of the back rooms. The difference between murdering, slandering and cancelling is only a matter of degrees.

But we also see a generosity of spirit that is astounding. How often I have watched one person pay for another's dinner on an evening when the budget didn't stretch far enough, only to see the compliment returned some months later when the boot was on the other foot. In a better country, each should bear his or her burden, but we should also bear each other's burden when the going gets tough.

9

Word Six: Life or Death

You shall not murder.
(Exodus 20:13)

I came that they may have life and have it abundantly.
(John 10:10)

I am writing this on the seventy-fifth anniversary of the Holocaust. I was twenty when I first went to Auschwitz in 1975. It was a grey winter's day. The camp had closed thirty years before, but there were plenty of people still around from both sides of the barbed wire. Poland was under communism, and the Russians who had liberated the camp were now seen as the oppressors. No culture, nation or person comes away clean when examining issues of oppression. It takes courage to hold the gaze of such a dark subject, because the mind's eye wants to avoid it.

I remember talking with a friend about the depression that lingered over me for weeks after my first visit. He told me I would not come to terms with it until I learned to recognise the anger, envy and hate in my own heart. Occasionally, I have remembered our conversation after moments of rage. Murder describes a reality from which there is no return, and murderous thoughts lurk in us all.

What Is Murder?

Murder is an act of ultimate domination that presumes absolute authority over another person's life. It resolves a difficulty by eliminating one of the parties rather than the problem.

Not all killing is murder. Soldiers who must defend their country do what no one should have to do and will carry their scars for life.[1] Those who rule legitimately have the heavy responsibility to take life in extreme circumstances for the defence and security of people under their protection. That said, the Decalogue applied to everyone, from king to servant. Murder done in the name of the government is still murder. You cannot reorganise society by destroying everyone who disagrees with you. Idealistic visions turn to totalitarian nightmares on both the left and the right. The twentieth century would have looked quite different had we understood this. There are enough examples of industrial-strength murder in recent history, from the Holocaust to the Gulag, and more recently from Rwanda to Srebrenica. It is easy to point the finger at others while we dehumanise groups that are inconvenient to ourselves.

The Economic and Social Costs of Murder

In the Café Now and Not Yet, people quickly list the immediate economic and social costs of murder, which are immense. Our taxes cover expensive police investigations, lawyers and judges, prisons, probation and rehabilitation, social workers, counsellors and medical costs – resources that might be used more fruitfully on education or exploration. We have not counted the loss of income and productivity or added the shock and grief in families and friends who never fully recover.

The psychological consequences of murder engulf neighbours with fear and anxiety about going out, and cause depression, loss of sleep, and concentration at work, and use of medication. The list continues, and we have not touched the smallest part of it. I assume it will not happen to me, but do I avoid dark alleys? Open the lens wider on society; consider the sanctity of every life – the trafficked, the enslaved and the unborn, separated from home and love, used and thrown on the scrap heap. Lives cut short on the altars of pleasure and convenience. The social costs of our casual attitudes towards others are profound.

The story gets worse before it gets better. Reflect for a moment on lives scarred by murderous attitudes.

That Man Is a Fool – Judgement as Murder

Thankfully, in many societies, murder is infrequent. Or is it? If murder is the elimination of one of the parties rather than the problem, is there a kind of murder that does not involve physically killing someone?

Once, while preparing for Easter, I used the Decalogue to examine my conscience. The first five words were difficult because there was much that needed repair. When I came to the sixth, 'You shall not murder', I thought with some relief, 'At least I haven't murdered anyone!' Immediately the faces of two people I was avoiding came to mind. A voice from somewhere said, 'They are dead to you, and you are killing the relationship.' It was mutual; they were killing it too.

Murder can take many forms. Consider the language we use to describe our interactions: 'He stabbed me in the back', 'She got thrown under the bus', 'Did he jump or was he pushed?' We talk of a 'cancel culture', where we banish someone because of disagreements on ideas or behaviour. Someone says of a neighbour, 'I will never speak to him again!' as she passes a death sentence on their friendship. It does not result in a knife in the back but a subtler, equally effective form of death, fuelled by fear, envy, dishonesty, aggression, pride, self-justification and more.

The first step towards murder is slander and gossip. The imagination we considered in Chapter 5 is aflame; an argument blows up in a mind full of destructive, violent thoughts that set the heart pumping and cause speculation seen as fact. Envy, which we will meet in Chapter 13, is that fiend of comparison that covets the other's status, capacities or power. Gossip, the acid rain of the soul passed from one mouth to another, is a more straightforward form of revenge. A subtle word here or there, backstabbing, slandering a reputation. The more intelligent, the greater the sophistication. Knives are drawn – not of steel but of words, and sharper for it.

Is someone dead to me, even though they are alive? Does the thought of them make my mind spin in endless self-justifying arguments? Who am I avoiding? How am I avoiding them? Do feelings of arrogance or pride cause me to dismiss another person as unimportant? Elimination is much easier than reconciliation and gives the illusion of superiority that reinforces a weak ego. Am I too busy to pick up the phone and face a void once filled with friendship? Murderous thoughts and destructive anger are wasteful, ineffective and enslaving. How thin, fragile and rigid relationships can be; people barely communicating, a little polite conversation or pleasantness, a thin veneer to cover fear and mistrust – less risky but less satisfying. Cynicism distorts judgements, which become shallow and hollow, and we feel dead inside. The cost is high and distorts reality.

We saw in the last chapter how we hand down the wounds of broken relationships and festering memories through the generations. Perhaps a simple lack of courage and social conformity stop many more physical murders than we realise. Would I kill if I could get away with it?

The instruction from the mountain in Sinai was a shadow, a limited version of God's standard for people with hard hearts. It was limited to physical murder. Christians believe that when Jesus came teaching about a better country, the lawgiver himself had become a man, and we learned of the infinitely higher standard of his character.

> 'You have heard that it was said to those of old, "You shall not murder; and whoever murders will be liable to judgement." But I say to you that everyone who is angry with his brother will be liable to judgement; whoever insults his brother will be liable to the council; and whoever says, "You fool!" will be liable to the hell of fire.'[2]

The man or woman might be a fool, but no one is *only* a fool. If I judge them as such, I have effectively killed all their other attributes, which are dead to me. I see only through my judgement and do not see the whole person. I have reduced them to my assessment of them and left no place for surprise or possibility.

Meanwhile, they feel trapped in the prison of my judgement and struggle for freedom.

Think of how we esteem someone as more valuable because they have more economic power or education; or the cultural prejudice that shouts, 'Keep your distance,' when people of different castes, cultures and races come supposedly too close. We defend ourselves at a high cost to the potential of the joy of knowing other people. The familiar and safe blind us to what is real and present.

Some relationships are no doubt so 'toxic' that separation is essential, at least for a while. But even if it is toxic for one or both parties, the attempt at reconciliation is better because, in the process, we confront the darkness of our hearts and can begin the journey to freedom.

We need to learn to hate murder in all its forms. Modern society sees hatred as the problem. Our experience of hatred is of the warped, irrational and destructive force that lashes out to destroy anything that threatens us. But like every emotion, hatred is emotional energy we can use appropriately or poorly. A healthy hatred of evil is constructive and informed by a love of the good[3] – not bitterness, resentment or revenge. It confronts the murderous thoughts and overcomes them while not avoiding the issues that aroused them.

Explosive Anger or Mature Anger

Today I read in the news of a son who murdered his mother with an axe in a leafy London suburb. Neighbours reported their shock at the unexpected violence of this quiet man, a tragedy of anger boiling over into violent hatred. He will spend the rest of his life locked up at a high cost to everyone. How much better if the young man had worked through his anger with a wise friend and learned that mature anger aims at reconciliation and not destruction.

Murder is untidy. It separates old friends and binds new ones in unhealthy loyalties. Emotions accumulate, bubble up and boil over; untended passions, like a garden full of weeds and brambles, lash out at anything in their way. Bitterness broods and memory lapses until a mere smell or misplaced word triggers old shame or anxiety attached to nothing we can recall. Then murder strikes, and someone is separated from the one they once loved.

In our daily lunch discussions at the learning community where I work, guests often raise the topic of anger. What is usually on their minds is the violent, quick-tempered, impulsive, explosive eruption of someone blazing away and out of control. Occasionally, someone might acknowledge other expressions of anger: passive aggression or sneaky, manipulative anger or internalised anger that eventually destroys the health of the one who holds it. They have encountered anger as harmful and painful and want to learn how to think about it. They intuit that anger must be wrong, but this idea seems inadequate or incomplete, so they are confused. Sometimes a more pious person might talk of 'righteous anger', but few know what that means, except that God must have it because he gets angry too.

The conflation of anger with explosive anger is so deeply ingrained in us that it is hard to think clearly about anger at all. Rarely do we ask: 'What is anger for?' or, 'What might good or mature anger look like?'

Anger against Injustice

Mature anger is the emotion that gives the energy to correct an injustice or a wrong. 'Be angry and do not sin,'[4] Paul wrote to the church in Ephesus. He recognised the need for anger and that anger does not have to be immoral, explosive or destructive.

Positively, anger is the *sustained* energy needed to stay focused on obtaining the resolution of the injustice over time. Mature anger seeks the resolution of a problem, not revenge for the pain caused by it. It supplies the power for sustained attention to resolving conflict and re-establishing trust. It is patient and persistent. First, it raises a flag that something is not right; then it asks what is wrong and what is needed as a corrective, who is the object of the wrong, and the reasons for it. Finally, it gives the courage, discipline and hatred of evil necessary for appropriate loving action.

Explosive, red-faced anger is defensive, disruptive, out of control and often anxiety-driven. Its energy is misdirected and ineffective; at best, it gives the temporary illusion of control.

Righteous anger points towards the one who provoked anger through their unrighteous act. Such anger aims at a constructive resolution of wrong, and reconciliation with the person who has wronged us or others.

Anger does not simply go away; it goes somewhere else. Healthy anger requires a clear object and outcomes. Is a woman angry because someone has bullied her, or is she merely an angry woman who needs to ask herself why she is always angry, to get to the bottom of her anger? In other words, does she have the courage to become specific about the cause of her anger, or does she let it bleed onto undeserving people? She might need to confront the person, and that will require courage and possibly the support of a friend, as the bully might be an overbearing manipulator.

Wisdom is required to direct emotional energy towards good outcomes. The problem must be named in order to find and implement solutions that do not involve eliminating someone. Sometimes, the parties may, sadly, need to separate for safety's sake. Repentance might not yet be deep enough, or forgiveness may not yet have done its work. Wisdom might indicate that it is not safe to trust. But we should never lose sight of the ideal.

If anger is the energy necessary for resolving some issues, what of those who do not experience anger or who deny they experience it? A counsellor listens to someone tell of an awful experience and asks what he has done with his anger. 'Oh, I am not angry,' he replies. He means it, but it is not true, nor should it be. Unrighteousness should evoke anger. In a case like this, cultural or family norms or fear of retribution have suppressed the anger to such an extent that it is not doing its job. Various cultures and families deal with anger in different ways. In many families, expressions of anger are punished rather than processed. The issues are avoided and wait like landmines for someone to step on them. In some countries, public outbursts of anger are a sign of moral or professional failure, and anger is swept under the carpet. In other countries, people take outbursts of anger less personally. While not ideal, it is at least honest and opens the potential for resolution. In those cultures, elaborate rituals and go-betweens are often in place to negotiate peace over time. Without appropriate and mature anger, people are powerless to resist abuse and are without agency to act.

Our anger is often linked to the pain of injustice and can give us a very partial perspective. Due process helps remove the emotion from justice to arrive at a true and right judgement. When operating correctly, the law's decision fulfils anger's rightful desire for justice.

People who exercise proper dominion over their lives have self-control.[5] They see the larger picture and clearly understand what is wrong. They use the energy of their anger to find a corrective – over an extended period if necessary. Their self-controlled anger drives them to patience and courageous action at the right time. Love directs their anger to good outcomes. They are willing to be proved wrong and are open to alternative solutions. It is not easy or automatic and best done with the help of wise counsel.

Someone might complain that they would get nothing done without domineering and intimidating anger. But the respect, loyalty and authority gained by disciplined self-control are far more potent than the resentment and passive resistance that result from abusive behaviour.

The Anger of God

Some people struggle with the idea of an angry God, but it helps to understand the relationship between anger and justice. A God who is committed to the flourishing of all humans must be equally opposed to all that threatens them. There is no necessary contradiction between love and anger. God's attributes, unlike ours, are not sequential but simultaneous and integrated. These are not mood swings from love to anger and back again. The anger of God is an expression of his persevering love. His sustained merciful anger is a model of self-controlled and focused energy towards loving ends, which is our reconciliation with him and restoration to right living and freedom. He would have been wholly justified in taking retribution for the destruction we have brought on his creation and those he loves, but that was not his aim then or today. Instead, he focuses his anger on a loving solution.

It was not only in cleansing the Temple that Christ showed the patient wrath of God on earth, but in all his encounters. Everyone he met fell short of his standard and was under his judgement, yet he treated them with truth and grace.

God's wrath is not the petulant anger of a frustrated will, nor the powerlessness of a deity outwitted by his creation. Instead, it is a patient, disciplined and focused will acting over time to restore love in the world. Hatred of murder means the pursuit of reconciliation.

'I Came that They May Have Life'

What, then, is God's will for his creation? What is his kingdom like? Jesus said, 'I came that they may have life and have it abundantly.'[6] But what is an abundant life? It is more than the biology of heartbeats and brainwaves. If death is the painful breaking of communion among people, then abundant life is deep communion, rich in trust and life-affirming. After all, what is more satisfying than the easy companionship of friends who can trust one another, where none has anything to prove, and each may be blissfully unconscious of themselves?

In one of his letters, the apostle John wrote to his friends, 'We know that we have passed out of death into life because we love the brothers. Whoever does not love abides in death. Everyone who hates his brother is a murderer, and you know that no murderer has eternal life abiding in him.'[7]

Eternal life is like a seed that germinates and begins to push out the old bitter ways as it grows and expands. Broken relationships should disturb believers who have the eternal life of God abiding in them. Of course, we are not perfect and make mistakes, but the general direction of travel should be towards reconciliation, trust and openness in relationships. In a better country, life is valued and the dignity of human life is recognised for all, regardless of age or race or disability or status or any other comparison of values. Each of us is valued fully by virtue of our existence.

The desire for communion is a sign that love is growing. A hardness of the heart points to an absence of eternal life. It is God's will to free us so entirely from murder and murderous thoughts that they would not cast the slightest shadow across the mind. A better country would be free not just from murder, but also from hatred of and between persons and groups.

This vision might feel distant and challenging. Reconciliation is a long and demanding road. Here the ideal confronts the real, and it is wise to be cautious, but we justify broken relationships too quickly. Dead relationships should cause grief, because they do not reflect the Trinitarian communion in God. As God works for our reconciliation, so must we. It is not merely a religious trait but a human one to want reconciliation. We feel the pain of separation as we close our hearts to others. The path to abundant life leads through humility, repentance, forgiveness and reconciliation. 'Impossible!' we shout and, of course, we are right; that is the tragedy of the human condition. We are dead until we have the eternal life of our Maker working in us.

The prize is worth the race, but the price is high. The death of Christ was a murderous act. It was a direct challenge to his authority and power. But it was overcome by the greater power of life, the communion within the Trinity.

Christ is risen. Our murderous thoughts and hearts have died with him; now they must die in us.

Coffee Break – Burnout

 Early every morning, customers rush into the café, down a quick shot of coffee to kick-start their day, then rush out again. These days, they often look haggard.

'You look tired this morning,' I occasionally suggest to someone I know and care for. 'You've been burning the candle at both ends, and the coffee is no longer working its magic.'

Nowadays, they talk about KPIs. That was new to me. Key Performance Indicators are management mantras of the modern age. One customer suggested to me recently, rather cynically, that his manager's KPI was: 'How much blood can I squeeze from a stone?' He was, he said, feeling burned out.

I recall a customer who suggested that it's not the work that burns us out but relationships. 'We overcompensate,' he said, 'In vain attempts to salvage our dignity, we become driven and drugged until we are depleted. We don't need rest; we need restoration.' Here the fragments of our souls are most unhelpful; envy, shame and anger sabotage our dignity, sap our sense of self and drive the slave within.

Some days I am left shaking my head as I watch another wounded road warrior set off, anxious for his mortgage and children's education, the bright candle of his youthful hopes and dreams spluttering in the dark. I often wonder as I give another hungry soul her coffee and croissant if we should not measure the quality of our relationships instead. They are hard to nurture, yet at the same time are what most make life worth living. Through them we get meaning, and when they are broken, life itself feels devalued.

We all need friends; there is only so much a cup of coffee can do!

10

Word Seven: The Possibilities and Problems of Love

'You shall not commit adultery.'
(God to Moses)

'I will never leave you nor forsake you.'
(Jesus)

'All You Need is Love,' sung by the Beatles, characterised the 'summer of love' in 1967. The great religions call us to love. Poets write of it. It is proposed as the ideal when discussing a better country. How could love possibly go wrong? My youthful question was simple: love might be all you need, but what is it?

I have divided this chapter into two parts to accommodate the complexity of love. In the first, I will describe our present situation, and in the second look at alternatives in the search for a better country.

Part 1: In Search of Love

The summer of love was one of those historical moments when subtle long-term shifts in perception come into plain sight; we saw reality through a new lens. Something had changed as the dust settled on the untold grief of two world wars, and we woke up to an identity crisis that followed the collapse of empires. Nature had replaced God as sovereign. Our senses governed supreme. We lived for *now*, free from the dead morality of a divine but absent landlord.[1]

Culture shapers were busy redefining the meaning and practice of *love* to reflect this new understanding. Technology and science enabled that first sexual revolution. Reliable contraception, in the form of the pill, and the widespread availability of abortion, made it possible for people to detach sexual pleasures from parenting responsibilities to a previously unimaginable degree. If those involved were consenting adults, why shouldn't people do whatever they liked?

Old cultural patterns like marriage, monogamy and family were wedded to old beliefs. Ancient forms gave way to new freedoms, and a growing individualism replaced communal life. Yet many family rhythms of life survived, albeit weakened and battered. It appeared that children needed stability, a place to *be from* and discover themselves, consistent relationships, security during their upbringing, and somewhere to call home after leaving. Strangely, the ancient cultural patterns offered advantages. Some paused and wondered if there wasn't a deeper magic in the universe we needed to rediscover. Were we throwing the baby out with the bathwater?

I knew what it meant to be attracted to someone, because I had had my share of attractions. Like many people, I had automatically associated love with warm feelings of excitement and acceptance. When those feelings disappeared, a person seemed to be no longer *in* love. I had assumed I would fall in love, but now I realised I might fall out of it.

What, I wondered, distinguished the exciting romantic attraction that drew people to each other from the mature love necessary to keep them in a meaningful and ever-deepening yet spacious relationship? Attachments based on warm feelings seemed too unstable to be of enduring value. This transient form of love did not seem adequate to bear the weight of the complexity of human relationships. Yet it was the message the entertainment industry, my primary source of knowledge, was vigorously promoting. I was painfully confused. Did no one have a deeper, more satisfying understanding of love?

More profound questions followed. Was love a response to something I had no control over and must blindly follow? Was it an emotion, a feeling or something I was supposed to do, an act of will? A minute's reflection showed its complexity.

The unresolved grief of two wars left people afraid of commitment. There was a massive spike in divorce rates after both wars. When we first lived in eastern Austria in the mid-1970s, we learned that most women in our district, many just young girls, had been raped by Soviet soldiers as the war ended. Trauma left people bitter, angry and powerless. Their sense of worth had been stolen. Something had been damaged deep inside; trust was broken, and grief made future attachments more tentative. If there was a deep cynicism about grand narratives, there was also a fear of giving and receiving love. Naturalism gave a more plausible account for the emotions people felt than the idea of a loving God, and it was shaping our understanding of relationships. But, by giving up on God, we lost the reference point that defined humanness and our understanding of love.

Nowhere were the fragments of human relationships more evident than in the search for the meaning of love. It was some time before I realised my experience of the fragments was shaping my questions and the answers society was giving. Love was in pieces. To understand it, the fragments had to be examined together. Could humans reach intentionally beyond themselves to each other in communion? Was this what it looked like when the fragments were whole?

Love in an Age of Individualism

When we returned to England after living for many years in Central Europe, my wife and I noticed a shift in the culture and language. 'Does your partner want some coffee?' said the waitress. 'She is not my partner,' I said involuntarily. 'She's my wife.' Both the waitress and I looked confused.

We spent months looking for a home and were surprised to discover nine out of ten houses were available because the partnership had dissolved. The average length of a partnership was then just over three years.[2] The builders who reconstructed our house had partners, but none lived with the mothers of their children.

Do shifts in language matter? We reflected on the assumptions behind the change in language and society. We supposed 'partnership' had replaced 'husband and wife' for many reasons, perhaps out of fear of offending couples who had chosen alternative arrangements or to emphasise an equality that my wife and I had always assumed.

As I write, the radio is on in the background. Someone is celebrating the blended family, loosely defined as parents and partners with children from earlier relationships. These form around one in three families, and will describe many of my readers. We can be thankful for every happiness we have, while accepting the inevitability of relational dysfunction that is deeply embedded in us all on many levels. Nevertheless, the fragments of longing, the divided loyalties and hidden injuries should sadden every feeling person, and we should be honest about them.

The long-term fallout from the 'summer of love' seems to be a fear of long-term commitment in relationships of any type, little knowledge of how to negotiate them well and few good models to learn from. We should not lose sight of the benefit of long-term relational commitment. Humans have a deeply held longing to belong. Tentative attachments are costly on many levels; commitment and communion have dropped from our consciousness. We sing to different rhythms and a less harmonic scale.

Love and Attraction

In contemporary culture, some understand love as the feeling the object (you) stimulates in the subject (me). Strong feelings seem convincing in a culture that prizes knowledge through experience. I am inclined to love my feelings because they authenticate my existence.

The cultural narrative, communicated through pop songs, rom-coms and boxed sets created by our culture makers, tells us to trust our feelings. In an ahistorical age, immediate feelings and experiences seem more authentic than long-term commitments to less exciting prior obligations.

We intuitively equate feelings of attraction with love and expect those feelings to be a faithful guide to future happiness. However, such assumptions give no framework and little guidance to evaluate whether an attraction is healthy and one to pursue, or harmful and best ignored.

Infatuation is easily mistaken for love. The experience of being trusted, heard, seen and enjoyed can be intoxicating; this is the appeal and danger of romantic love. Everyone is on their best behaviour and blind to negativity when they first meet. The results of unexplored but differing assumptions, incomplete knowledge or downright lies can be disastrous when not based on reality. Such a union is fragile and easily fragmented. When trust is violated, it feels like a betrayal.

Attractions happen for many reasons; some are positive and potentially a gateway to love, but many are far from loving in any meaningful sense. Consider these negative reasons for attraction: if I envy you, I might be attracted to the part of you I envy, and it would be easy initially to misread this as friendship. You might boost my ego and give me affirmation, comfort or approval. I might find comfort in how you manage my anger, anxiety or shame. None of these is necessarily wrong – any combination might feel exciting or satisfying – but over time they can be destructive if they are the foundation of the relationship.

Advertising has conditioned us to expect perfection in a society conditioned by consumerism. We return products that do not deliver. This attitude seeps into relationships, and dating apps increase the expectation: swipe left or right based on an image and an intuition.

Eventually, I will seek someone else if you stop stimulating feelings I associate with love, because it is ultimately the feeling I am buying. The clock is ticking, and time is running out. If this life is all there is, I have one shot at it. So why should I not have the glow the photoshopped advertisements promise? Life is too short to waste on failure.

But consumerism does not satisfy human longings. As we saw in our discussion on time in Chapter 7, every *now* derives meaning from the past and future. Our value comes from somewhere deeper than immediate satisfaction. A better country is one where people are valued for their existence as humans and not for what might be extracted from them.

Love and Sex

Our Western cultures place such a high value on sex that it is considered an essential element for human flourishing. I saw this in the early 1990s when working in Ukraine. Students were taught they would suffer mental neuroses if they did not have regular sex. Some were anxious! The narrative of materialistic communism led them to believe they were nothing more than matter and that their sexual drives were pleasurable but meaningless biochemical reactions. But they were hungry for kindness, dignity and self-respect. It became painfully clear that, in using each other in this way, far from giving them mental stability, this sexual activity emptied them of their sense of worth.

The sexualisation of relationships has strained friendships with other levels of intimacy. Watch the narratives of our popular culture, and you might think that falling in love and going to bed are the same. In a naturalistic frame, all this makes sense; attractions are merely biological, the satisfaction of a bodily impulse that *any* other body can meet. Both subject and object are instruments in which a relationship might be an inconvenience to manage rather than nurture. The means becomes an end, and gratification is the goal. We talk about *my* body, *my* rights, with little room for a communion of spirit and only the vaguest notion of what that might be.

An increasingly individualistic and naturalistic society reduces intimacy to sexual activity. But sex can act as an opiate to suppress more complex emotions and hide a deeper longing for a more profound but frightening intimacy. It is a modern myth that sexual activity is necessary for a meaningful life and relationships. That narrative is convenient for predators and traps many into consent by manipulation, from which they wake up feeling used, humiliated and abandoned. I question the naturalistic frame because of the loss of value and the hurt it has caused in people's lives.

Sex is not wrong, but on its own it is a fragment, stripped of its context of long-term commitment. We rush into the living room of each other's souls without taking time to know and love each other as whole people.

Fragmentation

Are minds really untouched by the faceless intercourse of strangers? Our fragmentation shows in how we use each other for physical fulfilment in the search for deeper intimacy. The discontinuity between psychology and biology, typical in contemporary life, has consequences. I find it hard to think that the frequency of anonymous sexual activity does not lead to anxiety, hardened hearts and a distorting suppression of memory.[3] It is a dehumanising burden for anyone who takes their life seriously.

In such acts, the immediate moment is separated from the flow of history, and memory is suppressed and fragmented because who would want to remember and compare former sexual partners? Hope is distorted because the act makes no promise to the future.

As I have noted throughout this book, modern people are primarily conscious of themselves as individuals, with the individual assumed to be the smallest indivisible unit possible. The contemporary individualistic narrative gives few answers to the fundamental question of integration of the self and the community. However, it does not offer solutions for the present epidemic of chronic loneliness in society.

The modern narrative dictates that individuals can treat physical, emotional, sexual and reproductive needs as unconnected fragments to be met separately and fulfilled in disconnected and impersonal ways through strangers or technology.[4]

Every technological advance is an expression and extension of human activity and reflects the dignity and depravity inherent in us. We may celebrate the benefits, but the downsides need to be named and mitigated. Relationships fragment under the pressures of modern life unless they are nurtured. We are experiencing a mental health crisis of epidemic proportions. Loneliness, identity issues and anxiety levels, to name a few, would be significantly relieved by long-term, loving relationships.

The Betrayal of Love

'To adulterate' has its roots in Latin and means 'to corrupt, weaken, add an impurity to something pure, water down, or mix inappropriately'. The seventh word of the Decalogue warns against adultery, which, in English, stems from the same Latin word.

When we lived in Austria in the 1980s, there was a scandal in the wine industry. After some poor harvests, unscrupulous winemakers added chemicals similar to antifreeze to enhance the taste of their wine. The adulterated wine tasted better but was less pure, and when drunk in large enough quantities could seriously damage your health. When the scandal broke, people were shocked and then outraged. The vintners had violated the promise of purity. Trust, won over centuries, had been betrayed. The wine industry recovered, but at a high cost to trust. The authorities destroyed over 27 million litres of wine, some of which, I read, they used instead of salt on the roads in winter, but that may be a myth.

Most people experience adultery as a painful betrayal, whether it is a breach of a marital promise or a betrayal of any relationship. The seventh word exists to protect us from ourselves and others when love fails, and until love recovers. What is it protecting? What is in danger of being watered down? Communion crashing on the shores of bitterness and hurt, and hearts hardening behind a protective shell of judgements that, in time, will seep into all other loves. Relationships of trust, love and intimacy need protection.

It is a tragedy that many people have lost belief in the permanence of committed relationships. Many of my most beneficial relationships are with people who have known me for a long time. They remind me of patterns in my behaviour and responses during stress. In working through our struggles, we learn, grow and confront the fragments of our being that need to be integrated into a coherent whole.

Love and Morality

Sexual abuse is cruel and damaging because it attacks the very essence of our worth and violates our personhood. What should be given and received voluntarily in a loving relationship has been stolen by violence or manipulation. The experience of sexual violation intrudes on future expectations of every other relationship and damages trust, dignity and hospitality.

Those who grew up in the 1960s and 70s came of age in a time of assumed sexual freedom, throwing off a rigid morality whose foundation they did not understand and their parents had forgotten. The dividing line between abuse and liberty was not always clear. In matters of sex, freedom and consequences are not equal. As Louise Perry has shown, the sexual revolution promised liberation for women, but enabled further sexual exploitation of women by men.[5] Later generations have paid the price in emotional and relational anxiety, a loss of trust and inner fragmentation.

The twenty-first century, by contrast, is highly moral and believes in justice, but it is a narrow justice. Few of its standards are shared widely. It frames morality narrowly as consent between adults, who must then parse whether consent is valid, given power imbalances and appeals to equality. However, it has no framework for forgiveness or restoration.

Modern views of law consider humans to be free rational decision-makers. Consent is enough for justice to have been fulfilled. However, agreement in the moonlight might seem less rational in the cold light of day. At which of those two moments is my word more mine? Especially when my peer group expects and even pressures me into sexual activity. Power is rarely equal, and a lack of resolve to say no is easily mistaken for consent.[6] The modern model does not offer real freedom or address the complexities of human interaction and, most importantly, short-circuits the process of building relational knowing and trust.

Both periods show that humans are moral creatures seeking a code to live by, as Crosby, Stills, Nash & Young sang in the 1970s.[7]

They were seeking a new form for sexual freedom, but I think they failed. Sex needs to be contained in a healthy, committed relationship. Neither generation has resolved the tensions raised by this new freedom or found a better form to meet the innate need for love.

Part 2: Growing in Love

We should not restrict our understanding of relationships to people in romantic love, or demand that such relationships fulfil all our needs. The idea that attraction *must* lead to romantic love is a recent phenomenon. Nor should we reduce love to sex. Deep and meaningful, albeit non-sexual, friendships seem to be a lost art, and we would benefit by rediscovering them.

It helped me to realise there are at least two kinds of loneliness that need different solutions. First, the *experiential* loneliness of finding oneself without friends is resolved by finding good company. The *existential* loneliness of a fragmented mind is resolved through the experience of being loved and by finding meaning. Sexual engagement can be as much a hindrance as a help. As I have pointed out in other chapters, individualism is too small a unit for human flourishing.

Individualism is not the same as singleness, but a state of mind also found in partnerships and marriages. A single person committed to relationships in a healthy community can be fully content. However, finding such a community is no longer as easy as it once was. Sustaining it requires the same time and commitment as any relationship.

Hence, much of what I will write in this chapter applies whatever *status* one might have: partner, married, single, celibate or some other. Committed love is not limited to people in certain unique or exclusive relationships. It can be found in various ways in any human interaction, different levels of intimacy, friendships of every type and community in general.

'It Is Not Good That Man Should Be Alone'

Let me take you back to the story of the first pair in the book of Genesis – a story I find both wonderful and strange. The ancient text tells us that God creates the heavens and the earth, and after each creative act, he says, 'It is good,' then suddenly he says, 'It is not good.' So, what is not good? 'It is not good that man should be alone.'

Why? All humans need relationships at some level, because without them we see life through our inner world. We need other points of view to see reality as it is and ourselves as others experience us.

There is another reason. It is not because the man gets lonely or needs help but because without the woman he is incomplete as the image of God. God is one in three persons. The man does not reflect the image of God without the woman. In our differences, we are invited to reflect the infinite intimacy, which is God.

God puts the man to sleep and creates the woman from him. Then he wakes him. The man sees the woman and sings. Then, strangely, God tells them they must be one flesh! If he wanted them to be one, why divide them? Yet being one is much more challenging when you are two than when you were one. It is not good that man should be alone, but how on earth can we live together?

The vision of a better country is one of a society of open-hearted, other-centred people whose commitment to relationships requires trust, the moderation and negotiation of power, and other-centred love. It differs substantially from the ideas of power that infuse Nietzschean or postmodern visions of society, which have no way of reconciling differences.

For many reasons, not all people marry, but they can still be in committed long-term friendships that reflect the love and communion of God and which are his intention for *all* relationships, married, single, sexual or celibate. Anything less is a distortion.

Relationship – Love, Trust, Knowledge and Personhood

Trust is the medium that enables free association among people and is the basis for healthy relationships and intimacy. Without free association, love is meaningless, relationships become controlling and domineering, and intimacy withers under fear and anxiety. As G. K. Chesterton said: 'If love is not free, it is not love at all.'[8]

As I wrote in Chapter 2, personal knowledge differs from scientific knowledge. Humans have an interior life that cannot be examined or accessed objectively by another person's rationality alone. The inner world of our ideas, assumptions, opinions, tastes, history and experience is hidden from others and awaits discovery but also needs protection.

While not scientifically verifiable, personal knowledge is genuine and proper knowledge. Personal knowledge is never complete or static, because we have unexplored depths and constantly grow and learn. Such knowledge is tentative, gathered gradually and only proven over time. We experience evidence of this daily; you may know the square of the hypotenuse by reason, but data will not enable you to know your friends.

Generous revelation is a self-giving activity that involves risk. We need a little trust to begin the process. With each step, the participants place faith in the trustworthiness of the other until they can rest in each other's company without fear and even in self-forgetfulness.

Another word for revelation is 'unveiling'. The continual unveiling of the mind in honest sharing of the inner life leads to an ever-deeper joining of hearts in commitment and attachment. The exchange should not be rushed or coerced because it raises questions of acceptance and the potential for ridicule. Trust and revelation work in a virtuous circle, in which we know and are known at deeper levels.

Without a common basis for trustworthiness, trust would be foolish. A commonly held objective standard protects against delusions and illusions. The wider it is shared, the deeper and longer lasting the communion will be among the greatest number of people.

We reveal ourselves to each other in stages, in ever more profound levels of intimacy and vulnerability. Patience is needed to tune in to each other and distinguish between the real and the illusion. It takes time to trust another enough to invite them into more intimate personal knowledge.

This circular dance of trust and revelation can frighten those unfamiliar with its rhythms; the unaffirmed, the tongue-tied, those who lack confidence or find small talk difficult! The dance differs from culture to culture. Such conversations usually begin with hesitation, but the steps can be learned.

Personhood develops in relationships. In turning to face each other, we see ourselves through new eyes, learning about our assumptions, fears, dreams and desires. As the other person draws out what is unique to me, I learn to become myself. Others experience me and tell me what they experience, freeing me to explore the external world in a new light. The encounter will be as rich as the honesty and generosity of hearts that accompany it. Other people confirm our existence and validate our worth by accepting and enjoying our presence.

Love and Emotion

It is common to conflate emotion and feelings and use the words interchangeably. While there is a significant overlap, I have found it helpful to separate them to understand the meaning of love. Not all feelings are emotions, and we feel emotions in various ways.

A mature emotion is the sustained *energy* needed to reach good outcomes. The key is in the word '*e*-motion', which implies movement towards or away from something. Fear, for example, is the emotion that tests for and responds to potential danger. Emotions need an object on which to focus and a moral direction to resolve whatever issue has aroused them. The object of my fear might be the bull in the field I am crossing. A good outcome might be to remove myself from the field. I will need energy to work out how to do it and to execute the plan. Mature anger, as discussed in

Chapter 9, is the energy required to stay focused on negotiating the best outcome for resolving injustice.

Feelings are bodily responses, either internal or external, to mental or physical stimuli and may not require any response. They enable awareness of our environment. A feeling does not have to move us to any action. Emotion must have resolution and direction somewhere; otherwise the energy could go anywhere, with unpredictable and destabilising results.

Emotions can have many feelings associated with them under differing circumstances. It is possible to suppress emotions and not feel them, especially if they were punished or scorned during childhood. That does not mean the energy is inactive, just that we are unaware of it. It is possible to be angry without realising it. We can also experience several emotions simultaneously, although we think of them sequentially.

These distinctions help us to understand love. At the emotional level, love is the energy to practise moral goodness towards others regardless of the loved one's condition. It may include various feelings. It may make me feel warm towards the one I love, but I might just as easily feel anxious, tired or jealous. The moral imagination guided by an ethical code like the Decalogue gives means to discern good outcomes.

Imagine it is 3:00 in the morning. The baby has vomited in his cot. Father is sick with (real) flu. Mother has an early start for work in the morning. She probably doesn't have warm, joyful feelings. She might feel slightly anxious about the child's sickness or about the fatigue she will feel in her meeting in the morning. She might sense a mild irrational irritation at her husband, whom she can hardly blame for his sickness, but her care for their child is no less loving. Love energises her to tend to the needs of their crying child.

What Is Love?

Mature love is a commitment to be other-centred rather than self-centred. It is a conscious and deliberate attachment of the heart, an act of moral choice to give direction and, at the emotional level, the energy to practise moral goodness towards others. It will include various feelings. It is also a continual series of choices to grow trust that leads to deeper intimacy. Finally, it will acknowledge the freedom of the loved one to be genuinely themselves and mitigate the impulse to dominate and control.

What do we mean when we say 'I love you'? Does my wife love me because I am lovely or because she is committed to love? We hope it is both! But there is greater security in her commitment to love, for although I may be lovely today, I may not be lovely tomorrow, and she will continue to love me (we have been married a long time, so I have evidence of this). It is a great relief because sometimes I am ugly. And I love her because I am committed to love; this is a relief to her, even though I know her well and find her amazingly lovely most of the time. We did not start that way but have learned it through many storms and deserts.

Other-centred love will inevitably lead to strong passions and deep feelings of affection. But these ebb and flow like the shoreline and the sea, depending on many circumstances. Love does not need such feelings to be present to act lovingly, but it joyfully embraces them when they are. The first few times the tide went out I was afraid, not knowing if it would return, but experience taught me that it does return, but unlike the tide it is not regular. We can enable it. It is not always clear what makes the tide of loving feelings turn; acts and words of kindness, understanding and grace, lots of forgiveness, thoughtful gestures, or mismatched expectations and mistuned assumptions, undiscovered wells of anxiety and need, and unkindness. It helps to keep short accounts, stay emotionally connected and keep communication open.

Other-centred love grows to know and respect the loved for who they are, not for what the lover needs them to be. I cannot make it up to suit me, nor form the person to suit my needs. I can only change what is in my legitimate power to change.

Wise people do not *fall* in love. They *grow* in love as they grow to know and respect each other, with their eyes wide open to reality and as trust grows. There is an external world beyond themselves, and the one they love is part of it. The real *I* meets the real *thou*, being one and accepting the difference. The rest is a continual negotiation. They dare to speak their mind, ask honest questions and test assumptions. They recognise feelings of attraction as a starting point for potential relationships of many levels of intimacy, from friendship to lovers.

The Bible gave me a helpful image to understand this: Jesus hanging on a cross. It is a strange and violent image, far from the romance of the modern age. Who would feel good under such conditions? As he suffered, physically and mentally, Jesus was concerned for his mother. He called his friend John to look after her, acting lovingly despite his feelings.[9]

Covenant Love

When I was twenty I spent some time in Egypt. Once, while attending a service in the Coptic cathedral in Cairo, I saw what I thought was a wedding ceremony in a side chapel. The bride was beaming, glowing in her white dress, while the groom was in his finest suit, and the guests had dressed to impress. When people moved to the reception, I asked my host about Coptic weddings.

'Oh, that's not a wedding,' she said, laughing at my cultural ignorance. 'They are getting engaged.'

It was a ritual larger than the couple. Families were making binding commitments – two histories woven into a tapestry. New loyalties and responsibilities formed. God was not only a witness but the one to whom all would be accountable. That evening I gained insight into a covenantal tradition mostly lost in the West, where marriage has become a legal contract between two individuals.

A covenant is a promise to go the distance, for better or worse, whatever the cost. It is hard work, to be sure, requiring a deep and growing knowledge of oneself and the other person. Covenantal love is demanding and no easy task, especially in its early stages. It requires the loosening and reordering of older loyalties, the courage of mutual truth-telling, mercy, forgiveness and acceptance, but it rewards the investment as intimacy grows. Many jump out too early and lock in their losses.

Of the many levels of communion, marriage is exclusive because we are finite and have a limited capacity for the deepest level of intimacy. The vulnerability of marriage is jealously guarded because it is risky. It holds out the potential of a union of the most profound intimacy and the danger of the most hurt.

The seventh word is protective of the vulnerability of the heart giving itself to another. Trust is hard to achieve and easily lost. The seventh word is the scaffolding that holds the marriage together as love matures.

This vision of marriage and union differs from modern ideas of a partnership between autonomous individuals in which sexual fulfilment is an enjoyable bodily need and children are a choice. Transactional love is more manageable. It says, 'I will be with you for as long as I benefit, and then I am gone.' Most of us are caught unaware somewhere between the two perspectives. Both are practised inconsistently and defended religiously.

Covenantal love goes beyond feeling or attraction. In attending to the good of others, we breathe on the embers of affection until they glow again. Meaningful love is powerful and requires a deep moral commitment to the good of the beloved. The writer to the Hebrews quotes Jesus as saying, 'I will never leave you nor forsake you.'[10] There is no limit to the depth of such love.

Intimacy and Communion

Our model for relationships is not just a partnership of two equal individuals. Partnership is inadequate to describe the *communion* we aim for. I know this idea may sound offensive and threatening to some but bear with me.

To enjoy communion, we give up individual sovereignty without giving up our uniqueness. It is, in some small way, a reflection of the Trinity. We have a loyalty and commitment to each other that is prior to ourselves. We are imperfect; our actions and ideals do not always align. We carry wounds that hinder our practice. We are hypocritical because our standards are demanding and we often fall below them, but we have learned in our repentance and forgiveness to turn towards each other and renew the journey.

When Paul the apostle wrote the words 'Husbands, love your wives, as Christ loved the church' to the followers of Jesus in Ephesus, he was not reminding them of something they knew but had forgotten; he was saying something new and very radical.[11] In the culture of ancient Greece, a wife was for having children and the preservation of the family line, and to take care of household management, while men went elsewhere for sexual enjoyment. Paul's announcement would disturb his readers.

More shocking were his ideas about mutual submission: 'The husband should give to his wife her conjugal rights, and likewise the wife to her husband. For the wife does not have authority over her own body, but the husband does. Likewise the husband does not have authority over his own body, but the wife does.'[12] The reader might have expected the part about the wife not having authority over her own body, but the last clause was staggering. That a man should love his wife and respect her as a person was revolutionary; for her it was liberating. One reason the message of Jesus was so attractive in the first century was the great liberation its sexual ethics introduced into a society that treated certain classes of people as sexual objects to be used at will.[13] Tragically it is something the Church has all too often forgotten.

Paul's teaching that the body is a temple of God also shows his high esteem for the physical world.[14] The creation is a gift from God, and our bodies are no exception. Not for him the Platonic idea that the material world is a problem from which we need to be freed.

The ancient Hebrews wrote that Adam *knew* Eve. Sex is a physical expression of an inner reality. Bodily knowing is part of personal knowing. Having trusted each other by revealing our inner being, we entrust our bodies to each other. The sexual act is so immediate and powerful that if it precedes the knowing of heart and mind, it will likely overwhelm and confuse the process.

If communion is to be mutual, there must be an equality of power – not of physical strength but of self-giving and self-renunciation. In its proper context, sexual intercourse is a most intimate and beautiful act of communion and hospitality. In giving and receiving, in self-abandoned trust, for a moment the lovers regain the fusion of inner and outer reality and complete other-centred giving that reflects the being of God and the life to come. The act expresses the inhabitation of mind and heart. As the marriage ceremony says, 'With my body I thee worship.' I acknowledge your worth.[15]

Consummation seals the union, expressing the abundant life that brings new life into the world in an act of creation that echoes something of the Three-in-One, whose infinite intimacy brought forth the universe.

11

Word Eight: Property and Generosity

You shall not steal.
(Exodus 20:15)

What do you have that you did not receive? If then you
received it, why do you boast as if you did not receive it?
(1 Corinthians 4:7)

In the Café Now and Not Yet the tables buzz with conversation
when it comes to thinking about theft. Maybe because everyone
has a story and a moment when their world was invaded. Theft is
easy to imagine – a stolen car or phone, a scam of some kind. Few
disagree that it is a problem, although many question the reasons
for it.

When I began to think about the Decalogue many years ago, I
had a dream in which I saw a pile of keys in the middle of Trafalgar
Square in London. It was a pile so high you could not see the top,
because it held all the keys and locks in that vast city. I tried in
vain to calculate the cost. I wondered about all those employed in
the security industry. My mind gazed over all the equipment and
technologies we need because someone wants to take what is ours.

Why Do You Have Keys in Your Pocket?

Wander through the city in your mind's eye; walk through the
shops and arcades. Do you see the security bars by the doors to
prevent theft? A security equipment salesman once told me he
made sales by monitoring the theft of clothes left on an unprotected

rack placed by the door. By the time the owners had lost 20% of the items, which happened quickly, they usually saw the need for security products. Look at the bars on the windows of our fine houses, decorated and beautiful, yet they hide the ugly truth that someone wants to steal from us.

Do you have keys in your pocket or handbag? We all have them, and passwords and PINs. There is only one reason we need to lock the house, car or office: someone wants to take our possessions. It is an irritant we take for granted and do not give a second thought to. I barely notice the mild unease as I lock my front door to leave for a few weeks, although I remember the violation I felt when someone burgled the house I was visiting. My anxiety grows when I forget my wallet in the café. If I ride my bicycle into the city, will it be stolen? How much must I budget for a good lock?

Larger examples come quickly to mind. The son of a friend started a company in Central Russia. It employed talented men and women to write computer code for foreign companies. One day he went into his office to find a stranger sitting at his desk. The stranger handed him a business card. It was a copy of his own card with the stranger's name as director. He was told he had a few hours to sign the company over and leave town, or he would face serious consequences. His was by no means a unique experience.

Dictators siphon off foreign aid into secret bank accounts. People are tricked and trafficked across borders for sex and fake intimacy, their very lives stolen from them along with their innocence. Officials demand bribes to turn a blind eye or extort a gift merely to do their job. Multinational companies shift profits globally to avoid paying what is due to the common purse. Governments set up systems with the best of intentions but unintentionally empower corrupt bureaucrats to take bribes.

Our modern consumer culture buys its culture and no longer creates it, stealing our agency and creativity as makers of culture by positioning us as passive consumers of culture. While modern technology opens many creative doors, children who grow up addicted to screens may know less of the joy of creativity and discovery – a subtle form of theft that suffocates and steals the desire to create.

Have I ever stolen a reputation through my slander or not given credit where credit is due? Have I given short change through my work? Have I left someone impoverished through my greed or disempowered through my misguided or uninformed compassion? Is the world a more trusting place because of my presence in it?

A Society of Trust

Remember my dream where every key and lock from every door and car was piled high in the central square? Add to that the safes, safety deposit boxes, miles of cable and CCTV. How high do you think the pile would be? What did it cost to extract the ore, smelt the metal, engineer, program, design and distribute the products? Imagine the energy and industry that went into their production; it is the carbon footprint of our protection and the cost of the management of our short-sighted choices.

Imagine the savings if society did not have to find the taxes to cover the cost of detection, prosecution and detention, paperwork and files, accountants, counsellors, security and police. Insurance costs would no longer drain the wealth from our bank accounts like a leaking tap. We would no longer have to factor in the time and cost to protect property.

Once, while visiting the United States with a group of Central and Eastern European friends, we were walking through a small town the evening before Independence Day. People were reserving space by placing sofas and armchairs along the route of the Fourth of July parade. My friends were surprised and a little confused as they looked, first at the very fine furniture that would stay out overnight unprotected, and then at each other to ask if it would be there the following day. The next day as we walked to the firework display, someone needed to return to the house where we were staying. He asked our host for the key. We were shocked to hear our host ask her husband, 'Do we have a front door key?' I am sure there are villages of high trust in Central Europe and places in the United States where the furniture would have disappeared. The level of trust was refreshing; people did not have to spend time and energy on the protection of their property. They did not even have to think of it.

The Decalogue simply says, 'Do not steal.' Imagine the levels of trust we would have if all society was free of the consequences of theft in all its guises.

The law is not naive and, sadly, keys are necessary. The idealist would call us to give up our keys and trust each other, but we know that is unrealistic. However, it places a point of tension, a boundary against which we measure ourselves, and it paints a vision of a world in which we might want to live. Every time you use your keys take a moment to pause and grieve.

Trust and trustworthiness have huge economic benefits. A world without the need for keys and all they symbolise would lead to a decrease in costs, administration and stress, accompanied by an increase in productivity and levels of trust that are presently unimaginable. We are signposted to a way of life that is liberating and opens the door for generosity.

Why Do We Steal?

In 1988, just before the fall of communism in Eastern Europe, I visited the largest state-owned printing house in the Balkans to see if it might be possible to print books that were illegal to own and that we had been smuggling, at great cost, into the country. After exchanging pleasantries about printing machines and the world price of paper, the director looked around to see that he was not being overheard and surprised me by saying he had printed nothing for years and that it was a cover for his real business. Having just had a tour of the plant, I was surprised. Large machines were printing newspapers and books. He clarified his position. 'Each man runs his machine as if it were his own business. I run an import/export business.' He had bribed various officials and, for the right money, could get anything through the Iron Curtain. This explained the racks of wine and the farming equipment that made his large office look like a wine merchant's or an agricultural showroom. A considerable proportion (over 50%) of the GDP of the country was generated in the shadow economy by creative risk-taking entrepreneurs who had no legal space but ran an unofficial free market within socialism. When the system finally collapsed, a friend told me, the revolution was not just against communism but against corruption. Many insiders had benefited, and now the rest wanted the same opportunities.

Under socialism in Central Europe, people were supposed to do what they were told and follow the five-year plan. Creative people and entrepreneurs were a threat to the system. The lack of alternatives forced people to create illegal supply chains and violate their conscience. Eventually, everyone understood how to work the system to their advantage, but it bruised their conscience and caused distortions that eventually led to the fall of the system.

While everyone had to work by law, there were a great deal of 'make work' jobs that had little real responsibility or output.[1] The range of salaries was limited. The salary differential between the doctor and the refuse collector did not reflect the difference in responsibility and time spent in learning the trade.

As utopian dreams collapsed into totalitarian dystopia, there was a saying, which I mentioned in a previous chapter: 'You pretend to pay us and we pretend to work.' As one of my friends said, 'Everyone gets paid a hundred dollars a month and spends two hundred.' Another saying went, 'He who does not steal from the state steals from his family.' People survived the chronic shortages of the planned economy through the theft of state property. The effect was morally corrosive, unproductive and generated mistrust.

Wealth creation is a moral issue. Beyond the generalisation that people steal because they are victims of oppression, there is a complex web of economic good and evil. It goes beyond the theft of material objects to the theft of ideas, plagiarism, or praise for work done by others. One sees it also in those whose labour is exploited but whose lives and communities are not enriched.

Advertising often taps into our deepest desires for meaning and significance, and misdirects them towards products that can never satisfy and soon wear out. It creates a false value structure in which, for a brief moment, a patent leather handbag can satisfy the hunger for identity or a pair of shoes that for affirmation. The products are not necessarily bad or evil; they are simply inadequate to satisfy the human longings for identity, status, significance and meaning.

We steal for many reasons: because we have a need, we are envious, or just because we can; for the fun of it, for the adrenaline rush; we do it out of revenge, spite or hatred, or because we can no longer stop the addiction. We steal because we are greedy, and everyone, rich or poor, can be greedy. We steal because we are impatient. Value accumulated through hard work is time-consuming. 'Take the waiting out of wanting,' said the credit card advertisement in the early 1970s. So we stopped saving and created value from the air as we borrowed from future generations.

When a person is valued solely by how much they can produce, when they are reduced and measured by a series of statistics, they become dehumanised, diminished and objectified. They have been fragmented – a piece of them has been used but not the whole. Both capitalism and socialism are guilty; it does not matter if it is communist theoreticians or the free markets. Something has been taken from them, but they are not truly richer for it. People suffer between the often-unpredictable gap in supply and demand. The responsibilities of employment go beyond the hourly pay rate.

People are disadvantaged for all sorts of reasons by limited access to or uptake of education, finance or other forms of social capital. Some are too ashamed of their lack of qualifications or culture to cross town to look for work; others have little encouragement and nurture from home. Ill-considered and hurried transitions in technology, imposed without discussion, result in impoverished communities. For example, thousands of Indian potters became unemployed when plastic containers made their clay pots worthless. Neither oppression nor idleness is the only reason for poverty. Slogans of the left and right provide inadequate guidance to correct problems.

The thief, in whatever form – individual, corporate or the state – takes the value you have accumulated and which you now steward. He violates and disrespects the process, stealing the worth of the work that enabled your purchase, appropriating the cost of your labour to himself. Your effort is unrewarded. His work adds nothing of value to the community. Instead, he lowers trust and adds costs. At a deeper level, the thief steals the value you have by virtue of your existence as a human. He empowers himself at your expense, literally; you are now poorer and he is richer. The total value has not increased; it has merely moved from one to the other.

Wealth and Generosity

In the circle of love there is generosity. Steal, and you have left the circle of love. We are free to choose how generous we are. By its nature, love cannot be mandated, only encouraged. Paul wrote the following to his co-worker Timothy:

> As for the rich in this present age, charge them not to be haughty, nor to set their hopes on the uncertainty of riches, but on God, who richly provides us with everything to enjoy. They are to do good, to be rich in good works, to be generous and ready to share, thus storing up treasure for themselves as a good foundation for the future, so that they may take hold of that which is truly life.[2]

Generosity is encouraged as a free act of love in which we mirror the generosity of God.

The rich life is much more than material value. True wealth is created in an environment of trust and trustworthiness. What matters is character, wisdom, maturity, humility and good relationships. Social capital includes curiosity, creativity, imagination, the ability to ask questions, the freedom to experiment and make mistakes, examine assumptions and think critically, education and skills. All these add the value necessary for a rich society. All this social capital can be shared and taught.

Wealth is created through creative ideas, hard work, risk-taking, tenacity, disciplined self-denial, character, wisdom, acts of generosity, developing trust with clients and suppliers, a good reputation, paying what is due to the communal good through taxes and gifts. To reduce wealth creation to power dynamics or owners of the means of production is to paint a very incomplete picture. History shows that humans can be amazingly generous or frighteningly oppressive, regardless of their political leanings. Oppression and exploitation are signs of the failure to respect and honour each other, and show the generosity to which all humans are called.

The financially rich enjoy more comfort, but to confuse material wealth, as comfortable as it is, with the real wealth of trust and relationship, is an illusion and another form of poverty. Financial wealth is relative and tentative.

Those who make money spuriously and with haste, rarely develop the long-term depth of character necessary to retain real wealth. Short-term profit made on the back of debt through greed that neither shares the benefits nor lifts others with it is not building a wealthy society but is paving the way for resentment and opening the door for envy to seek its revenge.

When the apostle Paul said, 'And you were dead in [your] trespasses and sins,' he was not being narrowly religious and judgemental. He was just describing the heart of the problem.[3] We are cut off from the source of ultimate wealth and from each other by the death of trust and generosity. It is not only the rich who are guilty of greed, and not just the poor who are guilty of envy. Our absolute poverty is that we are self-centred and inwardly focused, and we do not value other people as God values them and see them as equal worth to ourselves.

The problem cannot be solved by politics alone. For all their benefits, societies with free markets too often choose greed over generosity, while communistic systems coerce what must be freely given, eliminating both generosity and the motive to work. Economic freedom and generous economic justice are formed by an inner transformation to love and other-centredness, sharing the social capital presently unevenly spread but on which economic prosperity rests.

Failure to support the poor is not only a failure of government or the state but a failure of personal responsibility. You will not find a strong central wealth-distributing government in the Bible, in part because the technology and mobility did not exist to enable it. Moreover, as the dysfunctions of society and corrupting effect under communism in Eastern Europe showed, centralised government can greatly reduce personal responsibility and trust. Instead, the Bible calls every one of us to love our neighbour. A better country would be one where everyone was generous with their social and financial capital. While we need the communal purse to organise communal amenities, we must not outsource love.

Gleaning – the Balance of Power in the Act of Generosity

Love places obligations on us. A better country must be a country of generous hearts in which both giver and receiver are understood to be equal before the face of God, from whom all our wealth is derived. 'What do you have that you did not receive?' wrote Paul to the Corinthian church.[4] We are stewards of our possessions – only owners in a very temporary sense. My circumstances and hard work, giftedness or simply taking a risk at the right time may have established my wealth, and I should be thankful for it, but it does not add value to me. My value comes from the Creator who made me. Now I turn to my less advantaged friend to help him or her in whatever way is appropriate. I see this as a training ground for giving and receiving at a much more profound level.

Generosity is not without its problems and carries the potential for dependency, entitlement, resentment or envy. There are dangers for the giver too: feelings of superiority, the desire to direct and control in the name of stewardship, the hidden temptation to dominate rather than allow the recipient to exercise dominion. The question remains: does my generosity preserve the dignity of the recipient while meeting my obligation to serve? Love must be tempered by wisdom and humility.

The Old Testament principle of gleaning gives a helpful lens through which to view issues of power and generosity.[5] In that practice the landowner had to leave some grain for the poor to pick up. He was not to fully maximise his harvest. But neither was he to pick up the grain himself and hold a free distribution programme. The poor had to contribute productive labour to the process. Their labour in the sun preserved their dignity and responsibility. They had earned their food and no one else had the right to tell them what to do with it. They had contributed to the process of provision. Neither did the landowner give a percentage to the state in a distribution programme that collected the money from one source and gave it to another, breaking the relationship between giver and receiver, outsourcing responsibility and depriving each of the potential benefit of obedient compassion and creative productivity. It required that each confront their beliefs about the other.

Generosity is, in the first instance, not about transferring money from one to another but about giving the self to the other. I know what I write appears idealistic, but I have seen this sacrificial love in action in the Balkans, where an extraordinarily humble church leader spent many weekends digging sewerage systems for people in Roma villages. He was not interested in his personal prestige but in blessing his neighbour. The project was not without its problems. He was not naive but had great wisdom and patience. I was privileged to observe the fruit of sacrificial love in the joy on faces that had once been bitter with resentment and prejudice.

It would have been more efficient to have the harvesters do all the work, pick the field bare and then distribute grain directly to the poor. But such efficiency short-circuits other vital factors. It would also have allowed the landowner to boast about his giving. When the poor work for their living, the owner can hardly boast. It sorts out the motive: genuine compassion or mere prestige. While human dignity is not conditional on economic productivity, we recognise one another's inherent dignity by enabling those in need to be active participants rather than passive receivers. Am I willing to be a co-worker with the recipient? Do I see him or her as essentially equal, or is there a lingering prejudice?

Generosity and Hospitality

Absolute wealth comes from the ability to create something from nothing. A God who can speak existence into being is rich beyond description.[6] In the beginning was the other-centred generosity and hospitality of God who, without needing to, chose to create and share existence with something beyond himself.

Real value comes from being in a relationship with the infinite being behind all creation, and living out of his image, which in this case is generosity and gratitude. A better country is one of radical 'other-centredness'. It is rich in relationship, rich in trust, rich in shared knowledge, wisdom and kindness. Our responsibility is to receive the gift, appreciate it with thankfulness and share it with others.

It is a counter-intuitive truth that the more one gives, the more one receives. Imagine a world where generosity of spirit was ordinary, where no one was satisfied until their neighbour had enough economic and social capital and where our possessions did not possess us. It would go a long way to solving the problem of poverty. Imagine intentionally contributing to the prosperity of others rather than taking from them. We would alleviate many of our social problems if we understood that other people are infinitely valuable in the sight of God and should be in our eyes too. Trust in God liberates generosity, but God does not force it. 'Each one must give as he has decided in his heart, not reluctantly or under compulsion, for God loves a cheerful giver.'[7]

12

Word Nine: Reality or Illusion?

You shall not bear false witness against your neighbour.
(Exodus 20:16)

Do not lie to one another, seeing that you have put off the old
self with its practices and have put on the new self, which is
being renewed in knowledge after the image of its creator.
(Colossians 3:9–10)

'I am the way, and the truth, and the life.'
(John 14:6)

'You are fat,' said my young grandson, smiling. He was making
no judgement and meant no harm. He was merely observing,
comparing and speaking the truth, and I loved his innocence.
One of the wonders of the world is that humans can describe
and communicate their perceptions, feelings, emotions, concrete
descriptions and abstract ideas. Not perfectly nor exhaustively, but
substantially.

If the third word of the Decalogue was about language emptied
of meaning, the ninth protects the integrity between perception
and reality. It defends against deliberate distortions of reality and
the bending of perception to the advantage of one party. Our
freedom should be the freedom to live in truth.

Everyone lives by faith in the words of other humans, for who
could verify every word they hear? We expect a person's word to
align with reality and we feel violated when it does not. If the label
says 'cotton', most would feel cheated to discover the sheets were
made from polyester. Where there is uncertainty, we trust in social

systems and institutions to hold people accountable to their word. We want our newspapers to hold governments accountable and tell us when they abuse the public's trust.

Words tumble from our mouths in their millions, passing from one mind to another, half thought and half heard. They cover billboards, flow across the internet, advertisements and newspapers. They inform, persuade and describe reality – or reality as someone wants it to seem. Which words are faithful to reality, which enlighten and clarify, and which deceive, confuse or distract? Which allow greater participation in life and which diminish it?

The false witness bends their opponents' perception of reality to gain an advantage over them. They have more access to truth than those they leave in the dark, who are then unable to react appropriately. So populist politicians or progressive elitists repeat lazy slogans, black-and-white half-truths and generalisations, without context or explaining the large ideas behind them.

A lie is inherently unsubstantiated and weak. It must be remembered and sustained by repetition. Otherwise it evaporates like morning dew on a sunny day. It has only the energy of the liar to support it. Truth can be reconstructed from evidence and eventually comes to light because it contains the strength of the reality it describes.

Living with lies is a psychological drain on people and society. We need the light of truth to see where we are going, even if it is the painful truth about ourselves. When we dare to face and know the truth, we are most free to operate within it.

Reality

By 'reality' I mean simply what is. Reality is vast and complex. It includes the universe and all that is in it and beyond it. To assume one could know all of it would be foolish, but to think knowledge is impossible would equally be a mistake. The process of understanding is more challenging when someone is deliberately distorting the picture.

A truthful description of *what is* includes both objects external to me and my internal subjective responses. It acknowledges the distinction and relationship between the two.

Illusions *appear to be* but are not what they seem. Discernment between the two is simple when the question is, for example: 'Is it raining?' or 'Do you like chocolate cake?' It is harder to answer the question: 'Can I trust this person?'

How do we know what is real? Thinkers have studied this perplexing question since the dawn of thought. However, we should not be over-alarmed. In daily life, knowledge is rarely complete, but it is available and usually sufficient for most tasks at hand if we work at it with wisdom. My bank stubbornly insists on a relationship between my balance and the amount of money I can withdraw. My wife reveals to me some of what she is thinking and feeling. Young children learn to make sense of the world. When you ask someone to pass the salt, you can have a reasonable expectation that salt is what you will get.

That does not mean everything is straightforward. No one lives with a complete grasp of reality. It can be hard and sometimes impossible to know what is real and what is illusion. Anyone who has experienced psychosis will tell you how frighteningly thin the line between the two can be. Experience, intuition, reason and interpersonal revelation are the starting place for making sense of anything. We usually live with points of view, probabilities and uncertainties, and work with approximations substantial enough for reasonable communication and action.

Bending Reality – Large Lies

There is a lie behind many other lies that says the answers to the great questions of life require no further thought: do not doubt received dogma, do not think for yourself and do not raise questions or test assumptions. 'Just believe us,' say the elite, whoever they happen to be at the time. 'If you make your questions public, we will ridicule you, make life uncomfortable or imprison you.' It is a claim to authority in every religion, scientific field, philosophy and shade of politics.[1] It is a totalitarianism of method intolerant of other perspectives.

The prison of lies can be comfortable. It will leave you alone if you do not upset the apple cart of the prevailing orthodoxy. 'Life is wonderful,' it says. 'Up *is* down, even if the theory does not fit experience.' Beware of the blind man or the idealist who gives you directions. Beware when they massage the data to match the ideal. Beware when they maintain the argument through ridicule, slander or imprisonment. It is the sound of the lie spreading. In the moment you are silent, you have joined with the lie.

In late November 1989, forty years of communism in Eastern Europe had been over for two weeks. I was having coffee with an acquaintance in Brno, then in Czechoslovakia. 'How will this affect you personally?' I asked her.

'I will not have to ask myself who is listening every time I speak,' she replied.

I agreed with her then, but now I look back on her naivety with envy. Self-censorship is now common in the West, as my wife and I discovered when we returned to England. We had been customers of a bank for thirty years. In earlier years, my wife and I could speak for each other to arrange our financial affairs. Now we discovered we could only transact business on our joint account if the other partner came on the phone and gave their permission. It amused our cynical Central European minds that any female voice talking would be able to convince the bank it was my wife speaking. I complained to the customer service advisor and she apologised. 'Privately I agree with you, but it is more than my job is worth to speak out.' Listening to her self-censor her thoughts brought back memories of communist Eastern Europe.

We should not be naive, as if our democratic history had some sacred mantle of protection. Self-censorship is participation in the lie. It seems convenient until we read of how fear silenced people, and self-censorship became commonplace when the National Socialists rose to power in Germany in the 1930s.[2]

When President Putin began severely limiting opposition in Russia, a Russian friend asked me, 'Why do you need an opposition?' I had to stop and think for a while. The British political system has *His Majesty's loyal opposition*, because the discernment of truth and wisdom comes through open discussion, which generates new perspectives and fresh ideas. A free press is inconvenient and essential to good governance because it exposes lies.

For this reason, censorship and attempts to silence the opposition are dangerous. It takes humility to listen through the rhetoric to what is real in the opposition's argument. As I wrote earlier, to laugh at another person's point of view is to demonstrate that we have not understood it. To understand and even empathise need not imply agreement.

Propaganda is a form of false witness. Its aim is more to control than to persuade, and to intimidate by its ubiquity. Under communism, even the lamp posts were red. Newspapers were a state-controlled tool of propaganda. People learned to read between the lines. Newspaper headlines contained words like 'Truth', but no one took them at face value. News media did not hold power to account but were a tool of power to promote illusions. The search for truth became more urgent but also more difficult.

Vaclav Havel, who went from prison to become President of Czechoslovakia after the fall of communism, opened his first New Year's speech as president with these words:

> For forty years on this day, you heard, from my predecessors, variations on the same theme: how our country was flourishing, how many millions of tons of steel we produced, how happy we all were, how we trusted our government, and what bright perspectives were unfolding before us. I assume you did not propose me for this office so that I, too, would lie to you.[3]

Alexander Solzhenitsyn, a Soviet dissident, said:

> In our country, the lie has become not just a moral category but a pillar of the State. In recoiling from the lie, we are performing a moral act, not a political one, not one that can be punished by criminal law, but one that would immediately have an effect on our whole life.[4]

He also wrote in an open letter to the Secretariat of the Russian Writers' Union on 12 November 1969:

> It is high time to remember that we belong first and foremost to humanity. And that man has separated himself from the animal world by *thought* and by *speech*. These, naturally, should be *free*. If they are put in chains, we shall return to the state of the animals.
>
> *Openness*, honest and complete *openness* – that is the first condition of health in all societies, including our own. And he who does not want this openness for our country cares nothing for his fatherland and thinks only of his own interest. He who does not wish this openness for his fatherland does not want to purify it of its diseases but only to drive them inward, there to fester.[5]

These quotes stem from his experience of the totalitarianism of communism but would be true of any totalitarianism. In fact, one might say that being forced to self-censor and mouth lies is a sign of totalitarianism. The freedom to speak truth and examine truth claims is a sign of a better country.

Social media has made discernment of truth more complex. AI is making it much more difficult. News can be distributed quickly, but is also one-sided, distorted and censored. Fake news is straightforward manipulation, but algorithms reinforce prejudice.

In the Western world, everyone participates in a multi-billion-dollar advertising industry that bends reality to shape perception. The electronic icons in our pockets present us with glamorous and often unobtainable worlds. The perfection of their photoshopped illusions feeds on our longings and inadequacies. They set our standards of success but skirt around the edge of truth. They confuse legitimate desires for beauty and glory, comfort, pleasure, belonging and worth, but rarely deliver on their promise. Instead, they hold up demanding, unreal and unsustainable ideals while selling short-term benefits at the cost of long-term consequences. Meanwhile, click-bait curiosity eats away at concentration while feeding greed and envy. The onslaught awakens our emotions but leaves our critical faculties numbed and confused.

The illusions we create are not limited to the advertising world. We should take to heart the observation of Jesus when he spoke to the religious leaders of his time: 'You are of your father the devil, and your will is to do your father's desires. He was a murderer from the beginning, and has nothing to do with the truth, because there is no truth in him. When he lies, he speaks out of his own character, for he is a liar and the father of lies.'[6] Lies bend reality to the advantage of one person or group over another. Truth respects everyone.

The Limits of Illusion

In 1948 many Czechs believed in communist ideology. They did not consider it a deception. It made sense in its historical context and the aftermath of the Nazi occupation. The longer the system continued, the more obvious it became that the fundamental economic and social assumptions of communism were not in line with a deeper reality. People were simply not as good or equal as socialist theory assumed them to be. The entrepreneurial spirit was crushed, corruption was widespread, and a new elite emerged. The Party maintained a large-scale deception to stay in power.

In 1988, just before the collapse of socialism, a friend who was a computer specialist worked for a giant steel company and, like all companies, it was state-owned. His job was to take the actual company data from the computer and massage it to fit the five-year plan of the state when it was printed. They had to cover up the discrepancies between reality and illusion. Management knew the data was false, and the state bureaucrats responsible for the five-year plan knew it was false. The *appearance* of reality was enough. When the socialist system finally collapsed, the gap between illusion and reality had become too vast to sustain.

Centralised planning and enforced equality were social constructions incompatible with human nature over time. The illusion took forty years to unravel in Eastern Europe, and longer in Russia, a more communal society that is still wrestling with the place of personal rights in society.

Reality is the wall where deception and illusion crash when ideals and desire collide with the givens of life. Soccer is a social construct; humans make up the rules and can change them. The distance between the earth and the moon is not a social construct and is subject to greater forces than humans can muster. However, there are many grey areas in between. What are the limits of our freedom? It is not always easy or obvious to know where the boundaries fall. For example, is marriage a social construct or an expression of a divinely ordained institution to protect human sexuality and its fruit? Is sex determined biologically, or psychologically through the environment and early childhood experience, or something in which biology and psychology must be combined?

Many social constructions exist because millennia of trial and error have shown them to be the most effective way of living. Taboos develop to protect society against social practices that have failed in the past. It is easy to forget the reasons for them. Societies go through cycles of idealism and illusion until the boundaries between social construction, nature or the law of God reassert themselves. Violate the taboo, and after some time, if the original reasons are still valid, they will re-emerge. With time we will discover the relationship of gender to sex and whether marriage has roots beyond human construction. In the meantime, we will live with the consequences of our beliefs and actions.

Bending Reality – Small Lies

The primary understanding of the Decalogue concerns truth-telling before a judge, bearing witness to the truth for the sake of justice. Those living under corrupt legal systems feel powerlessness: justice is bartered to the highest bidder. When a person bears false witness, justice is impossible. My father was once in a driving accident. The other driver hit his car so hard that it turned his vehicle to face in the wrong direction. It took some time to convince the court of his innocence. A well-meaning young friend asked why my father had not named him as a witness. 'You were not there!' replied my father. The man found it difficult to understand why this was important.

Lies make discernment unnecessarily complicated; verification is costly and time-consuming. The consequences are often less convenient in the long run. The cheat who bribes the tutor in an exam, or the plagiarist who covers his ignorance, lowers the standard for everyone. The student goes out into the world less prepared. Lessons remain unlearned, and education has produced less real value. The qualification looks the same, but it contains less knowledge or skill.

An Austrian friend told me of bricklayers he was employing from Eastern Europe. Just before the holidays, as they were going home, they asked him what skills he would need next. 'Electricians,' he said. The following month the same workers arrived from home with electrical certification. He was reasonably sure they would have had plumbing certification if he had needed it.

Some lies are more subtle but no less damaging to integrity. The person given to hyperbole leaves the listener unsure of his or her genuineness. Another boasts of strength or exaggerates weakness by curating their identity on social media. The compliant person implies agreement when there is none.

When I was young, I met Brother Andrew, famous among Christians as the first Bible smuggler behind the Iron Curtain. When I asked him, 'How are you?' he looked at me with piercing eyes and replied sternly, 'Will you give the rest of your life to my answer?' It was an important reminder to take what I was saying seriously and question the value of my words.

A statement of truth is an act of commitment to a relationship. It says: 'I can trust you with this truth. I believe our relationship can bear this.' In the film *The Invention of Lying*,[7] people always tell the truth and expect it from others. For a moment, one gets an insight into society without false witness.[8] While withdrawing money, one of the characters goes to a bank and realises that people will believe his lies. He becomes wealthy as he manipulates people's perceptions; at the same time, he becomes very lonely. In gaining a life of ease, he loses the relationships of trust that give life its meaning.

Whereas the false witness confuses and destabilises society, those committed to truth add value and strengthen perception of reality; all words become more trustworthy. Imagine an immigration officer at a border saying, 'I don't need your photograph and documentation; your word will be enough.' Consider the cost and time savings in the massive bureaucracy needed to produce documents to verify identity, ownership and competence. Think of the administration and tools no longer required to monitor the truthfulness of our words: passports, fingerprints, photos, facial recognition verification at the border, driving licence, and the notary to verify a signature on a contract. The endless verification of documents required to replace trust should sadden us. Each adds hidden costs in time and money to every transaction and movement. If only we could trust each other and be trustworthy.

Bending Reality – Self-Deception and Personal Integrity

To lie to another person is a skill we can master with practice. To deceive *ourselves* is a skill that requires ingenuity, and we all do it. Reality can be challenging and too painful to acknowledge. Shame, disappointment and failure can make illusion preferable to the truth. Humans are self-justifying. We bend our perception of reality to fit the narrative we need. We deny the truth about our inner life through exaggeration, lying or dissembling. But the result is the internal fragmentation and stress of keeping two versions of the story separate in the same mind. We should listen for the lie in our hearts. It is not always easy to hear the truth amid the clamour of self-justification.

Truth is the starting place of integration. It is liberating to give up the burden of dissembling and undo the web of deceit woven to cope with life's disappointments. To name truth for what it is and to walk towards it can be humbling, but it is the beginning of maturity.

Discerning Truth

Children live in a polarised world of good guys and bad guys. The rest of us live in a world in which good and evil are deeply embedded in each other. Solzhenitsyn's well-known thought that the line dividing good and evil cuts through every human heart tells an uncomfortable truth with which each of us must come to terms.[9] The writer to the Hebrews in the New Testament said something similar when he warned his readers that it takes practice to discern between good and evil. 'But solid food is for the mature, for those who have their powers of discernment trained by constant practice to distinguish good from evil.'[10]

The Bible repeatedly encourages its readers to 'test everything; hold fast what is good'.[11] It does not encourage blind faith but critical thinking. Those who are quick to judge or judge superficially will get their judgements wrong. Humans are morally ambiguous. James wrote, 'The wisdom from above is first pure, then peaceable, gentle, open to reason, full of mercy and good fruits, impartial and sincere.'[12] He encourages reasonable faith and trusts in the God who created an existence that can be examined and considered.

Discerning truth is demanding work; those who try find that the deck is stacked against them. It is not difficult to manipulate perception with fake news and augmented reality in a digitised world. Communal pressures exist to make us conform. From our most formative years we hear 'Don't rock the boat' and 'Curiosity killed the cat'. It takes courage to face reality and resist the lies by developing discernment and acknowledging the truths and half-truths embedded in all sides' arguments.

Discernment cannot be decoupled from character and the virtues of patience, humility and wisdom. The faithful witness to truth must look, listen and understand other points of view, teasing out reality from illusions and idealism, exploring all the angles by entering the grey world where good and evil are entangled and hard to distinguish. 'A false witness will perish, but the word of a man who hears will endure.'[13]

Complexity in Truth-Telling

When learning Slovak, it took hardly any time at all to learn the words 'yes' and 'no', but it took ten years before I could *hear* their meaning. When we invited new friends to visit, they would say 'yes, thank you', but we were confused when they did not come. They were rarely deceitful and did not intend to be rude. Desire and possibility were merely different. Sometimes yes meant 'I would love to, but I cannot' or 'I would like to, but I would feel uncomfortable, so I won't'. It is no different among the English, who have hundreds of ways of saying yes when they mean no. If society is to be free to trust, we must be able to trust each other to keep our word. That does not mean blurting everything out unfiltered. But politeness or conflict avoidance should not lead to deception. Healthy relationships lean on reality.

God himself does not reveal everything. If it meant telling all the truth, we would not be able to contain all the information he could show. And who could bear to hear all the truth about themselves?

Access to truth is not an automatic right. In ethics courses, students hold theoretical discussions about the morality of telling lies to save someone from the concentration camps of the Holocaust. The soldier demanding to know if you have hidden Jews is intent on injustice. Powerful people who abuse their authority forfeit their right to truth.[14] Are they looking to administer justice or merely seeking power to destroy their opponents? We should not contribute to the violation of justice by truth-telling. There is a time for silence and patience. Wisdom bides its time until those listening can receive truth without calling judgement on themselves.

Truth, Love and Courage

When writing to his friends in Ephesus, Paul encouraged them that 'speaking the truth in love, we are to grow up in every way'.[15] To tell the truth in love means, at one level, to speak painful but important truth in the context of the good truth so that the hearer can keep perspective and proportion. The intention is not just to give a person a piece of my mind but to give all of it lovingly, with patience and understanding, knowing that everyone needs correction sometimes.

Speaking the truth requires courage and risk because there is the possibility of misunderstanding, rejection, contempt or indifference. Reveal your dreams and visions, love and hate, joys and fears, desires and needs with caution and reflection. More profound levels of trust and deeper revelation are possible when the listener receives them. In a society of truth-tellers who have mastered 'telling the truth in love',[16] life will be richer and freer.

Living in Truth with Eternity in Mind

When the Spirit of truth comes, he will guide you into all the truth.
(John 16:13)

'If you abide in my word, you are truly my disciples, and you will know the truth, and the truth will set you free.'
(John 8:31–32)

Trust in the word of others is a basic unit of human interchange, the oil of a good community. The deeper the trust, the wealthier and freer the society. A trusting community is alive with potential and the community without trust is dead. But trust cannot be forced; it must grow as people prove themselves trustworthy.

Across human societies, religions and philosophies, people recognise the benefits of truth-telling, as much as they are tempted to put it aside when it benefits them. Imagine the tradesman who came on the day and at the time arranged, the advertisement that delivered on its promise, the insurance company that paid out on its commitment, or that an oath was not necessary in court.

Imagine if everyone took the time to discern truth; that they would never dissemble and could always speak truth to power and live without fear of retribution. Imagine lovers whose self-revelation was a mutual unveiling of honesty and whose self-knowledge was genuine and not an illusion.

A stable word is one you can trust enough to lean on. On the first page of the book of Genesis, we repeatedly read of God, 'He spoke… and it was… and it was good'. Word aligned with action; God did what he said he would do. In other words, 'You can trust me to keep my word.'[17] Valuing truth is far from unique to Christians, but if the bedrock of reality is a God who is true and trustworthy, we should have confidence that truth available to us is knowable and liberating.

Jesus sat with his closest followers at supper just before his death and said, 'I am the way, and the truth, and the life.'[18] He spoke of truth this way, not only because he was talking about personal and relational truth, but because, like his father, there is no discontinuity between what he says and does. Many might speak truth, but there is no other person but the creator whose nature is *truth*, whose speech and actions create reality. There is no lie in his voice. Christ invites us to a life of integration, to become such masters of ourselves that our word and deed are one. We are invited to participate in a kingdom where everyone keeps their word and where each word is trustworthy, unambiguous, loving and worth its weight in gold.

13

Word Ten: Envy – Dominion or Domination

You shall not covet your neighbour's house; you shall not covet your neighbour's wife, or his male servant, or his female servant, or his ox, or his donkey, or anything that is your neighbour's.
(Exodus 20:17)

For the whole law is fulfilled in one word: 'You shall love your neighbour as yourself.' But if you bite and devour one another, watch out that you are not consumed by one another.
(Galatians 5:14–15)

Do nothing from rivalry or conceit, but in humility count others more significant than yourselves. Let each of you look not only to his own interests, but also to the interests of others.
(Philippians 2:3–4)

When I was a poor student in Austria, I craved a camera. On my way to and from German classes, I would pass an auction house and spend too much time gazing at cameras in the window. My longing was eventually rewarded when someone gave me enough money to buy an Olympus OM-2e. Looking back, it is strange that I can remember the name of the camera but not the person who gave the gift! Shame on me. The camera is long gone, but one powerful lesson stayed with me. Seeing my new camera, a friend said, 'I am so thankful that you have that camera.'[1] And he meant it with all his heart. He was happy that I prospered.

How easy it is to see others prosper and become envious of them. We talk of the grass being greener on the other side, being green with envy, and getting ahead, but ahead of what or whom? It is easy to use our power, mental capacities, physical strength and cunning to diminish others so they stay one step behind us.

Jealousy or Envy?

Envy is an inversion of the positive emotion of jealousy that we explored in Chapter 5. In the second word of the Decalogue,[2] we saw how jealously God protects his image from the distortions of the imagination. Envy and jealousy are interchangeable in modern usage, but there is a difference. Jealousy is protective, while envy craves possession. God is jealous for the goodness of the world; the satanic spirit envies his power and grasps after it at every opportunity.

Closing the Circle

If the first word was an invitation to draw near and prioritise God, this final word completes the circle concerning our neighbours.

A better country should be better for everyone. A place where relationships are rich, and everyone can reach their full potential without fear of envy and truly delight in the prosperity of others without feeling diminished. In such a community, the demand for equality becomes irrelevant because people know they are of equal worth; an equality that comes from the one who called them into being and ascribes immeasurable value to each and all. This makes sense considering the spirit of generosity I spoke about in the last chapter. We want our neighbours to prosper, and we do not feel diminished if they get ahead somehow. It adds nothing to our neighbour's essential value and takes nothing from us.

Negatively, the tenth word addresses the temptation to empower ourselves by disempowering others. Viewed in this light, this is possibly the darkest commandment because it exposes the shadowy motive of envy behind our most corrupting behaviours.

This instruction is often misunderstood to be against desire, but desire can be directed to good as well as evil, though desire must be rightly ordered, as Augustine pointed out. After all, Jesus encouraged his followers to 'hunger and thirst' for righteousness.

Remember the bright red sports car from earlier in the book? Imagine my friend has one and I have been longing for exactly that model and colour. My desire for a lovely, red, electric car is not wrong.[3] There is nothing wrong with buying one just like my neighbour's. The issue lies in the smouldering craving to diminish the other person by taking what is theirs. The object is not always physical; I might envy their status or reputation. So let's look at how it works.

Worship – Comparison and Competition

All humans worship:[4] this simply means that we assign worth to people and objects and put them in a hierarchy. But, as we shall see, the wrong ordering of worth has far-reaching consequences.

Children ask, 'What am I worth?' unconsciously before they can think or even articulate. They observe the world closely and repeat what they see. 'Am I worthy of your attention?' is the question behind the relentless attention-seeking of children. They must know they are loved, because their lives depend on it. 'Am I more important to you than your work, play or mobile phone?' is a demanding question. Those who grow up uncertain of their worth go through life with a question mark lurking in their heart, a hesitation in the way of every relationship.

As we grow, we ask, 'Who or what is worth my attention?' Because time and energy are limited, we must choose who or what we give them to. That question – 'How much am I worth?' – soon becomes 'Am I worth more than you?' We learn fast from a young age to establish equality and fairness by comparison with our neighbours. Jack complains that Leila has more sweets. Harry tells everyone that he is taller than Yasmin. My dad is bigger than yours. Who is the most intelligent? We even do this with attributes that weaken as we age, such as physical strength or youthful zeal, like building sandcastles by the sea.

First, we learn to compare and then we learn to compete. Some competition drives creativity and improvement – lacking it can feed laziness and self-satisfaction. However, competition and a diminished sense of personal value can fuel an envious spirit.

Behind the comparison and competition hides the question of who is the strongest and most powerful. Being weaker raises the spectre of vulnerability and the potential of subjection, shame or humiliation. To survive I must be equal to, if not stronger than, my neighbour.

The command says, 'You shall not covet your neighbour's house; you shall not covet your neighbour's wife... or anything that is your neighbour's.' This is much more than repeating the instructions about stealing or adultery. In my coveting, something more is at play. I do not just want a shiny, red sports car *like* my neighbour's; I want my neighbour's car. Either I have it or my neighbour has it, but both cannot have it. Taking the car increases my worth, prestige and power while diminishing my neighbour. It is more than just wanting the vehicle; I do not want them to have it.

Covetousness hates that they are getting ahead. I envy their prospering and flourishing while I feel weakened. And, if I do not have the courage or capacity to do something about it, I smoulder with resentment; my imagination manufactures all kinds of reasons why my neighbour is evil, a threat and now possibly an object of hatred. This is not a great foundation for a better country, but it is the world we live in today.

Covetousness describes a desire that is out of control and uses my neighbour for my benefit and against theirs. I want to enrich and empower myself by dispossessing, thereby disempowering, my neighbour. For this reason, many people are slaves to success. So rather than enjoying their work and relationships, they fight their way up the career ladder only to discover it is attached to a long slide.

Feelings of anxiety can easily slip into paranoia and distorted judgement. You watch your neighbour closely. Think of the person behind the twitching curtain, the pressure of 'keeping up with the Joneses', or the young person glued to the internet following powerful influencers half their age and apparently many times more successful. Although these examples are about individuals, they could just as easily be about clubs, communities or countries. Are the other powers benevolent or cruel? Threats come in all shapes and sizes, from the bully in the school playground to the empire next door.

Our Rage against Ultimate Power

This primitive lust for power is the craving to achieve ultimate control – in effect, not just to be *like* God but to *be* God. I trust no other and allow no equal.

We look out into the dark universe and crave the power of the unknown and unnamed impersonal god or gods, at whom even atheists shake their fists; the infinite, faceless, impersonal force behind our existence, on whom we project our shattered human image and who we blame for our misfortune, weakness and inadequacy.

There can be only one god, and we will crush every potential rival. Our envy manifests itself in the envy of other people. We sense his image in them and envy their intelligence, creativity, body image, authority, status, poise, position and possessions. It is the wound of Eden, whispered in the hiss of the snake that tempted Adam and Eve by awakening their envy, the venom that poisons the heart of humankind, the pride from which all wrongs derive.

Do you think this is too dark? Many people judge others who have this problem, but not themselves. Until I have seen this in my own heart, I have not begun to understand or know myself. What Christians often call 'sins' are merely the fruit of this dark attitude. Our attempts to correct those behaviours can even be a way to avoid seeing the darkness behind them. The tenth instruction protects love against this inverted, envious self-love.

A Closer Look at the Covetous Heart

Covetousness is an inversion of love. Afraid of trust and intimacy, and envious of other people's relationships, the person who covets turns inward, becoming the object of their own love. They are attracted to the strengths of others and want them for themselves. Other people's strengths and attributes, real or imaginary, *are* attractive. The attraction seems genuine and can, perversely, be mistaken for 'falling in love'. Not all attractions are what they appear to be. Rather than being glad for the other person, the covetous person wants their attributes. Inverted love does not empty itself for the other but eventually empties the other for itself.[5] Listen to the apostle Paul in his letter to the church in Galatia:

> For you were called to freedom, brothers. Only do not use your freedom as an opportunity for the flesh [life lived disconnected from God's Spirit], but through love serve one another. For the whole law is fulfilled in one word: 'You shall love your neighbour as yourself.' But if you bite and devour one another, watch out that you are not consumed by one another.[6]

Paul speaks metaphorically, but the metaphor contains something real. The ultimate act of coveting is cannibalism! Historically, cannibals did not eat other humans for calories but to acquire the life force in their victim; this is the heart of envy. I gain power by disempowering the other. I will take your life, your wife, your property, your ideas, your credit, your status, your identity and your reality. I will empty you to fill my emptiness and secure my existence.

Covetousness is active and aggressive, although it can hide its tracks well. The apostle James wrote honestly to some friends: 'You desire and do not have, so you murder. You covet and cannot obtain, so you fight and quarrel.'[7] I have no idea if an actual murder had occurred in his congregation or if he was speaking metaphorically, but covetousness lurks below our restlessness and conflicts.

Life can be confusing and disorienting for those who are envied, as conflicts have no readily identifiable root, and attempts at reconciliation are fruitless. The symptoms painfully distort our sense of reality and are hard to spot. The community has a sense of discomfort and confusion; solutions feel elusive. It is like trying to catch a wet bar of soap, because the problem changes shape to hide the fundamental issue of envy behind other matters. These might also need addressing, but they are not the root cause. The guilty party, full of comparison and contempt, secretly gossips and has a cynical and controlling spirit, a sneer, a hard heart and ingratitude. All this might be delivered with a smile. Anger, even rage, is well hidden for the most part. But in the inner life, it hides speculative and unfounded judgements or irrational and destructive thoughts directed at other people.

It is hard to acknowledge envy, let alone admit to it, because humans are self-justifying, and it disturbs our self-image. But, like its cousin shame, envy can become a blinding, all-consuming and obsessive emotion that energises destructive, intrusive thoughts and irrational behaviour. Workaholism, promiscuous sexuality, drug-taking and other addictions can be the symptoms of a need to suppress or redirect brooding resentment.

We hide covetousness in social convention, behind pleasant smiles over the garden wall, in the barbed observations at the academic dinner table, or in supposedly objective peer reviews. The gossip and backstabbing symptomatic of envy are common in spiritual communities, village hall meetings or higher halls of power. It invades the best of intentions and the noblest of causes. We do not like to admit to it in ourselves, and if accused of it we defend ourselves vigorously.

Because we are discussing who is most powerful, it should be no surprise that the covetous heart manifests itself supremely in the subject of power to which we will now turn.

Power – Dominion or Domination

How are we to think about power? Power is essential for change of any kind to occur in the world. Everyone needs a little energy to get up in the morning. It is necessary, in various forms, to take the train to Paris or to reorganise the train network. We tend not to think much about it until we experience humiliation or domination; these negative encounters distort our picture. A gun pointed at your head is rarely conducive to clear thinking. Or we tend to be cynical and suspicious of power, seeing corrupt power everywhere, hyper-aware that 'power corrupts, and absolute power corrupts absolutely'.

Power can be administered positively by love, and by law when love fails, but negatively by a demanding fist – in other words, by dominion or domination. Let me explain what I mean by these two words.

Domination

Domination is the tyranny of unmediated power. Its oppressive abuse is at the heart of all slavery; those who are dominated are dehumanised and devalued. It is a curse that diminishes the joy of life.

Domineering leaders are controlling, and diminish the potential of others.[8] They indoctrinate rather than educate. Their followers become infantile and subservient and function below their ability, and they miss the opportunity to mature by exercising responsibility. Questions and doubts remain hidden for fear of being accused of being rebellious or not submissive. Communication becomes speculative and subversive. For example, I once visited a church where people often began private conversations by whispering, 'I know we are not supposed to say this, but…' Fearing criticism, shame and blame for mistakes, some followers manifest indifference, passive aggression and low commitment, initiative and creativity. They avoid responsibility, stop volunteering and only do what is necessary. In extreme cases, they will even sabotage outcomes. Others, fawning to get praise, will suffer humiliation and blame themselves for poor results.

Domination can even masquerade as sacrificial love. Hidden in the velvet glove lurks a controlling fist that allows no dissent, difference or shared responsibilities. A mother, envious of her daughter's youth, insists on accompanying her on holiday. Mother alone knows where to go, what to do, eat and wear. She complains about her sacrifice, when the daughter would much rather be with her friends. The daughter feels suffocated and cannot breathe without correction.

One day, when living in Slovakia in the immediate aftermath of communism, I observed the long-term impact of domination when I needed to register a car. I stood outside the appropriate office in a long queue. At that time, old and new attitudes were still competing in a clumsy bureaucratic system. The law required busy owners of companies to sign the documents personally rather than send a delegate. These entrepreneurs were busily talking on their newly acquired and expensive mobile phones. A young officer appeared and shouted an order. I was surprised at how quickly they fell silent, heads down, conditioned by years of humiliation by petty bureaucrats in uniform who held power and could demand yet another document or notarised signature. Each demand was a hidden request for a bribe – corruption threatened to squeeze the entrepreneurs' vitality and energy. How wasteful the controlling domination and the envy behind it. How much more fruitful when there is dignity and respect on all sides.

Dominion

Dominion, as I am using the term, is the exercise of power in the first place over oneself before exercising authority elsewhere. As I explained in Chapter 3 on freedom, dominion is being self-controlled enough to implement your yes and no, a prerequisite for healthy communal co-operation, best served by negotiation towards mutual benefit.

We should neither abandon responsibility to exercise power nor use it in ways that would diminish the dominion or humanness of others. Everyone has some power. We see this in our diverse abilities and capacities. Some are clever or bright; some are strong or fast; some can make money, manage risk or influence others. Some have a stable upbringing and access to education, finance or culture. Capacities are not evenly distributed; my wife can concentrate longer than I can and pays more attention to detail. The unequal distribution is not a problem in a community where people accept the differences and complement and celebrate one another.

Leaders exercising dominion empower those who follow them. They restrain their own power, where necessary, to benefit others, stepping back so others can step forward and sharing honour where it is due. Under such leadership, people can think for themselves, ask questions, raise doubts, explore and exercise curiosity and seek wisdom. People are free to take personal responsibility, negotiate, exercise initiative and creativity, and have the courage to engage in honest face-to-face encounters.

In the book of Genesis, God commands humans to exercise dominion over the earth in shared responsibility – not in domination and exploitation, but through good stewardship.

In the New Testament, Paul describes self-control as a fruit of the work of the Spirit of God, enabling his followers to grow in exercising dominion over themselves, mastering their impulses and their response to external stimuli.[9] The work of the Holy Spirit leads to self-control, not Spirit-control, in keeping with God's will that his creation share dominion with him. Good leaders reflect the Spirit of God when exercising healthy authority, sharing power and building consensus.[10]

The Power of Love

There is none so self-disciplined as God, the ultimate authority and power in the universe, who has chosen to share dominion with his creation in outward-facing, other-centred generosity and hospitality. God exercises sovereignty but does not dominate, nor is he overbearing.[11] Even in his apparent absence, his restraint enables our maturity and freedom.

God's absolute power is safe because he is morally good. He will be satisfied when the object of his love flourishes. Human power and authority are derivative, dependent on God's wisdom, and given for the love of his creation.

Humble Yourself – The Way of Freedom

Communities and even whole societies are organised around ambiguous concepts like fairness or equality in vain attempts to keep covetousness in check. Policies and procedures may limit the damage and manage the symptoms, but they do not treat the underlying cancer. What is missing is a generosity of spirit that desires the prosperity of others.

The depth and darkness of envy are difficult to recognise and harder to acknowledge. Humans are interdependent but we rebel against dependent relationships because they have been the cause of past hurt and humiliation, and we aim to avoid them at all costs.

It was shocking and made me fearful to discover covetousness in my own heart. At first I could not understand why I was so irrationally angry and even felt hatred for a friend whom I otherwise cared for profoundly and owed much. My deep affection for him and gratitude for his help made me question the disturbing anger that kept bubbling up in my imagination towards him. It happened at a time when my own life seemed unfruitful and difficult. He was working fruitfully in an area I considered my domain and expertise. I suddenly saw my envy at his fruitful life. It was shocking but liberating because, in naming it, I could own and turn from it. I learned to hate it rather than him and realised I was trying to fill my hunger for meaning and significance from the wrong source. The change was gradual, and it took a few years to realise that some of my most religious activity was driven by that covetous spirit. It occasionally still rears its ugly head, but experience has taught me to recognise it for what it is.

Freedom from covetousness comes through radical personal honesty, listening to the heart and understanding why I am comparing myself to others and for what end; acknowledging both their worth and mine, seeing the other person for who they really are and practising gratitude for their gifts, while seeking their best. This kind of humility is a strength, not a weakness. It is an acknowledgement of worth, not a denial of it, and it is practical wisdom, whatever a person believes about ultimate reality.

But there is a further step for those who believe in transcendence. The Decalogue is a helpful signpost to the transcendent and ultimate object of worth in the universe. When I compare myself to him, I find myself wanting. When I stop comparing myself with others, I begin to see them for who they are. The New Testament writer, Paul, discovered this to his benefit. Such examination opened his way to freedom, however painful in exposing his corruption. 'Yet if it had not been for the law, I would not have known sin. For I would not have known what it is to covet if the law had not said, "You shall not covet.""[12] The commandment gave a name to his experience, and painful self-acknowledgement enabled him to realise his need to turn from the distorted and fragmented shadow he had become to recover the true image of God in himself.

The way to life sometimes feels like dying (and grieving) and, in a way, it is. Paul encouraged Christ's apprentices to 'put to death therefore what is earthly [disconnected from the eternal] in you: sexual immorality, impurity, passion, evil desire, and covetousness, which is idolatry'.[13] The covetous heart grasps for life in all the wrong places.

Each of these fragments of life contains something good but has been warped and has no integration point, direction or end goal. If we want wholeness, we must surrender the fragments. It may sound negative, but Paul is saying we must put to death those things enslaving us so that we can be free. To know the earth alone is to know one part of reality; submit to the eternal Spirit, and we will have eternity and the earth.

If the first instruction of the Decalogue calls for humility before the ever-present and active Creator to whom we must answer, the tenth calls us to humility towards everyone else. The apostle Peter reminded his friends, 'Clothe yourselves, all of you, with humility towards one another, for "God opposes the proud but gives grace to the humble".[14] Humility before others is the proper ordering of humanity – each preferring the other's good to his or her own.

In a better country, fairness and equality are too small a goal. Instead, God calls us to consider each other's benefits above our own. If everyone did this, there would be no lack, but it is hard for cynical hearts to believe. Humility is often misunderstood as a weakness or putting ourselves down, but this is a misunderstanding. Humility is the proper ordering of worth in life. Compare yourself with God, and all other comparisons become irrelevant.

Moses and Paul knew something about this. Both were strong and known for their power and zeal, attributes rarely associated with humility. How could men of such commanding authority be humble? The Bible says, 'Now the man Moses was very meek, more than all the people who were on the face of the earth.'[15] Paul wrote that he was 'serving the Lord with all humility'.[16] Moses had seen the glory of God on the mountain when he received the law. Paul met and heard the risen Christ on the Damascus Road and described other transcendent encounters with God to his friends in Corinth.[17] Having seen God's power, glory and goodness, and compared themselves with him, they gained no significance by comparing themselves with others.

We are made in God's image; comparing ourselves to him is humbling and dignifying. Seeing ourselves in relation to God reminds us that our value does not come from what others think about us or the worth they ascribe. We are the objects of our maker's deep affection, which allows us to recognise the deep and inherent value all humans have by virtue of existence as objects of his desire.

Humility is a sign of great strength and a radical de-centring of the self. It acknowledges the worth of others without denying our own value. We need no longer be the centre of attention, blow our own trumpet or puff ourselves up.

The sign of humility is contentment, gratitude and worship. Now in part but later in its fullness. Contentment, not as resignation, but as a recognition that genuine joy comes from trusting relationships. Each of us may become who we are gifted to be without fear of ridicule or grasping. Gratitude is not merely the outward act of saying thank you but the inner state of being permeated with gratefulness. Rather than feeling envy, we are thankful for everything our neighbour has and will have in the future. We rejoice in their prosperity, and they are grateful for ours. Humility enables true worship as recognition of the goodness of God's character, his supreme worth and value, and setting all other values below him.[18]

When Time and Eternity Meet

'In the beginning, God created the heavens and the earth' – a demonstration of power beyond our wildest imagination, unlimited but not unrestrained; God's hospitality and generosity given precisely to make space for our freedom and maturity. His power is disciplined and controlled by virtue, his dominion is infinite, and his intentions for the flourishing of his people will be fulfilled. Those who deny God because of the suffering in the world have mistaken patience for powerlessness or injustice. Their equation is incomplete. God will deliver justice and right every wrong, but first he will have people who love and do good from their own hearts and not by force.

In Jesus we see that God himself is humble. Jesus' death on the cross was not an expression of powerlessness but of staggering restraint, necessary to show his absolute power over death. In this, Jesus showed up all other powers for what they are, in effect saying, 'Destroy my biological substance, but you cannot take my life because life is more than matter alone.' He showed his humility in his incarnation and death. He has all the power in the universe ('Do you think that I cannot appeal to my Father, and he will at once send me more than twelve legions of angels?'[19]), but he did not call on it. He gave up his life, among other reasons, to demonstrate the righteousness of his Father, whom he trusted to judge him rightly and raise him from the dead.

The strength and resolve needed to recreate us in God's image come from Christ himself. He said, 'Whoever feeds on my flesh and drinks my blood abides in me, and I in him.'[20] There is a kernel of truth in the distorted understanding of the cannibals, as in all religions. At one level, Jesus was talking symbolically. But the symbol points to something real. Jesus reminded his followers that if they were to have life, they must remain connected to the source of eternal life; they must feed on him, the source of life. The connection, maintained by trust, is not merely a theological concept to which we give intellectual assent, but actual participation in the life of God.

God offers us communion. There is nothing as hollow as a self-made man, nothing as fulfilling as taking up the yoke with Christ. It is a great relief to lay down the burden of ultimate authority. God does not want puppets, however, but men and women willing to stand up and participate with him in good governance. First, though, he must remake us in his image.

The exercise of authority and power is part of the meaning of being humans in the divine image. The Father sent, and the Son came into the world, yet the Son is equal with the Father. The Spirit led Jesus towards temptation in the wilderness. Jesus willingly went without undermining the equality of Father, Son and Spirit. Authority exercised without diminishment of position. The proper administration of authority is a distinction of function, not of status or worth. The Son is secure in the love of the Father; he is coequal with the Father. He said, 'I and the Father are one.'[21]

When the eternal Son became human, he did not need to grasp the equality he already had with God his Father. Though Christ 'was in the form of God, [he] did not count equality with God a thing to be grasped, but emptied himself, by taking the form of a servant, being born in the likeness of men. And being found in human form, he humbled himself by becoming obedient to the point of death, even death on a cross.'[22] There is no covetousness or inverted love within God.

We can live with open hands when connected to the one who created everything out of nothing. Of course, death was not the end of the story. In the Christian narrative, resurrection is where the fragments finally come together to make the whole. And the whole is much more than the sum of its broken parts.

14

Written on the Heart: The Way of Love

'Truly, I say to you, whoever does not receive the kingdom of God like a child shall not enter it.'
(Luke 18:17)

I will put my laws into their minds and write them on their hearts, and I will be their God, and they shall be my people.
(Hebrews 8:10)

Imagination in Search of a Better Country

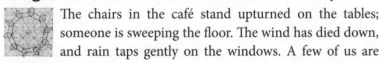 The chairs in the café stand upturned on the tables; someone is sweeping the floor. The wind has died down, and rain taps gently on the windows. A few of us are reflecting and winding down after another evening of discussion while you have been reading.

Sit down and join us. We have been talking for quite some time, so you are joining us mid-conversation. Marco was just explaining that the sculpture is in a circle to symbolise how each of the Ten Words connects to all the others. People often read them as ten separate instructions, as if they were stand-alone rules for individuals. But their strength is in seeing them as a unified whole – ten towers combining their wisdom to protect the freedom of the community. Let's listen in.

'Of course, the version from Moses' time was for a people with hard hearts – "stiff-necked", God called them. Jesus' expanded version was for people hungry for right living and whose hearts were

225

softening. They express something more profound than murder, theft or lies,' Marco says. 'Jesus summed them up by saying, "Love God and love your neighbour as yourself."'

Anna-Liisa asks, 'You mean the Ten Words are a description of love?'

'Yes, a summary of what love looks like in action. That is what David, the ancient songwriter, saw when he wrote that they tasted like honey and shone like gold.'

Suddenly a cold blast of air fills the room. Nadia has returned from somewhere. She looks worried. 'Do you have any news?' she asks. The rumours have proved genuine: war has broken out just a few miles away in the neighbouring country. Anxiety is running high. People are fleeing a tyrant whose lust for power covers a national shame. Chaos and confusion fill the airwaves. We are deeply concerned.

'This is why we need truth,' Tibor says angrily. 'Propaganda distorts reality – theirs or ours. That man is a dictator and delusional.'

'Aren't all dictators delusional?' asks Anna-Liisa, but she expects no answer.

Tibor is old enough to remember the distortions and lies of an earlier regime. 'Do you remember how we used to read between the lines of the newspapers if we wanted to know what was going on? Words bent to the will of power.' He sighs. 'Thinking about a better country raises emotions and questions I prefer to forget.'

'What questions?' asks Marco.

Samat speaks up. 'Why resist? Why not live passively in peace under their oppression?' He is speaking for many like him who, coming from a country with limited freedoms, have little experience of freedom and no choice except to leave home.

'You mean a world of suspicion and little trust? Where life is cheap, and humans are disposable?' replies Tibor with resentment. 'To resist is a daily decision.' He is unrelenting. 'In the old days, finding a good book was like fresh air in the fog of mental pollution.'

'How did it come to this?' asks Maria, who is younger and cannot remember the former regime.

'I often ask myself if there is any meaning beyond the daily fight for survival,' sighs Tibor, whose despair starts to show. 'With respect, Marco, I find your dream about rumours of a better country hard to believe. It's wishful thinking.'

Marco speaks to calm the emotions. 'You might be right, but obviously I don't think so. Partly because you care so passionately, if I may say so, and that must mean something. I might hazard a guess that your anger is driven by longing for something better.' He reaches out and touches Tibor's arm. 'You are right to be angry – we all are – but if you can, point your anger in the right direction.'

'Well, maybe, but I don't want to lose what we fought for in our own revolution. The years since then haven't been perfect, and I was hoping for more, but life is better now than under the old regime,' Tibor replies.

Rumours of the war make us nervous. We feel our powerlessness.

'It's early days yet,' says Marco. 'There is word that help is coming.' After a pause he continues, 'Our assumptions shape our expectations.' He looks around at the large old café, and his gaze rests upon the imposing old mirror he used to dislike but has now come to appreciate. 'If life's beginning was matter, energy, dust and chance – I mean, if it was just empty space and endless time – then everything just is and has been for ever, and nothing means much.'

'But then why do we love and fight for our freedom?' asks Tibor.

'Why indeed,' says Nadia, catching Marco's eye and pointing to the glasses behind the bar. 'That love must come from somewhere.'

Samat speaks. 'Don't we just pass through life like water in a waterfall? Existence is the curve, but we are nothing. Then who cares what the dictator does with his power?'

'I care,' Tibor almost shouts, clearly irritated by Samat's resignation. He catches himself and turns to Samat. 'I apologise.'

Samat nods his appreciation.

'I am happy that you care,' Marco replies, standing up slowly. 'There is so much more than the curve! Samat, the river flows *from* somewhere *to* somewhere; the curve is beautiful as an experience but finds its meaning in the source and destination of the water.' He walks behind the bar and returns with two bottles of wine in one hand and an opener and glasses in the other. 'Nadia,' he asks sheepishly, 'do we have any cheese?'

Her frown is half-hearted, her affection complete; they have been together for a long time. Of course they have cheese, pickles, sausage and olives enough for every late-night longing. She is trying not to be his conscience. She goes into the kitchen and returns to the table with a tray.

Marco cuts cheese and passes it around with crackers and bread. 'If the beginning was personal and good, intentional, not accidental, then the act of creation, whatever the process, was a gift of immense generosity and hospitality. One to be shared and enjoyed: light for the eyes, beauty and colour. Ears to hear, sound and music, rhythm, and bodies to feel and dance.' He stands and dances a little, his eyes slightly closed, as he opens the first bottle with practised hands. 'Taste in infinite variety. Life's a gift to explore and discover, to be recreated, formed and reformed in millions of ways.' He seems to be talking to himself as he moves, stops, offers everyone a drink, and points to the food. 'It's on the house.' He smiles.

'Why does this all-knowing, all-singing Being feel so distant?' says Tibor, breaking a cracker a little too vigorously.

Marco acknowledges his pain with a nod and a sigh. 'It is hard to feel much when fear and suspicion drown out other voices. The word "God" calls up such black feelings in some people, who see everything through the mist of pain. The darkness has been carved into our minds through years of mindless conformism. It took me years to trust it experientially.'

Anna-Liisa picks up her glass and drinks, then asks, 'You think we have been wrong all along? That the hand reaching toward us is not dark, but light to be invited and not feared?'

Tibor brushes the crumbs from the table and picks up a broom to sweep the floor.

'I suspect it *is* to be feared. But not in the way most people think. There is a humbling fear, but in that moment it is liberating and loving,' says Marco.

'What went wrong?' asks Maria.

'A good question,' says Anna-Liisa.

'Our pastry chef is a master of his craft, a genius of creativity.' Marco looks over at the vitrine; one of the kitchen staff is removing pies and cakes to a cool room for the night. 'He makes the very best pies imaginable: cherry pie, pecan pie, pumpkin pie, blueberry pie, blackberry pie, peanut butter pie, lemon meringue pie, lime pie, banoffee pie, custard and cream pie, coconut pie, fudge pie, carrot pie, even a Brussel sprout and cheese pie for those with not such a sweet tooth, chocolate pie, mincemeat pie, and yes, apple pie, and that's just the Anglo-Saxon pies. There is something for every food group, for vegans and for every kind of food intolerance. Imagine someone has given you a coupon that says, "Eat as much pie as you want, as often as you want."'

'It would be like winning the pie lottery,' laughs Tibor, recovering his smile as he sweeps the floor a few tables away. Samat joins him and picks up chairs ahead of him as Marco continues.

'Imagine among the pies there is a most attractive and colourful pie box. A label on it reads: *To be eaten later!* You open the box, and the pie is uncooked and the contents are raw, but you can see its potential. This is not any old pie; it is larger, its crust is thicker, and the layers of sugar sparkle – the mother of all pies. In your imagination, you can already smell the aroma coming from the oven. But there is a warning: *Stop! We must cook and eat this pie together. I must bring a special ingredient. Eating it raw will make you deathly sick, and I do not want you to die.*'

'What is the point of a pie we cannot eat?' asks Anna-Liisa. 'What a waste!' The potential of this pie has driven the abundance of all the pies we *can* eat from our minds. 'I think it must be an apple pie,' Anna-Liisa continues. 'I may have heard this story before.' She laughs at her joke.

'Perhaps it is the freedom pie,' says Marco.

Confusion is written on everyone's faces, and perhaps it is on yours too.

'Remember freedom requires the ability to implement your *yes* and *no*. Saying yes is easy; you may say yes to all the pies, but how will you learn to say no? Without no, you will be slaves to your appetites. Without the ability to wait, you may become a slave to the immediate. Eat this pie too soon, and you lose the possibility of learning no, or persevering. Life is more than eating pie; you must be able to say *no*, or *later*. Learning to say no to this pie frees you to say yes to everything without being enslaved by it. Learning to say "not yet" means the freedom to enjoy something that needs time to mature – like a good cheese.' Marco holds up a very old Gouda imported from Amsterdam as it crumbles in his hand.

'More than that,' says Nadia, 'can we love properly without mastering *Yes* and *No*?' She lifts her empty glass and signals Marco to fill it. 'Love coerced is not love at all; love must be freely exchanged. Love requires patience. It matures as we grow to appreciate each other.'

'How do we know what to say *yes* and *no* to?' asks Anna-Liisa. 'How do we distinguish good, better and best?'

'Isn't it a question of perspective?' says Nadia. 'Imagining the consequences might help, but all the imagination and experience in the world could not help us grasp good and evil. We need help from beyond the world. Love depends upon it. The mind is not large enough, and once we experience it, evil colours judgement like ink in water.' Nadia drinks from her glass. 'Doesn't one of our old proverbs say: "There is a way that seems right to a man, but its end is the way to death"?[1] Wait and eat the pie with the master baker; you will have all the perspective you need. That is the special ingredient he brings to make the pie safe to eat.'

Marco has taken over sweeping from Tibor, who sits and eats more crackers and cheese, but he looks as though he is dreaming about an enormous pie.

Marco is a little short of breath as he speaks. 'So, the story goes, in his infinite generosity and hospitality the Creator planted a garden. The man and woman could eat fruit of every type and flavour, just not from the tree of wisdom; apparently, wisdom comes through a relationship with the Creator, who alone has perspective from outside the creation, not merely from inside.'

'And you know what happens when you get ill!' Tibor sounds as though he is speaking from bitter experience.

'You think about yourself. At least I do.' Anna-Liisa laughs. 'Our pain becomes so large we can think of nothing else.'

'We become self-centred rather than other-centred!' says Tibor, seeing the distinction clearly for the first time.

'Exactly,' says Marco. 'And look where that gets us! A prison of bureaucratic rules and regulations in a vain attempt to bypass trust and trustworthiness, rather than learning to exercise wisdom based on the elementary principles we discussed this evening. God's desire is simple and straightforward: love God and love your neighbour.'

'Then why are we so powerless to do it?' asks Tibor. 'Why do we endlessly fight and oppress each other? Why are we so selfish and short-sighted?'

Marco leans on the broom and looks at the ground, pondering how to reply. 'Imagine you made it to the high jump at the Olympics,' he begins thoughtfully. 'All the competitors are eager. They warm up, they run and jump, but almost right from the start jumper after jumper fails. *How strange*, think the spectators. Then up steps an athlete who makes the jump every time. The bar goes higher and higher, and he leaves the other competitors behind, languishing in defeat. The camera pans back; we see the larger picture. If it were not so tragic, it would be laughable. The reason for the failure is clear to the spectator, if not to the participants. Each competitor is blue in the face, panting and weak; symptoms of heart disease are everywhere. They barely crawl to the bar, let alone jump over.' Marco is smiling at his thoughts. 'More practice won't help; they are too blue. They need radical heart surgery, a new heart to replace a heart of stone, calcified by years of insufficient use, too much good pie, too much *yes* and not enough *no*.'

You may not believe in Adam, an apple and a garden, but you know your heart,' says Marco. 'Where can we find a new heart, one already connected to the life source of the universe, ready to pump the blood of divine love through our body? We look at the one who jumps so effortlessly and so high. Does he have the vitality to carry us with him? Dare we believe he has a new heart for everyone who asks? We cannot jump over, but in that moment we see the glory of the one who can.'

'Perhaps they need more exercise,' suggests Samat, 'or a better trainer.'

Marco continues, 'At some point, more exercise is not an option; we need a new heart, as the one we have is too damaged. The Decalogue is a helpful diagnostic tool. Only when I feel the full weight of the sickness do I cry for help.' He looks up sadly, breathes out and says, 'Help will come.'

'But you can't rewrite human nature – or at least I'd need pretty convincing proof that it's possible,' says Tibor,

'The proof of the pudding is in the eating,' Marco responds. 'The Decalogue for hard hearts was carved on stone tablets. Its instructions for soft hearts are written on those very hearts. An altogether more delicate operation.'

We sit in silence. Minutes go by, and the candlelight flickers against the wall and mirror. We avoid each other's eyes.

Nadia smiles and breaks the silence: 'How our questions pile up! And reasonable minds must think them through. When Jesus talked about faith, he meant we should trust a person, not believe in a system.'

Marco has been deep in thought but looks up as Nadia continues. 'Belief does not mean blind faith or thoughtless submission. Trust looks for solid evidence from history. It examines our longings to see where they might point. There is evidence. Not the certainty of scientific study, but the confidence of relationships with people. Belief in God is not one decision but a thousand moment-by-moment steps of trust, some more confident than others. We are bound to hesitate occasionally; all Jesus' followers did, even while he was with them. Many very gifted people have followed the evidence and found it worthy of respect, but when they met God, they found him worthy of worship.' He has been leaning on the broom; he turns and starts to sweep the floor again.

Nadia continues: 'The ultimate evidence is in the person of Jesus. He was either a monumental egomaniac or what he claimed to be. He said, "Truly, truly, I say to you, whoever hears my word and believes him who sent me has eternal life. He does not come into judgement but has passed from death to life."[2] To grasp this, read the writings of those who knew him and willingly suffered for it later. We can choose. Do we want freedom, trust and love? When I chose to love, I quickly discovered how hard it was, and I felt the depth of my fear and envy. I discovered my slavery to impulse and immediate gratification. Our obedience must not be the passive, reluctant compliance to a tyrant who will beat us if we get it wrong, but the willing response of love to love. Jesus himself said we must receive his kingdom like children, not being childish but childlike. Don't children talk excitedly as they wonder at the world? They receive life as a gift and contribute with imagination and creativity. They ask the most profound questions and ponder the answers. They observe relentlessly, wondering what is just around the next corner or over the next hill. The people of the better country have rediscovered their childlike trust, their sense of curiosity and marvel, but they are not naive.'

Marco brings water and a plate of apples that he cuts into wedges. Tibor finishes his wine and takes the last bit of cheese. 'Is it possible,' he asks, 'to recover innocence? So many uncharted assumptions sit deep in me and govern my reactions. I feel generations of hurt stored in my body.'

Anna-Liisa speaks. 'If there is any justice in the world, we must pay what we owe and repair the damage.' She pauses for a moment. 'Without judgement, there is nothing to forgive nor innocence to restore.'

'We can't be entirely innocent!' says Maria, although she is too young to fully understand what she is saying. 'Anyway, what is forgiveness?' she continues.

Nadia replies, 'If you had a coffee here and walked out without paying, you would leave a debt. Forgiveness is about who pays the debt. It seems to me our debt is large.'

Marco picks up the theme: 'I am not sure if we can recover innocence, nor am I sure it would be wise to be that naive, but maybe we can be reconciled to the past if we accept the judgement. What is the point of a new heart if it is going to get sick again?'

Marco finishes sweeping the floor and restoring the chairs to their place. Tibor and Maria offer to help. 'Thank you, but I am happy to do it,' he says. 'When our builder constructed that arch,' he continues, pointing vaguely towards the arch that divides the two main parts of the café, 'he first made a wooden frame on which he put the bricks and cement. Then, when it had hardened, he removed the scaffold. The Decalogue is a kind of scaffolding for our moral life. It describes the rule of love. Not the sentimental or romantic attachment of early attraction, but the courage of disciplined covenantal love through thick and thin. The persevering love that sometimes feels good, sometimes disorienting and tiring, but is always clean. I don't know if you ever pray, but when I pray "Your kingdom come, your will be done, on earth"[3] I am asking for *this* world to be run according to the principles of love Jesus showed in his life.'

Nadia stands up, carries the broom to a cupboard, and then begins gathering the plates on the table. 'Marco and I were asking ourselves if there was a better way of living when we read that King David meditated on the Decalogue day and night. So we started to ask what would change, economically, relationally and socially, if everyone in our community practised even a couple of the instructions of the Decalogue, not because they had to but because they wanted to. That was when the lights went on, and we started to understand why people called it good news. But it also showed up our debt towards God. Here was a kingdom, and more importantly a King, who had these characteristics. Before then, we had used the term "good news" like a cliché one never thinks about.' She clears the table, fills a tray with dishes and walks to the kitchen.

'But those laws are not for everyone, are they?' says Maria. 'I mean, we can't require people who don't believe to submit to them. It wouldn't be normal, would it?'

Marco pours himself another glass of water and sits down. 'You know, I was shopping at the market one day. The farmer weighed out a sack of potatoes. Then it hit me that the scales are an external measure and the same for every shopper. I began to wonder what "normal" means, and realised it has two meanings: what is *average* in our behaviour, or a *norm* by which we measure something. If you mean average, then we have average now – everyone does what they can get away with, and we are graded on a curve. But if you mean a norm, we are weighed in God's balance and found wanting. Truth be told, everyone is a hypocrite. Our own scales find us wanting because no one even lives up to their own standards.'

'It is humbling to admit that you are not what you thought you were; to realise that life's wounds have made you callous, cynical and blind,' says Tibor. 'It's humbling to reach out and ask for help.'

Nadia replies, 'And to discover your debt. Which of us can pay? I don't think we have scratched the surface of how large it is. Until we do we will not understand the death and resurrection of Jesus. We must listen to him if there is to be hope at all. Life's delights are beautiful, but its burdens can be heavy. Jesus said, "Come to me, all who labour and are heavy laden, and I will give you rest."[4] She walks over to the coat rack and picks up their coats. Anna-Liisa, Maria and Samat follow her lead. Then she says, 'He didn't say it is easy, just that it is possible.'

'Well, we must be off,' Marco says, putting on his long woollen coat and holding his wide-brimmed black hat. 'It has been a long day, and we want to catch that last tram. But one final thought. Our family home sits below a wooded hill that climbs steeply to the village above it. In late April, the woods are full of bluebells. One spring, when we had first arrived and were unaware of the landscape, I walked up to the village to cast my vote in an election. The air in the woods was as fresh as paradise. The sunlight shone through the trees on the blue carpet swaying like waves in the gentle breeze. I came to a fork in the path and chose randomly to take a long path up a steep cliff. After casting my vote, I meandered back, exploring a different way, and discovered a valley I had not known existed. Suddenly I came to a place which seemed utterly familiar, yet I had no idea where I was. It was like returning to a place I had never been. As I stood, puzzled, it slowly dawned on me that I was back at the fork in the path. Now from a different angle and with the sunlight behind me, everything had a different perspective. I suspect the better country is like this. For those who have learned to hunger and thirst for what is right and good, it will be like coming home to a place they have never been, and yet a place where they have, in some strange way, lived all their lives.'

Marco opens the door for Nadia and puts on his hat. You can hear the rhythm of their shoes on the pavement getting quieter as they walk to the tram stop.

Anna-Liisa, Maria and Samat get ready to leave. 'Have a good night,' I call after them, but they are deep in discussion. If you want, I can get you something to drink. Tibor often stays and reads at a table by himself until very late. A waiter is here all night to offer coffee and comfort to those who need it.

I hope you have enjoyed your visit and heard a rumour or two to ignite your imagination. Seek out others who have stumbled across the rumours for themselves and pray for strength to live together as its citizens now. May I wish you a very good night.

Light glows, illuminating the sign above the door, because the Café Now and Not Yet never closes.

Notes

Prologue

1 It is hard to imagine now, though it existed until 1989, but a literal 'iron curtain' made of barbed wire, guard towers and machine guns once separated Europe into two political spheres. It ran from the Baltic to the Balkans. People from the East were not often allowed to travel to the West, because it was feared they would not return.

2 It is a great sadness that in the intervening years it has not been possible to obtain even their own worthwhile and significant dream.

3 Quotations from Mao Tse Tung at: www.marxists.org/reference/archive/mao/works/red-book/ch05.htm, (accessed 30 May 2023).

1 An Invitation to the Café Now and Not Yet

1 Leon R. Kass, *Leading a Worthy Life: Finding Meaning in Modern Times* (New York: Encounter Books, 2020).

2 Psalm 1:2.

3 Jesus did this in his Sermon on the Mount, which you can read in the writings of Matthew (chapters 5–7).

2 My Search for a Better Country

1 The Prague Spring was a short period of political liberalisation in 1968 in Czechoslovakia when people called for 'socialism with a human face'. It ended with the invasion of Soviet troops, who moved in to suppress the reforms.

2 I lost touch with Teg-Chin Go, but if I recall correctly, he moved to California and married. I have no idea how he went about it!

3 One reason for the collapse of the system was that productivity was very low. Removing all personal incentives resulted in low work rates and thus more time for relationships. Mutual help was necessary for survival. In the post-communist environment people had new

opportunities, which absorbed their time and energy and left little time for old friendships.

4 The number of people living alone in the Western world has risen from around 4% in 1955 to 33% in 2018. This mirrors the growth of the rise in the percentage of GDP committed to the State sector. While correlation does not equal causation, it is worth asking if there is causation. Levels of isolation, loneliness and associated problems of mental health and addiction have reached such a level that in 2018 the UK government appointed a Minister for Loneliness.

5 There are several ways to understand the fragments. The older way was belief in an absolute standard from which we have wandered and to which, with help, we might return. The materialists and naturalists believe the parts are a long series of mutations, mindless forces at work in random ways. We can harness those forces a little, but should not expect more. The German Romantics in the eighteenth century, followed by the existentialists and the postmoderns, thought that life is what it is; there are no rules. Create the world however you like by the strength of your will. But whose will prevails? (See Isaiah Berlin and Henry Hardy, *The Roots of Romanticism* (London: Pimlico, 2000); Rüdiger Safranski and Robert E. Goodwin, *Romanticism: A German Affair* (Evanston, IL: Northwestern University Press, 2014).)

6 I have read many versions of this story in Jewish literature over the years, but cannot find a definitive origin for it. When I first read it, I was a frequent traveller in parts of Europe from where large numbers of Jewish villages had vanished into the Holocaust. A culture had disappeared, leaving memories distorted by pain and guilt.

7 On our return to the UK after thirty-five years in Central Europe in 2008, we noticed that trust was lower in some parts of society than it had been in the past, but still high in other parts. Open a bank account or buy a mobile phone and you confronted the complex form-filling bureaucracy enabled by impersonal centralised computer and data management systems, which were an attempt to replace trust with a form of absolute knowledge. In traditional institutions people still trusted you. In multicultural areas trust was lower and suspicion higher, while among homogenous ethnic

groups of every kind, trust was higher because assumptions and expectations were better understood. Professionals employed in the State sector complained of not being trusted, but of being controlled by check boxes and time-consuming measurements that were tangential to their professional goals. It was vaguely reminiscent of life behind the Iron Curtain.

8 A covenantal relationship is one based on a commitment to the person regardless of personal benefit. A transactional relationship is one where the benefits of the relationship are more important than the relationship itself. This does not have to be negative. You do not go to the butcher to have a relationship with them, but to buy meat. But it can be negative if the parties to the relationship have committed to a loving relationship and have different understandings of it, and if one party is using the other for their own ends.

9 Compliments to Daniel Raus. See his website: www.danielraus.com.

10 (Matthew 6:10) The immediate reason was that a priest, Václav Malý, led the meeting. The prayer was risky, because the outcome of the chaos was not yet clear. Many people could not remember the words of the prayer, but a surprising number could.

3 Out of the Land of Slavery – The Way of Freedom

1 Exodus 20:2.

2 See: www.dancinghousehotel.com/en/home/, (accessed 10 May 2023).

3 Francis A. Schaeffer, *The Complete Works of Francis A. Schaeffer: A Christian Worldview* (Wheaton, IL: Crossway Books, 1982). The idea of form and freedom appears frequently in Schaeffer's work.

4 Francis Fukuyama, *Trust: The Social Virtues and the Creation of Prosperity* (New York: Free Press, 1995); Geoffrey A. Hosking, *Trust: A History* (Oxford: Oxford University Press, 2014).

5 *Tradition and legalism*: Discussions about law and freedom inevitably raise questions about tradition and legalism. Traditions are caught as well as taught; we learn them by watching our elders and by taking part in the rhythms of life. They are the accumulated wisdom of group experience, passed on through storytelling and

social memorials that keep memories alive through the generations. Traditions are the informal glue that binds a social group; habits of collective cultural memory liberate because social conventions need not be reinvented. That is when they make sense, and the memory of those reasons is alive.

They become oppressive meaningless dogma, and lose their pull and power, when the link between meaning and memory has died, changed or become irrelevant. An older generation might attempt to impose them on another to maintain communal cohesion.

Unexamined traditions can be costly. I once heard a story, which may be apocryphal, of how, during a cost-cutting exercise, the British army examined ways to reduce the number of men in the artillery. Two men moved the gun, one loaded it, another aimed and fired it, but one man stood back behind them and did nothing. On inspecting the records, they discovered his role was to hold the horses, but they had not used horses for over fifty years.

Communal loyalties have historically been essential for survival. Collective anxiety is aroused where tradition is questioned, which is one source of the inter-ethnic tension as communities share space in our hypermobile modern times.

Individualist societies wrestle with issues of identity because there is limited communal memory or narrative to form a common bond. A society without a shared identity has limited access to its history, and interpersonal knowledge is often lower.

Legalism to maintain a communal identity: There are two types of legalism. The first is to maintain group loyalty and cohesion. It prioritises the communal will over the individual and demands conformity as the price of belonging. It is common in any community that perceives itself as a minority – religious, ethnic or social.

The communal identity is enforced by gatekeepers, who dominate others and create a toxic atmosphere in which dissent is discouraged or punished and their particular moral or cultural standards are established as normative. Such legalistic rules are often poorly thought through, inconsistent and overly concerned with image and conformism. The community is quick to judge outward signs such as language, deviant ideas, different clothing and music. Curiosity is suppressed, and creativity, initiative and wisdom are actively discouraged as a potential threat. Such rules are not essentially about morality, but about conformity and control. The rules – in whatever form they take – are used as a marker to discover who is included and loyal and who is a potential threat to community cohesion. Questions are answered with clichés and stories rather than reason. Objectors are marginalised, then squeezed out through gossip and slander. Dissenters feel demotivated and disempowered until they are denounced and eventually cancelled. The benefit of living with such a standard is a sense of belonging and the protection of a closed community, but it is a small and suffocating world that falls far short of being fully human.

Legalism as a means of self-justification: The second kind of legalism has two cousins: self-justification and self-righteousness. They are found together in religious communities, but if you look hard enough, you will find such people in every club and workplace. They are the conscience of the society, but it is a false conscience, stealing the freedom of everyone who disagrees with them. They reduce the standard to a low but attainable level for people with a strong will. Superiority and domination replace humility.

Here we see the corrupt influence of the so-called Pharisee, ancient or modern, who, in their self-righteousness desire to be justified in their own eyes and the eyes of their peers, lowers the high standard of love to easily measurable outcomes.

But legalism never results in a righteous life; the standard is too low. Jesus said, 'Unless your righteousness surpasses that of the Pharisees and the teachers of the law, you will certainly not enter the kingdom of heaven' (Matthew 5:20). Jesus' point was that genuine morality isn't a matter of outward conformity to a rigid code. Real goodness requires wisdom that understands the deeper realities to which the moral code points. To lower the standard is to reduce the relational richness of life. Legalism mistakes old boot leather for the best steak.

Law as letter is a cardboard cut-out, externally imposed and fragmented; it is mechanical, demanding and performative, with the goal of self-justification. *Law as spirit* is internalised and integrated. It emanates as wisdom in the pursuit of other-centred love for the best good and freedom of all.

6 Simone Weil, *Oppression and Liberty* (London/New York: Routledge, 2001), p. 81.

7 Matthew 5:37.

8 Perhaps this is one of the meanings of the tree of the knowledge of good and evil in Genesis 3. Where would the man and woman learn the discipline of saying no when placed in a garden of delight and abundance with permission to eat from all the trees except the one forbidden them?

9 Havel went to prison after he wrote this piece.

10 Václav Havel and Timothy Snyder, *The Power of the Powerless* (London: Vintage Classics, 2018).

11 Ben Lewis, *Hammer & Tickle: A History of Communism Told through Communist Jokes*, UK edn (London: Weidenfeld & Nicolson, 2009).

12 Marleen Hengelaar-Rookmaaker (ed.), *The Creative Gift, Dürer, Dada and Desolation Row*, The Complete Works of Hans Rookmaaker, vol. 3 (Carlisle: Piquant, 2021).

13 See 'religion' at: etymonline.com.

14 1 Timothy 6:15–16.

15 Galatians 5:1, 13.

4 Word One: An Invitation

1 Exodus 20:3.

2 We tend to speak of belief as if it were binary. This mechanical and somewhat idealistic understanding of belief is almost certainly not real. The progression towards confidence and trust is a process of clarification. It is more honest to say that we have many levels of conviction based on our understanding at the time. Rational and clearly articulated beliefs coexist with intuitions, approximations, desires, loyalties, doubts and suspicions – even confusions – which ebb and flow depending on various states of mind.

3 This understanding has more in keeping with the words of Moses, 'For what great nation is there that has a god so near to it as the LORD our God is to us?' (Deuteronomy 4:7–8), and with the creation

narrative of the God who brought life into being and the animals to Adam so he could name them (Genesis 2:8). It is more in keeping with one of the last prayers of Jesus, 'And this is eternal life, that they know you, the only true God, and Jesus Christ whom you have sent' (John 17:3).

4 John 17:20–26.

5 Peter J. Leithart, *Traces of the Trinity: Signs of God in Creation and Human Experience* (Grand Rapids, MI: Brazos Press, 2015).

6 Science is concerned with understanding material existence. The scientific method is about the construction of hypotheses and the design of experiments to falsify them. Hence, scientific 'truth' is open and represents understanding at a given moment in time. Science has no tools to explore beyond the material world. But it would be a mistake to say there is nothing to explore.

7 See Thomas Nagel, *Mind and Cosmos: Why the Materialist Neo-Darwinian Conception of Nature Is Almost Certainly False* (New York: Oxford University Press, 2012).

8 Hebrews 1:3.

9 See Deuteronomy 6:5; Leviticus 19:18; Luke 10:27.

10 In our individualism, we are likely to emphasise the persons of the Trinity over the union within it; to emphasise the three-ness, possibly even so much as to be tri-theists who believe in three gods. Those from a more communal culture fall off the horse on the other side and emphasise the union at the expense of the persons so much as to become monists.

11 Philippians 2:1–11.

12 Christians believe that every relationship is mediated through Christ, who facilitates the complexities and tensions of our life together through the extension of grace and forgiveness, by both the divine presence in every moment and by his example in the Gospels. See Dietrich Bonhoeffer, *Life Together and Prayerbook of the Bible*, ed. Gerhard Ludwig Müller et al., vol. 5, Dietrich Bonhoeffer Works (Philadelphia, PA: Fortress Press, 1996).

13 Job 38:1.

14 Job 42:5–6, italics mine.

15 Exodus 32:1–6.

16 The Tower of Babel – a story from Genesis 11:1–9. The symbolism of the story is important. The people of Babel tried to make a city that had its top in the heavens. They feared their wanderings were separating them and they needed something to bind them together. But separation was the fruit of turning from God. Their own efforts would not re-establish the bond that binds man together. This was the lesson that Abraham had to learn in the next section of Genesis.

17 Luke 9:28–36.

18 Genesis 22:1–20.

5 Word Two: What Do You See? Image and Imagination

1 When social anthropologists look back at the shaping of the Western mind, they may discover that binge-watching TV box sets and streaming shows shaped the modern consciousness. Brilliantly produced and emotionally engaging stories shape our assumptions and expectations; half-truths airbrush the consequences of actions while promoting a consumer agenda in which the hero has desires very much like ours.

2 This is not merely personal memory, but also communal memory handed down through generations.

3 My grammar checker suggested I replace 'prejudice' with 'racism', but racism is a sub-set (albeit an important one) of the wider category of prejudice or pre-judgement, which can happen towards *any* difference. To end racism the underlying impulse to *any* prejudice must be examined and addressed. If we conflate them, we are in danger of losing the tools to test and correct wrong judgement.

4 Children learn continually through observation of the world around them. Absorbing images and experiences, and watching the behaviour of other people, profoundly shapes how they interpret reality in later life.

5 See Thomas Nagel, *Mind and Cosmos: Why the Materialist Neo-Darwinian Conception of Nature Is Almost Certainly False* (New York: Oxford University Press, 2012).

6 See Iain McGilchrist, *The Matter with Things: Our Brains, Our*

Delusions, and the Unmaking of the World (London: Perspectiva, 2021).

7 Luke 5:27–28.

8 Matthew 19:16–22.

9 Luke 7:36–49.

10 Ephesians 1:18.

11 Matthew 5:6.

12 Deuteronomy 5:9.

13 Colossians 1:15.

14 John 1:14.

15 John 14:9.

6 Word Three: What Is Your Name?

1 My justification for the broad interpretation of the Decalogue comes from the Sermon on the Mount in Matthew's Gospel (chs 5–7), in which Jesus immeasurably expands the scope of the Decalogue. It also comes from the book of Hebrews, which describes the Old Testament law as a shadow of a larger reality of God presently not visible to us. God's eternal name includes the attribute *creator*, through which 'every family in heaven and on earth is named' (Ephesians 3:15) and is the source of all other names. The Decalogue is a description of the moral character of God and a comprehensive map for human relationships.

2 Human language is nuanced and complex. It enables communication between people in ways machine language cannot, however powerful the machine. Humans are not calculating machines but have complex, ambiguous and unquantifiable attributes like trust, will and emotion. We bring capabilities and interests irrelevant to our relationships and tasks. We bring our joys and worries to work. We share the football scores or our interest in gardening or pressing concerns about a sick child. While it may seem like a disadvantage to humans, it is the imperfections and unpredictability that make life beautiful and interesting. The vibrations of strings that produce beautiful music all contain small elements of imperfection. Irritants in an oyster result in the formation of pearls. Imperfections in many materials make them stronger. Unpredictability is a double-edged

sword: while it can cause harm, it can also lead to wonderful surprises.

Robotic machines usefully replace humans in many tasks precisely because they have no concerns irrelevant to the task and because they do not tire. The machine is predictable, but you could never have a meaningful exchange of views with a machine about taste based on experience, because the machine does not have experience. It knows nothing of enjoyment, fear or disappointment. In fact it *knows* nothing at all because it is not a knower; it is an information processor and information is not the same as knowledge.

The essential difference between the machine and persons is in the consciousness and personhood. In the machine, names must be converted to numbers for calculation and pattern recognition; names exist only to make the product of calculation intelligible for humans and have no meaning in themselves for the machine. Machines are very efficient at mining patterns from a vast array of data, with great promise of benefit and potential for abuse because they reflect the moral capacity of their human makers.

When made to appear human, the machine is mere magic, giving an illusion of familiarity and connectedness. However, it contains the assumptions, moral categories and worldview of the magicians. The machine can never know in the sense that humans know. It has no skin in the game. It loses nothing if the relationship fails. The subject has no *awareness* of the object. It is blind, deaf and dumb to the object of calculation, and the calculations have no meaning to it at any point. It has no telos external to its programming, nor can it create one. The machine does not have a mid-life crisis; it will not mourn when you die. It is pure logic, pure rationality without imagination, emotion, appetite or a will beyond that of its creator. It has no ambiguity of memory. While computer memory is selective, it never forgets unless erased by accident or external authority. It cannot show discretion, mercy, empathy or compassion. Emotion is embodied sensation that energises humans towards a necessary outcome or action. The machine has no emotional content. It has no desires, nor can it feel pain or have embodied experience; at best it is programmed to simulate feelings for the benefit of the human observer.

The ability to name, describe and participate in a maturing relationship of trust is unique to humans. The biological interface is essential to being human and gives signals necessary for relationships. Our skin is the medium through which we feel pain, the warning sign that all is not well; through which we experience the intimacy of touch, are affirmed and know love.

3 Genesis 1:2.

4 Genesis 2:19.

5 See Matthew 5:22–23.

6 Martin Buber, *I and Thou*, 1st Touchstone edition (New York: Simon & Schuster, 1996).

7 William Shakespeare, *Romeo and Juliet*.

8 I am speaking here grammatically. In referring to people as objects I merely mean as external to oneself and do not imply objectification. Each 'object' is also a subject with their own history, thoughts and feelings.

9 Luke 8:26–39.

10 John 1:12.

11 Revelation 3:12.

7 Word Four: What Disturbs You? Finding Sabbath

1 David Brooks, *The Second Mountain: The Quest for a Moral Life*, 1st edn (New York: Random House, 2019). Brooks helpfully explores the theme of success.

2 Genesis 4:13–14.

3 Genesis 2:2.

4 Saint Augustine, *The Confessions*, trans. Henry Chadwick, reprint edn (Oxford: OUP, 2008), Book 1.

5 This is a slight abbreviation from Goethe, who wrote: '*Wer nicht von dreitausend Jahren, Sich weiß Rechenschaft zu geben, Bleib im Dunkeln unerfahren, Mag von Tag zu Tage leben.*' ('The one who will not reckon with the last three thousand years, appears to be living on from day to day, in a blind, benighted way', which is often quoted as, 'He who does not live from three thousand years of history is living from hand to mouth.')

6 Genesis 2:3; Exodus 20:11.

7 Job 38:7.

8 Ephesians 5:16; Colossians 4:5.

9 Deuteronomy 5:15.

10 I am thankful to David W. Gooding, Professor of Old Testament Greek at Queen's University, Belfast, for this observation.

11 Galatians 4:7.

12 I say 'the habit of worship' because merely attending a service or singing, which is sometimes called 'worship', is not the same as standing in awe of the worth of the Creator and ordering one's life accordingly.

13 Psalms 95:2; 100:2; 105:4.

14 Leonard Cohen, 'Sisters of Mercy', 1967.

15 Acts 17:28.

16 Matthew 11:28–30.

17 Hebrews 4:11.

18 Isaiah 58:13.

19 Mark 2:27.

20 See Francis A. Schaeffer, *The Complete Works of Francis A. Schaeffer: A Christian Worldview* (Wheaton, IL: Crossway, 1985), especially Vol. 3, 'True Spirituality'.

21 Galatians 5:25.

22 George Verwer, the founder of Operation Mobilisation, gave me a gentle kick with this thought when I was young.

23 John Donne, *Holy Sonnets* (10): 'Death, be not proud'.

8 Word Five: A Reckoning with History

1 Matthew 7:3–4.

2 2 Samuel 18:33.

3 1 Corinthians 5:1 (It is not clear from the text if she was his mother.)

4 1 Corinthians 13:4.

5 1 Corinthians 13:11.

6 Matthew 19:13–14.

7 See 'Early Masters', under 'R. Zusya (1718–1800)', in Martin Buber, *Tales of the Hasidim* (New York: Shocken Books, 1947), p. 251.

8 See Lekë Dukagjini, Shtjefën Gjeçov and Leonard Fox (eds), *The Code of Lekë Dukagjini* (New York: Gjonlekaj Pub. Co, 1989).

9 For a very helpful explanation of this in Albania, see 'The Law of Kanun' at: www.varsity.co.uk/culture/7628, (accessed 20 May 2023).

10 Matthew 6:10.

11 Romans 12:19; see also Deuteronomy 32:35; Hebrews 10:30.

12 See Ellis Potter, *3 Theories of Everything* (Vaud: Destinée Media, 2012).

13 John 10:30.

14 Matthew 3:17; Mark 1:11.

15 Luke 9:35.

9 Word Six: Life or Death

1 Pacifism expresses a longing for something profound, but I think it is an idealism, even a temptation, those looking for a better country must resist. While violence and war are a last resort, we also have a responsibility to resist evil and protect those we love.

2 Matthew 5:21–22.

3 Hebrews 1:9.

4 Ephesians 4:26.

5 Galatians 5:23.

6 John 10:10.

7 1 John 3:14–15.

10 Word Seven: The Possibilities and Problems of Love

1 Of course, God and his objective morality had been on notice long before those wars, but war made it personal and visceral.

2 Though many went on to marry.

3 Eva Illouz, *The End of Love: A Sociology of Negative Relations* (New York: Oxford University Press, 2019).

4 Michel Houellebecq and Frank Wynne, *Atomized* (London: Vintage, 2001).

5 Louise Perry, *The Case against the Sexual Revolution: A New Guide to Sex in the 21st Century* (Cambridge: Polity Press, 2022).

6 Tom Wolfe, *I Am Charlotte Simmons* (London: Picador, 2005).

7 'Teach your Children', track 2 on *Déjà Vu*, 1970 ('You who are on the road'). Look up the words if you are interested.

8 G. K. Chesterton, *Stories, Essays and Poems*, Everyman's Library Series, no. 913 (London: J. M. Dent & Sons Ltd, 1946). 'On Evil Euphemisms', p. 209.
9 John 19:26–27.
10 Hebrews 13:5.
11 Ephesians 5:25.
12 1 Corinthians 7:3–4.
13 Tom Holland, *Dominion: The Making of the Western Mind* (London: Little, Brown, 2019). This describes Roman attitudes towards sex and sexual abuse, which is one of the reasons the Christian message was so appealing and liberating at that time.
14 1 Corinthians 3:16.
15 An old version of the wedding service in the Anglican Book of Common Prayer – a prayer book that guides the liturgy of worshippers.

11 Word Eight: Property and Generosity

1 Those interested in Universal Basic Income (UBI) might usefully look at the impact on the sociology and psychology of Central Europeans of similar wage structures in Central Europe during the socialist period.
2 1 Timothy 6:17–19.
3 Ephesians 2:1.
4 1 Corinthians 4:7.
5 Leviticus 23:22; Ruth 2.
6 Hebrews 11:3.
7 2 Corinthians 9:7–8.

12 Word Nine: Reality or Illusion?

1 One reason for the polarisation of our times, and the shrill discussion that goes with it, is that we have no means to reconcile and arbitrate who has the authority to describe reality beyond who has the most power. Humans are not merely chemicals or physics – properties that can be analysed or measured accurately. Our subjective interactions are infinitely more complicated. Modernism prefers the objective, measured and defined (loosely called scientific);

it tends to be dismissive of the subjective. Postmodernism prefers the subjective, intangible and not-easy-to-pin-down. It is more commonly found in the softer sciences: psychology, sociology, cultural anthropology and, more recently, gender and media studies. Here the measurements, if they are measurements at all, are not hard and fast and are difficult to replicate. It is less interested in and has doubts about objective reality. The epistemological divide has been present for generations. But as the postmodern discussion about morality as social construction and language as power has begun to dominate public debate, the divide has become broader and more visible. It remains to be seen how the discussion will end. In the meantime, the sides either ignore each other or shout to drown out reasonable argument. I understand both object and subject are part of reality.

2 Julia Boyd, *Travellers in the Third Reich: The Rise of Fascism through the Eyes of Everyday People* (London: Elliott & Thompson Limited, 2018).
3 Vaclav Havel: New Year's Address to the Nation, 1 January 1990.
4 Alexandr Solzhenitsyn, *The Oak and the Calf – A Memoir* (London: Collins and Harvill Press, 1980), Appendix 32, p. 533.
5 Solzhenitsyn, *The Oak and the Calf*, Appendix 13, p. 494.
6 John 8:44.
7 See: www.warnerbros.com/invention-lying, (accessed 25 May 2023).
8 Why the film should portray people who tell the truth as gullible and naive is not clear.
9 Alexandr Solzhenitsyn, *The Gulag Archipelago 1918–1956, I-II* (New York: Harper & Row, 1973).
10 Hebrews 5:14.
11 1 Thessalonians 5:21.
12 James 3:17.
13 Proverbs 21:28.
14 See Romans 13:1–10. The good is not defined by the ruler but by God.
15 Ephesians 4:15.
16 See Ephesians 4:15; 25.

17 Hebrews 1:2.

18 John 14:6.

13 Word Ten: Envy – Dominion or Domination

1 Nigel Spencer gave me an unintended lesson that has richly rewarded me ever since.

2 'You shall not make for yourself a carved image, or any likeness of anything that is in heaven above, or that is in the earth beneath, or that is in the water under the earth. You shall not bow down to them or serve them, for I the LORD your God am a jealous God' (Exodus 20:5).

3 This instruction is often mistaken for a warning against desire, as if desire was wrong. As C. S. Lewis wrote, 'It would seem that Our Lord finds our desires not too strong, but too weak. We are half-hearted creatures, fooling about with drink and sex and ambition when infinite joy is offered us, like an ignorant child who wants to go on making mud pies in a slum because he cannot imagine what is meant by the offer of a holiday at the sea. We are far too easily pleased' (C. S. Lewis, *The Weight of Glory and Other Addresses* (New York: HarperOne, 2001), p. 26). *The Weight of Glory* by C. S. Lewis © copyright 1949 CS Lewis Pte Ltd.

4 Worship is a larger concept than the reductive idea of attendance at religious services.

5 Philippians 2:5–8.

6 Galatians 5:13–15.

7 James 4:2.

8 Those who submit may be complicit in the process through lack of courage or compliance.

9 Galatians 5:22.

10 Philippians 2:2.

11 In the face of our cruelty, God's restraint must be an act of immense patience and self-discipline. If I were God, the temptation to act against the evil in the world would be strong. We often demand justice and ask why he does not end the evil and suffering in the world, but we do not realise that we are all bent towards selfishness, which is the root of evil. If our demand were met, God would have

to judge every human heart, because no one is free from acts of violence however subtly they are hidden.

12 Romans 7:7.
13 Colossians 3:5; see also James 4:2; Galatians 5:24.
14 1 Peter 5:5.
15 Numbers 12:3.
16 Acts 20:19.
17 1 Corinthians 12:1–3.
18 Psalm 73:3–13.
19 Matthew 26:53.
20 John 6:56.
21 John 10:30.
22 Philippians 2:6–8.

14 Written on the Heart: The Way of Love

1 Proverbs 14:12.
2 John 5:24.
3 Matthew 6:10.
4 Matthew 11:28.

Further Reading

Allender, Dan B. and Phyllis Tickle, *Sabbath*, Nashville, TN: Thomas Nelson Inc., 2009.

Brooks, David, *The Second Mountain: The Quest for a Moral Life*, London: Random House, 2019.

Buber, Martin, et al., *I and Thou*, 1st Touchstone edn, New York: Simon & Schuster, 1996.

Burnside, Jonathan P., *God, Justice, and Society: Aspects of Law and Legality in the Bible*, Oxford: Oxford University Press, 2010.

Heschel, Abraham Joshua, *The Sabbath: Its Meaning for Modern Man*, New York: Farrar, Straus and Giroux, 2005.

Leithart, Peter J., *Traces of the Trinity: Signs of God in Creation and Human Experience*, Grand Rapids, MI: Brazos Press, 2015.

Lewis, C. S., *The Great Divorce: A Dream*, San Francisco, CA: HarperOne, 2001.

Lewis, C. S., *Mere Christianity*, San Francisco, CA: HarperOne, 2001.

Lewis, C. S., *The Abolition of Man Or Reflections on Education with Special Reference to the Teaching of English in the Upper Forms of Schools*, San Francisco, CA: HarperOne, 2001.

Licona, Michael R., *The Resurrection of Jesus: A New Historiographical Approach*, Westmont, IL: IVP Academic, 2010.

Meek, Esther L., *Longing to Know: The Philosophy of Knowledge for Ordinary People*, Grand Rapids: Brazos Press, 2003.

Meek, Esther L., *Loving to Know: Introducing Covenant Epistemology*, Eugene, OR: Cascade Books, 2011.

Potter, Ellis, *3 Theories of Everything*, Vaud: Destinée Media, 2012.

Potter, Ellis, *How Do You Know That?*, Vaud: Destinée Media, 2016.

Potter, Ellis, *Comprehensive Spirituality*, Vaud: Destinée Media, 2023.

Safranski, Rüdiger and Robert E. Goodwin, *Romanticism: A German Affair*, Evanston, IL: Northwestern University Press, 2014.

Further Reading

Watson, Thomas, *The Ten Commandments*, Edinburgh: Banner of Truth Trust, 1999.

Willard, Dallas, *The Divine Conspiracy: Rediscovering Our Hidden Life in God*, San Francisco, CA: Harper San Francisco, 1998.

Willard, Dallas, *The Great Omission: Reclaiming Jesus's Essential Teachings on Discipleship*, Oxford: Monarch Books, 2006.

Willard, Dallas and Jan Johnson, *Hearing God: Developing a Conversational Relationship with God*, London: IVP Books, 2012.

Acknowledgements

These ideas have been over thirty years in the making and began with a seed planted in a week-long study in Holland in 1983. David Gooding reminded his audience that when King David wrote in Psalm 1, 'How I love your law, it is my meditation all the day', he was talking about the Decalogue. As a chronic insomniac I decided that I might give at least some time to it. In those nights the enormity of the scale and implications of the Decalogue slowly dawned, and the goodness and love of God began to move from abstraction to reality.

It was possibly on a train somewhere in Russia that Marc and Kara LiVecche helped design the Café Now and Not Yet. Miro Jurik provided helpful input. Ellis Potter has served as a waiter in many of our cafés, and his ideas are present throughout the book. Many students listened to early talks at SEN in Slovakia. Sarah Liechty ran the café countless times and organised the transcription of lectures given at L'Abri Fellowship in the UK, with whom we have partnered in the years since moving from Central Europe.

Thank you to past and present workers, especially Josue and Lili Reichow, who read many chapters with me and gave honest criticism. Artur and Mika Metz, and Thorsten Marbach read the whole text and a large and revolving reading group of students at L'Abri helped rethink various drafts, especially Leland Taylor. Wendy Houston, Brian Corns, Zdravko Voynov, Barry Seagren, Linda Procter, Fliss Mackenzie, John Webber, Jessamin Birdsall-Saunders, and Richard Emmens all read drafts and contributed critical insights. Thanks also to Howard and Roberta Ahmanson for putting me in touch with Andrew Frisardi and enabling his editorial guidance when my head was 'pot-bound' between idea and text. Thanks to Jesse Voth for his tireless work to cut or connect the rabbit trails. My niece, Ginny Mašinović, who loves literature, fruitfully challenged my use of middle-class Anglo-Saxon characters in the café. Adrian Petrice of Graduate Impact in Romania was a great encouragement, our week with Liviu Mocan in Cluj was delightful. Thanks also to Vee San Cheong for her clarity of thought, good questions and grammar, and to Caleb Woodbridge for his editorial wisdom.

Our friends in Leicestershire have put bread on our table faithfully since 1983. Thank you to Adrian and Marilyn Parkinson, Brian (who now knows the reality of it) and Molly Beardsworth, and all our many friends there for your trust. And more recently, Phillip and Christa Johnston and so many friends in Greatham and Petersfield, who have cheered and waited patiently from conception to birth, especially to Richard and Pat Evans, Tom and Lizzie Smiley, John and Claire Kirby, Ken and Boopie Cope, Mark and Sue Harvey, Pat and Mimi Baines, Tricia Porter, Jim Smith, and Richard and Jane Winter, in whose wonderful garden I found those moments of Sabbath. With all these we gather for comfort and joy most weeks when we are home. Thanks for your immense encouragement.

Andrew Fellows, Brian Jose and Tim Oglesby provide accountability and requested this book. Their wives Helen, Audrey and Judi are kind enough to give them the time. Herb and Terry Schlossberg have been a great encouragement and an example to follow; it has been a joy to benefit from their wisdom. Thank you, Robert Mullins, for your regular email encouragements. Thanks to Julo Nagy for teaching me how to read art on our trip to Vienna. I thank Liviu Mocan for his sculpture and the hours of meditation on it that continue to be so helpful. Thank you to Lauri, Owen, Ira and Anna, whose chats have been highlights over the years.

I am a visual and lateral thinker. It is a struggle to put pictures into words. I sit to write in the mornings because by midday my head is so full with the noise of life that clear linear thought is no longer possible. Every morning Tuula brings coffee and encouragement. She practises much of what I write. In this we are a good team.